BELIEVING
IN
AMERICA

BELIEVING IN AMERICA

Congressman Bud Shuster

WILLIAM MORROW AND COMPANY, INC.
New York   1983

Library of Congress Cataloging in Publication Data

Shuster, Bud.
  Believing in America.

  Includes bibliographical references and index.
  1. United States—Civilization—1970-
2. United States—Social policy—1980-
3. Unites States—Economic policy—1981-
4. United States—Politics and government—1945-
I. Title.
E169.12.S517   1983   973.92   82-21693
ISBN 0-688-01834-3
ISBN 0-688-02494-7 (pbk.)
ISBN 0-688-02495-5 (leather bound)

Printed in the United States of America

  2 3 4 5 6 7 8 9 10

BOOK DESIGN BY BERNARD SCHLEIFER

To
My children: Peg, Bill, Deb, Bob and Gia—
and their children's children—who someday
might fly to the stars because their ancestors
hacked a path through the Pennsylvania wilderness

Where it might prove embarrassing, or even dangerous in the case of Soviet citizens with whom I have met, the names of persons have been changed.

CONTENTS

9

BELIEVING
IN
AMERICA

INTRODUCTION

AMERICA. For some, the great Satan, imperialist war-monger, capitalist exploiter; a flag to be burned, a building to be bombed; a land of violent crime, where people walk dark streets in fear, street gangs snatch purses from the elderly, and rioters loot and kill.

America. A nation at the public trough, with one out of every three people receiving some form of federal largesse —twenty-three million on food stamps, nine million living in subsidized housing, twenty-one million carrying Medicaid cards, ten million collecting government aid for dependent children—approximately twelve million out of work.

America. A land of greed and narcissism, where having means more than being, taking more than giving, consuming more than saving, being loved more than loving, satisfying more than sacrificing.

America. Savage to the world—defoliating jungles, massacring innocent villagers, toppling unfriendly governments, propping up dictators.

America. Streets lined with porno flicks and drug pushers, cities decaying and families disintegrating.

America. The Devil's Sodom.

But for others, the very word *America* transmits a tingle down the spine, goose bumps on the skin when Kate Smith sings "God Bless America," or a spiffy high-school band plays *The Stars and Stripes Forever.*

America. A land of opportunity, the one place on earth where dreams can still come true.

America. That mixture of mountains and valleys, prairies and deserts, teeming cities and sleepy towns, religions and nationalities, all coming together to produce a cornucopia of freedom and opportunity, peace and prosperity.

America. God's promised land.

Which America is America? The answer, of course, is that all of it is America, plus much more between the two extremes: respected and hated, loved and feared, free and oppressed, independent and dependent, selfish and unselfish, prosperous and poor, idealistic and cynical, responsible and irresponsible, decent and despicable—God's land *and* the Devil's Sodom.

The threshold question is not simply one of clear-cut good or bad; rather, it is more complicated: How much of America is good and how much bad? How much is right and how much wrong? If many of the answers are gray, are they almost white or nearly black?

The thesis of this book is that the good so vastly outweighs the bad that America stands alone—preeminent. When compared with the world around her, America sparkles.

Producing more than twice the gross national product of any other country, providing a standard of living virtually untouched by other regions of the world, protecting not only herself but allies too, permitting speech, belief, and travel unfettered by official chains, and making higher education available for all who choose to reach, America has achieved that of which others only faintly dream. Compared with her past, today's America stands at the summit of her own majestic mountain, but even from that pinnacle, she has an almost infinite capacity to build still higher toward the heavens.

Despite her shortcomings, which are real and sometimes heavy, America is worthy of belief. Americans can believe in their country, not out of naïveté or chauvinistic patriotism, but because the hard evidence shows that America is deserving of belief. Americans should believe in their country, for belief is the father of a free and prosperous future, disbelief the harbinger of decay.

The world, too, can believe in America, not out of blind friendship but because America offers the best hope for a free and prosperous world. Indeed, the world ought to believe in America, because the alternative is starkly visible for all who choose to look.

Rather than being embarrassed by their country's shortcomings, Americans have solid reasons to be proud of her strengths. Too long have some Americans listened to the drumbeats of the negativists and nihilists, to those who choose to see the worst, finding perverse satisfaction in flagellating what is nearest, in tearing down rather than building up. But the pessimists who scrape their jagged fingernails across the steel muscle of America merely grate, rather than destroy, for they are dealing with an optimistic people who, from earliest days, have built their lives around belief, not disbelief, who have made America the object of that belief and, by so doing, have made America special. Fashioned by hybrid vigor—with people of different temperaments, talents, and convictions—America is made, not of spineless conformity, but of intertwined diversity. Rooted in a past that has believed in their country's destiny, Americans have made that destiny come true.

To forget what Americans gave, in blood and steel, that freedom might survive; to forget what Americans gave, in technology and tools, that prosperity might be born; to forget what Americans gave, in law and values, that representative government might flourish where dictatorships once ruled, would be to curse a blessed past and condemn a bright tomorrow.

By virtually any standard one chooses, except Utopia, America shines.

It is the purpose of this book to seek out the sources of that light; to explore and analyze, to quantify and estimate the causal basis of America's strength. And in the end, to make the case, rationally rather than emotionally, factually rather than conjecturally, that believing in America is both a duty and a dream.

Rooted in reality, the belief itself becomes the propellant for soaring still higher, for healing lasting sores while fashioning a future more free and prosperous than even we have known.

Believing in America: a vision of what can be, because of what has been.

I

BELIEVING WASN'T ALWAYS EASY

It was the best of times,
It was the worst of times. . . .
—CHARLES DICKENS

THE ELEVEN-YEAR-OLD lad trudged through the deep new snow. Wrapped in a brown paper bag, an old hand-painted shaving mug was tucked tightly in his left arm. It was 1943. His grandfather, the barber, had recently died. Except for the collection of shaving mugs, there was little of value in his half-century-old barbershop. Painted by the boy's grandmother around the turn of the century, each mug featured its own individual flowery design and color scheme, with the patron's name ornately lettered in the center. For years the mugs had been good only for decoration; the days had long since passed when men got lathered out of a shaving mug for a barber's straight-razor shave. The names on the mugs, however, told a story of the little town the boy's grandfather had helped lay out in lots in the year Colonel Teddy Roosevelt had led a charge up Cuba's San Juan Hill.

While cleaning out the barbershop, the boy's grandmother had come across the shaving mug that had belonged to Asa Weiss, a Jewish immigrant who had died without knowing that one day his son, Sammy, would be elected to the Congress of the United States. Congressman Weiss lived only two blocks from the boy, and his grandmother thought he would be pleased to have his father's shaving mug.

Apprehensive about knocking on the congressman's door, yet excited at the thought, the lad set out on his errand on that cold December night, during a time when the little town, along with the entire country, ached. Nearly half the houses along the way displayed small, red-bordered white banners in their front windows. Most featured a blue star in the middle, some a silver star—and one a gold star, from which he turned his head as he hurried past, subconsciously unwilling to acknowledge that war could claim someone he actually knew.

The boy thought about the congressman who traveled back and forth to Washington each week, helping make decisions that would surely win an awful war. There could be no doubt. In the boy's innocent eleven-year-old world, good always triumphed over evil, and the difference between the two was always clear to see.

He remembered the day he stood on his tiptoes among the crowd at the town's main street corner watching the first round of draftees being packed into streetcars—more streetcars than he had ever seen, crammed with young men filling the seats, standing in the aisles, and hanging out of windows. Although the streets were jammed with townspeople standing shoulder to shoulder, a somber silence blanketed the crowd, except for intermittent sobs and the screams of a Polish mother in her black babushka who tried to run after one of the streetcars as it pulled away. The congressman was there, standing on a bunting-draped flatbed with a half-dozen others, all with faces of stone, waving slowly, silently.

The boy also remembered how he had stood behind the bench at an old-timers' baseball game as the congressman rushed through the gate, pounding his glove, apologizing for being late, explaining that he had just got in from Washington where they had been rushing emergency measures through the Congress. It seemed as if he was in the middle of the world's greatest undertaking, yet still he was one of them, with his battered glove, rolled-up pants, and faded sweatshirt.

To the townspeople he was more than a congressman, more than the highest elected official who had ever come out of their small town. He was hope—the link, their lifeline with the fearsome world beyond; he was the one last person to whom they could turn for help when all else failed; and turn to him they did—by the hundreds. He was their protector—the one man with both power to make things happen and heart enough to care. He did more for their small community than its priests and preachers combined. And now the boy was on his way to give the congressman a very special gift—something that couldn't be purchased in a store.

When he arrived at the congressman's outer office, which adjoined his comfortable stone home, the boy seated himself on one of the straight-backed wooden chairs along with the other people who were waiting their turn. Through the thin wall the boy caught the rhythm of the procession: a shriveled, ashen-faced woman, whose homemade dress of widow's black hung beneath her tattered coat, asked in halting, broken English if her only son might be brought home from overseas because her husband had died; the corner service-station proprietor told how he could not fulfill the ration-card requirements of his customers unless his gasoline allotment was increased; the high-school halfback, sitting between his parents, explained why he wanted to go to West Point. To those requests and many more, the congressman listened patiently and replied that he would try to help.

When the boy's turn came, he took a deep breath, felt a mingled surge of excitement and fear as he entered the congressman's inner office, made his short speech just as he had practiced it, and handed the shaving mug to the smiling recipient.

Telling the boy how much it meant to have such a remembrance of his father, the congressman placed the mug in a prominent spot on a nearby shelf.

Beaming, the boy shuffled backward out of the office, pulled his tasseled cap down over his ears, and with his heart pounding wildly, plunged into the lonely darkness of the snowy night. Although the cold, raw wind stung his face, the afterglow of his encounter suffused the rest of him with mellow warmth. It had been the most exciting few moments of his short life. For one shining instant, his world—a worn-out fuliginous valley of dreary steel mills and frightened people—had been transmuted into a magical room where a single man possessed the ability to right the wrongs being inflicted upon good people all about him.

As the boy neared his own home, he stopped suddenly, knee-deep in snow, and earnestly announced aloud to the stars in the frigid winter sky: "Someday, I'm going to be a congressman!"

Almost three decades later, with the boyish dream long since faded, he picked up his morning paper to read that a newly created congressional district included the county of his adopted home. Staring at the words, a spark deep inside him rekindled his boyhood dream. He thought of all the intervening years, first hard, then full beyond his fondest hopes. He reminded himself that he had never run for public office, that, not being a professional politician, he lacked the normal political ties seemingly so essential for such an undertaking. Driving to work, he turned over the possibility in his mind. "Why not?" he asked himself. Then a few minutes later he smiled and, speaking aloud, proclaimed: "Now's the time!"

Fifteen months later, after shocking the political establishment with his challenge, and tirelessly knocking on thousands of doors with his family, friends, and campaign helpers; after carefully planning every small detail and working from six in the morning until late at night; after studying the issues, learning about the media and advertising, using telephones, computers, speeches, and posters to tell his story—and after totally throwing himself and his savings into the task, he stood on the floor of the U. S. House of Representatives. Flanked by his children, he raised his right hand to take the oath of office as a duly elected member of the Congress of the United States.

The all-but-forgotten dream of an eleven-year-old boy had actually been fulfilled. For him, there could be no question: America was a land where dreams could still come true.

While his dream was turning into reality that noon of January 3, 1973, as he swore to "support and defend the Constitution of the United States against all enemies," others across America—men and women, fathers, mothers, young and old—had also captured at least some pieces of their own dreams during the years that had pushed America from anguished depths to soaring heights.

*   *   *

When the high-school class of 1950 gathered for its thirtieth reunion, the biggest surprise was not that one of them had served a prison term; it was that only one of that year's 108 graduates had gone to jail. It wasn't easy growing up in a mill town of mostly first- or second-generation Polish or Italian immigrants, in a depression eased only by a terrible war.

Betty Dobshinski symbolized that portion of her grade-school class who were regularly sent home when the dirt and bugs became too much to tolerate. She was lucky. Her parents shaved her head. Some days the classroom smell would be so bad that the worst offenders would be sent to stand in the hall—not because of poor conduct or even willful neglect but because it wasn't easy not to smell when you had only one or two ragtag dresses and came from a home without running water.

Then there was Ron Belko, who solved the problem by simply refusing to go to school, explaining to the truant officer that he was too embarrassed by his hand-me-down clothes. His Sunday-School class quietly sold chocolate Easter eggs and turned the profits over to the owner of the local clothing store, who called Ron in and told him that someone from out of town had asked him to outfit a deserving boy for Easter.

It was not surprising that the offspring of the town's early settlers, the minority in the Class of 1950 who had gone off to college, had succeeded. They had been least scarred by the Depression, and even when scrimping was required, everyone knew that they would get an education. In a nation where the standard of living had more than doubled since the day they crossed the high-school platform to receive their diplomas and stand to sing their alma mater for one last time, getting on was easy for those who could get in. Their success was not the big news of that thirtieth class reunion. The big news was the success of Betty Dobshinski, Ron Belko, and others like them.

Betty was the neatly dressed wife of a plumber, and a mother of two. They had just burned the mortgage on their home. Ron was a bookkeeper in the steel mill. His suit was new.

The Polish and Italians who came from first- or second-generation immigrant families, and who in many cases were raising third-generation Polish-Italian-American children, were decent, hardworking, thoughtful, well-dressed, home-owning, considerate citizens. They were helping make America go: as plumbers, bookkeepers, policemen, air-traffic controllers, civil servants, crane operators, clerks, truck drivers, salesmen, homemakers, newspaper distributors, and caring parents. Perhaps most important, they were typical of millions across America who thought it perfectly natural to expect a better life for their children because they were living one themselves.

From the beginning, Americans believed they were special. Americans thought they saw the proof of God's protection in the success of their Revolution against Great Britain and took great care to provide in the federal Constitution for the free exercise of religion. Every state, save one, acknowledged God in its constitution. Every President, in his inaugural address, acknowledged God in his own way. America relied on God—believed that God would bless America.

The Civil War sorely tested that belief, but in the end, after the nation had been torn in two, it healed together again. America not only endured, it grew and prospered further, proving once again that America surely must be blessed. Some even talked of the coming twentieth century as the American Century and used terms such as manifest destiny.

By the turn of the century, the wounds of the Civil War, economic and psychic, were healing, and the nation was looking ahead with confidence.

John Gutelius and his sons, typical of small businessmen across America who satisfied the needs of a growing but still rural country, had no inkling that those needs would swiftly change. When Gutelius and his sons paraded out their buggies from their shop in Mifflinburg, Pennsylvania, for display at the County Fair in the summer of 1900, they thought they owned a secure and prospering business. For them, the world, already good, held nothing but even greater promise.

Along with other local buggy makers, they employed more than three hundred men from their small community as carpenters, blacksmiths, stitchers, painters, and pattern-makers to turn out high-quality buggies which they sold for $100 each.

What John Gutelius did not know as, under sunny skies, he contentedly moved his buggies over rutted roads to the County Fair, was that a different kind of buggy maker was at work some 440 miles west, in Detroit, Michigan.

Henry Ford had been tinkering for half a dozen years with his dream of a horseless carriage—a buggy pulled not by a horse but by an invention known as the internal-combustion engine. Once he found a tougher steel to take the terrible beatings his vehicles would suffer on the crude roads, he would be ready to revolutionize the way America moved. John Gutelius's buggy-making days were numbered. By 1908, Henry Ford had found his steel and introduced five versions of the Model T, pricing the least expensive at $825, about half that of other cars coming on the market. Even more important than his acquisition of stronger steel was his introduction in 1914 of the concept of the continuously moving assembly line. By 1924, Henry Ford had driven down the price of his least expensive model to $260, and by 1927, had produced over fifteen million cars. A revolution was occurring. The concept of mass production had been devised. Soon it would be applied throughout America to provide a whole new range of products. Coming first within the range of upper-income Americans, automobiles, electric lighting, indoor plumbing, central heating, refrigerators, and radios would eventually become affordable to almost all Americans.

Across America, some adjusted to the times and prospered in their new endeavors; others, standing pat, eventually sank, to be superseded by those with energy, intelligence, and the willingness to take a chance. John Gutelius could have been one of the many who had laughed at John Jacob Astor when, in 1903, he predicted that the gasoline engine could be used to provide a new age of air travel for America. Public outcry had been heard just a few years earlier when Congress had "wasted" taxpayers' money by appropriating $100,000 to build an engine-powered flying machine. When the Wright brothers flew their flying machine on December 17, 1903, at Kitty Hawk, North

Carolina, most Americans thought it had no practical application, except perhaps for carnivals and county fairs, to which people could travel in John Gutelius's buggies to be entertained by daring aerial stunts.

But some believed.

Airplanes, automobiles, and assembly lines became part of America, and none too soon, for America was about to be called upon to satisfy more than consumer wants.

When Gavrilo Princip, a Serbian terrorist, gunned down Archduke Francis Ferdinand of Austria-Hungary on June 28, 1914, at Sarajevo on the Balkan peninsula, most of Europe may have sensed the war clouds gathering, but to America, it was just another example of the constant European turmoil with which Americans could be thankful they were uninvolved.

America watched, an ocean away, detached and disgusted, as war spread across Europe. The old world was at it again, and America would stay out of it.

By the spring of 1915, however, the Germans had sunk the British passenger liner *Lusitania*, drowning almost 1,200 people, including 114 Americans. That, coupled with the use of poison gas, got America's attention, but sending American soldiers to fight a European war was still unthinkable. Europe was a tired old man, burdened by the blood feuds of ancient families, on whom a youthful America did not intend to dissipate her blessings.

Bloody battles seesawed into the winter of 1917 when German submarines began sinking neutral ships. When Germany ignored America's protests, America, reluctantly, went to war.

By the spring of 1918, with the Germans only seventy kilometers from Paris, General Pershing, commander of the American Expeditionary Forces, knew he could no longer keep his troops in reserve for training. At Château-Thierry, American divisions were committed to battle for the first time on the European continent, and together with French and British troops, they stopped the German advance. By summer the Americans were driving the Germans back through the Argonne Forest and across the Meuse River at Verdun. America had made the difference.

Over 1 million American soldiers participated in the engagement that finally broke the back of the German resistance and ended the war. With a regular army of just over 125,000, America had called almost 5 million men to arms. America had spent $28 billion on the war and had loaned her allies almost $10 billion, much of which would never be repaid. Over 53,000 Americans had been killed in battle, and another 70,000 had died in Europe of illness and other causes. Over 200,000 Americans had been wounded in battle. The direct financial cost of the war was forty times the annual cost of running the entire U.S. federal government. The war was paid for by new income taxes and over $20 billion from American subscriptions to Liberty and Victory bonds: a burden which, of course, would eventually have to be paid with interest.

As heavy as the price was to America in blood and dollars, the toll on Europe was crushing. Over 8 million had been killed and over 20 million were wounded. Over $200 billion had been directly expended by the nations involved, and the productive capacities, especially of the vanquished, were decimated.

America emerged not only victorious but demonstrably the strongest nation on the Earth. The price she paid for victory was lighter than that of any of the other major combatants. American land had not been scarred, and the insatiable appetite of the allied war machine had driven America to build new factories, shipyards, and transportation networks which would be in place to serve a peaceful nation.

Once again, the evidence mounted. America seemed destined to be a world power—a special hand of Providence surely was steering the course of this great land.

To Americans who looked across the Atlantic to see the postwar convulsions of Europe, the contrast made America sparkle. In 1924, when Germany was unable to make its reparations payments, America agreed to help by developing the Dawes Plan which rescheduled German payments and made possible an international loan backed by the United States. America's modest involvement filled a dejected Europe with hope.

The war had turned European nations into debtors, and a generation of future leaders lay buried beneath the weakened land. Professor Laurence LaFore observed that by the early 1920's, "paralysis, inflation, strife, depression, confusion and vengefulness contorted the Europe that ten years earlier had run the planet."

The British pursued an economic policy aimed at stability through balancing the budget, raising taxes, depressing wages, and reducing investment. What they got was stagnation and breadlines.

While Europe writhed during the decade after the "war to end all wars," America's prosperity bubbled over into sumptuous plenty. America was the most prosperous, successful, wonderful nation in the world. Uncle Sam was first, and America knew it.

When the crash came, it seemed as if, overnight, America had gone from first to last.

Nippsy's Candy Store was a ramshackle cracker box across from the high school, where the little boy, on his tiptoes, could press his nose against the candy case to inspect fireballs, root-beer barrels, licorice sticks, and other one-cent, sweet-tooth bargains. He would linger at the store listening to the grown-up talk of high-school students.

One day he asked his mother for a nickel so he might splurge at Nippsy's. Hesitantly, she took her change purse off the shelf and emptied it on the kitchen table. From the dozen or so coins, she pushed two pennies toward him, then burst into tears. He was startled for a moment, but when she quickly wiped her eyes, smiled, and motioned him toward the pennies, he scooped them up and ran off thinking only about the hard but happy choices that lay ahead.

Asking his mother about the incident years later, he discovered that she remembered it vividly. The problem, she mused, was that those few coins were all that was left. She didn't know how she was going to feed her family.

They were lucky compared to millions of other families during the Depression. They were sheltered by their modest, though remortgaged, home and by the love of a close-knit family and caring friends—found most frequently in the heart of small towns and old neighborhoods where roots run deep.

Across America people were being devastated in a dozen different ways.

What was wrong with America? Had God deserted her? Or was the belief in America's special destiny just the figment of self-centered, wishful thinking?

The people standing in the breadlines of 1932, or the parents plucking dandelions for soup or picking coal from railroad tracks to heat their homes would have thought it incredible that one day their children would have more food than they should eat, while living in comfortable climate-controlled homes.

The bottom had fallen out of their world. When Herbert Hoover became President in 1929 the country had been booming for a dozen years: National income had increased 45 percent; production had grown 25 percent; 3.5 million new homes had been built; 9 million more homes had electricity; there were 6 million more telephones, 7 million more radios, and 14 million more cars. Mr. Hoover had predicted that, soon, "poverty will be banished from this nation." Yet, within months, the stock market collapsed, common stocks lost 90 percent of their value, savings evaporated as banks failed, industrial production plummeted by half, 12 million Americans were without jobs, unemployment compensation, or welfare, and people's homes were wrested from them by bank foreclosures.

By 1932, 17 million were without jobs, 34 million had no means of support, and 273,000 families were evicted from their homes. For those who had jobs, the average weekly wage was $16.21. Two million Americans, wandering in search of work, set up hobo camps across America, begging food, riding the rails, and making midnight visits to farmers' chicken coops.

Having listened through a slightly opened back door to a vagrant's plea for "just a dime to buy some soup," one mother spoke for many when she advised her son: "Never give them money, but never turn them away without something to eat." Then, routinely, she would hand the boy a peanut-butter sandwich, or a bowl of soup, to be given to the poor fellow, never realizing that the boy, wide-eyed and tense, feared being kidnapped or diseased by making contact with the bedraggled beggar. Years later, when the lad saw a picture of Walt Whitman, with his shaggy unkempt beard and hair, he was certain that the poet must have been one of the hobos walking the alley of those boyhood years.

The calamity was unbelievable.

What had gone wrong? How could this happen to America? How could this happen to families who had worked hard, saved religiously, and tried to be good citizens and neighbors?

While Americans were stunned by the sudden crash of 1929, they were numbed by the decade-long duration of the Depression. Most unfathomable was the hard reality that despite valiant efforts—families scraping to make ends meet, fathers walking miles in search of any kind of a job, government creating massive new programs and public-works jobs to alleviate the misery—nothing really worked. In 1939, 17.2 percent of America's workers remained unemployed.

Under New Deal policies, only war would put America back to work again.

While America suffered, Europe disintegrated.

The wounds of World War I continued to fester and weaken the continent. The Depression dried up America's loans to Europe, and U.S. tariff walls impeded commerce. In January, 1933, Adolf Hitler promised glory to a nation with 43 percent of its working people unemployed, pulled Germany out of the League of Nations, and put Germans back to work building roads and cars and guns.

Gambling that Europe would not resist, Hitler occupied Austria, Czechoslovakia, and Poland. Emboldened, he continued to march: into Denmark, Norway, the Netherlands, Belgium, Luxembourg, and France which, by June 1940, had been crushed in a month's time. Having won his gamble that Western Europe would fall before his Blitzkrieg, and confident that Britain would surrender under the incessant pounding of his Luftwaffe, Hitler took his most fateful gamble: On June 21, 1941, he suddenly turned eastward against the Soviet Union. At first the Hitler gamble paid off, but as

American Lend-Lease aid began to flow into Russia, and as German forces drove more deeply into that vast landmass, the more obvious it became that, in turning eastward, Hitler had grossly misjudged the Russian willingness to resist and the American capacity to rally herself from the crumbling of her once mighty economic house. As Hitler began too late to realize, America was by no means finished; beneath the economic rubble of the 1930's her firm foundations had endured.

Although still mired in economic depression in the autumn of 1941, on the eve of a new conflagration that would soon envelop the world, America was stronger than she or others knew.

Despite the ravages of a seemingly unending economic catastrophe, despite the doubts about her own abilities, despite the near destruction of confidence in government, despite the fears for the future of her children, there remained beneath the surface a resilience that would not die. America had left the comfortable shores of sure belief, had stood upon a shaky bridge of doubt, but had refused to cross over into the land of disbelief.

While America had been badly crippled by the collapse of her economic and governmental institutions, other life-support systems, some uniquely American, had kept the country breathing. The family, supported by neighbors, church, and community, had provided the faith, hope, love, and security that sustained Americans through those most insecure of times. At his thirtieth high-school class reunion, one man, reflecting on growing up during the Depression, put it this way: "We didn't know how bad off we were because everyone was in the same boat and we all cared about each other. We had nothing but each other. Our parents made our childhood days happy by letting us know how much they loved us and by spending time with us. Love and time were all they had—and they gave them to us, probably more so than I do with my children today. They hid their problems from us, saving them for late-night talks behind closed doors after we were tucked in bed. I didn't realize how bad things were until years later."

Relatives moved in together, and old folks, instead of being shunted off to nursing homes, remained part of the ebb and flow of family life.

People made their own fun by visiting nearby friends or relatives, by playing cards or games such as dominoes and Pick Up Sticks. Families would religiously gather at the same times each evening to laugh at Amos and Andy or Lum and Abner, to follow the exploits of the Lone Ranger almost as if he might ride out of the sky at any moment to set things right for them, and to shiver with patriotism at the opening strain of the national anthem. The hit songs of the Depression years (e.g., "Some Day I'll Find You," "Wrap Your Troubles in Dreams," "It Happened in Monterey," "Let's Have Another Cup of Coffee," "When the Moon Comes Over the Mountain," etc.) showed that the nation still could believe in faith, hope, love, and romance.

Part of that belief stemmed from far beyond the families and communities of the day. It was rooted in the American system. Freedom was a commodity that did not crash on Black Friday in 1929. It was a faith, a spirit, a tradition, that had made America different from the very beginning. Some in those dark Depression days were descendants of the early pioneers who had hacked their way through the wilderness, fighting Indians, animals, pestilence, and the elements to make a better life for themselves, or at least for their children. They had known what freedom was and had passed that feeling on to their descendants. Others had fled Europe or had heard the stories from their parents or grandparents, and they too knew what made America different. In 1774, Michel de Crèvecoeur, a Frenchman who settled in America, had written:

> What then is this American, this new man? Two hundred miles formerly appeared a great distance, it is now but a trifle. He no sooner breathes American air than he sets out on projects he never would have thought of in his own country. Here individuals of all nations are melted into a new race of men, whose labors and posterity will one day cause great changes in the world. . . . The American is a new man who acts upon new principles and entertains new ideas.

Rather than being diluted, his words had been strengthened by the challenges of the intervening years. The taming of a nation, the clash of a Civil War, the test of American leadership on the blood-drenched soil of Europe, and the agony of economic deprivation had tempered both the nation's mettle and the excesses of the easy prosperity that had led it into darkness.

As Hitler prepared to plunge the world into a long night of hell, America was ready to emerge, battered but not broken; weakened materially, but strengthened spiritually; still floundering collectively, but dedicated individually. America had survived the Great Depression. The tears of a million mothers had watered the flowering of their sons and daughters, and the sweat of their fathers had transmuted them into steel.

II

CONFIDENCE REGAINED

Destiny is not a matter of chance, it is a matter of choice. It is not a thing to be waited for, it is a thing to be achieved.
—WILLIAM JENNINGS BRYAN

ON SUNDAY AFTERNOONS, if you were under twelve, you could see a double-feature movie for only eleven cents. One penny went to pay an amusement tax, but nothing was amusing one Sunday afternoon in December 1941, when a group of children walked out of the dark theater into the brilliant sunlight of an uncommonly warm winter day. While they had been cheering Gene Autry and booing Humphrey Bogart, their world had changed forever.

Pearl Harbor had been bombed.

Eight U.S. battleships had been destroyed and other ships damaged; six air bases had been hit and most of their planes wiped out as they sat unattended on the ground; 2,800 Americans had died in the sneak attack in which the Japanese had lost only 55 men, as Japan's special envoy, Saburu Kurusa, sat in the U.S. State Department explaining that America stood in the way of peace in East Asia.

Confirming the real Japanese message of death, Tokyo quickly followed through later that afternoon with a formal declaration of war on America. On Monday, the United States and Britain responded by declaring war on Japan. Within three days, Germany and Italy declared war on America, and Congress reciprocated. America was in it again. A three-and-one-half-year struggle for survival had begun. Pearl Harbor had proved that, this time, the two oceans were not impassable moats. This time it was not going to be a war to "make the world safe for democracy." It was kill or be killed. No imagination was needed to translate newsreel pictures of German soldiers marching through the Arc de Triomphe into visions of their marching up Pennsylvania Avenue. So, once again, America gritted her teeth, set her jaw, and dug in to do what had to be done.

General Douglas MacArthur, saddled with meager forces in the Philippines, withdrew southward to Australia and began to build his new Southwest Pacific Command.

First in the battle of the Coral Sea in May 1942, and a month later at Midway Island, 1,149 miles from Pearl Harbor, America made her stand. A Japanese invasion force, planning to use Midway as a base for air raids on Hawaii, was met and defeated. The destruction of four of its aircraft carriers and nearly three hundred of its planes cleared the skies under which America could begin the bloody drive toward Tokyo. As American forces battled from island to island, names such as Wake, Guadalcanal, Tarawa, Saipan, Kwajalein, Guam, Iwo Jima, and Okinawa became household words, both feared and revered. At Iwo Jima alone, U.S. Marines paid the price of 5,931 killed and 17,382 wounded as they took Japan's most heavily fortified outpost, desperately needed to protect American bombers flying from Saipan and Guam, and as a safe landing place for those that got in trouble. But take it they did, as America bombed and bayoneted her way back across the Southwest Pacific toward Tokyo.

In Europe, meanwhile, Britain had become the staging area for the American-led Allied thrust toward Berlin as British and American forces fought their way across North Africa, through Sicily, and up the Italian boot while the Russians drove the Germans back to the borders of Poland.

Achieving what may well have been beyond the skills of even Washington, Grant, or Napoleon, General Dwight David Eisenhower held together a temperamental, strong-willed, multinational command, forging the successful strategy for freeing a tortured Europe.

On the morning of June 6, 1944, the largest invasion force the world had ever seen crossed the English Channel and left over 10,000 casualties on the sands of Normandy as the awful price of beginning the new march toward Paris. As those forces slashed their way across France, another 1.5

million troops were poured in behind them. By September
they had entered Germany, and on March 24, 1945, they
had crossed the Rhine. On April 30, as Russian guns con-
verged on Berlin, Hitler, deep in his bunker, put his gun to
his head and cheated the hangman's noose.

Within a week, the Third Reich surrendered uncondi-
tionally. In early August, mushroom clouds over Hiroshima
and Nagasaki finally blotted out the Rising Sun. Japan surrendered aboard the battleship *Missouri,* in Tokyo Bay, on
September 2, 1945.

After 1,365 days, it was over. The Axis had been destroyed, but the costs had been crushing.

Of nearly 16 million Allied troops killed in combat,
America had lost nearly 300,000; the Soviet Union, 13.6
million; France, over 200,000; Great Britain, nearly 300,000;
Poland, over 300,000; and China, 1.3 million. Of 4.7 million
Axis troops killed in combat, Germany had lost 3.3 million;
Japan 1.1 million; and Italy 262,000. In addition, nearly 38.6
million civilians had been killed, including 7.7 million in the
Soviet Union, 6 million in Poland, 1.3 million in Yugoslavia,
over a million in China, nearly 600,000 in Germany, 155,000
in Greece, around 300,000 in both Hungary and Estonia,
nearly a half million in Romania, 173,000 in France, 60,000
in Britain, and nearly a million in Japan. Among the dead
were over 6 million Jews who had perished in the world's
most monstrous program of systematic human extermina-
tion. All together, nearly 60 million had died.

One of them was Rudy Knezavitch. He was so tough that in
a high-school football game, playing with his arm in a cast,
he collared a runner with his one good arm and broke the
runner's neck. He was smart, too. His older brother was on
his way up, to become a medical doctor. But Rudy was soon
to be on his way up into a Marine gun turret aboard the
battleship *New Mexico,* off the shore of Okinawa. When a
Japanese kamikaze pilot zoomed in on him, just after sunset
on May 12, 1945, all he could do was watch. The suicide
plane crashed into the turret, engulfing it in flames. Nothing
was left but charred remains.

He might have been a great coach, or a writer, or a

doctor, or a good husband and father. He might have been the man to save a city or turn a child away from crime. But what might have been was not to be, for him and sixty million others whose lives were forfeit to the madness of war. As it was with them, so would it be also for uncounted millions in decades yet to come—children who would never be born because potential fathers had been struck down; women whose lives would be forever scarred because sons or husbands lay in distant graves. That atrocity called war had robbed not only those whose lives it had claimed but also those whose lives it had blighted or had kept locked in barren wombs.

Would the dust of sixty million lives taken in the world's most epic struggle to free the spirits and bodies of billions of their fellowmen be scattered for nothing across the sands of time? Or would they feed the earth so fields of humanity might flourish anew to produce better men and women who, thinking and feeling, would have the wisdom to know what was right, and the strength not to do what was wrong?

The military costs of World War II exceeded a trillion dollars, and the destruction of property approached another trillion. The Allies' direct military cost exceeded $676 billion, of which America spent over $317 billion. Germany spent almost $273 billion of the $423 billion Axis expenditure. In 1981 dollars the costs would have to be multiplied five times.

Once again, America made the difference. The United States supplied itself and its Allies with $186 billion in munitions. In 1941, America had 1,157 combat planes and a similar number of tanks. By 1945, America had produced 297,000 planes, 86,338 tanks, 17.4 million rifles and sidearms, 64,500 landing craft, a quadrupling of the U.S. merchant fleet and a tenfold increase in navy firepower.

Under Lend-Lease, America transferred $49 billion to her Allies, 60 percent of which went to Great Britain and 22 percent to the Soviet Union. By mid-1944, Allied production, led by America, was four times the Axis production. Nearly thirteen million Americans worked in war industries to feed the Allied juggernaut.

But it was two bombs, dropped two days apart from two B-29s in August of 1945, which brought the war to a sudden halt. Seventy thousand died at Hiroshima. Another sixty thousand were wiped out when the second atomic bomb was dropped on Nagasaki. The two apocalyptic clouds rained a temporary fallout of reason and restraint on a world conditioned to death. The world had quickly forgotten that eighty thousand had died in Tokyo the previous March when conventional incendiary bombs, dropped from B-29s, had blackened sixteen square miles. Millions of Japanese civilians had been left unprotected and starving after the Allied blockade of Japan had cut off food and fuel. Two atomic bombs had exorcised the demons of war and given Japan a new chance at life.

First in Europe, then in Asia, America had crushed her enemies and saved her Allies. America stood alone—preeminent in the world.

No longer did America alone believe she was special: The world believed!

On the morning of September 2, 1945, when Mamoru Shigemitsu, the Japanese foreign minister, dragged his heavy wooden leg up the gangplank of the battleship *Missouri*, anchored eighteen miles out from the port of Yokohama, he expected MacArthur, the great Allied conqueror, to extract his just revenge.

Shigemitsu and the other members of the Japanese surrender delegation were surprised and skeptical when the general announced: "It is my firm purpose, in the tradition of the countries I represent, to proceed in the discharge of my responsibilities with justice and tolerance. . . ." They heard their conqueror acknowledge their emperor as a symbol of their continuity rather than as a target for destruction as the symbol of a defeated nation. With starvation threatening millions of Japanese, MacArthur ordered his forces to stop consuming local food so it could be available to the desperate civilian population. Along with supplies rushed from the Pacific Theater for American Forces, 3.5 million tons of food were provided through army kitchens for the Japanese people.

General MacArthur set forth America's occupation policy in striking clarity:

> First destroy the military power. Punish war criminals. Build the structure of representative government. Modernize the constitution. Hold free elections. Enfranchise the women. Release the political prisoners. Liberate the farmers. Establish a free labor movement. Abolish police oppression. Develop a free and responsible press. Liberalize education. Decentralize the political power. Separate church from state.

Between 1945 and 1950, General Douglas MacArthur, acting for America, gave the world and posterity the most brilliant, constructive, successful occupation ever imposed by a conquering nation upon a vanquished foe. Exercising restraint, MacArthur brought only twenty-five major war criminals to trial. Each was found guilty, and seven were executed, including Tojo, the wartime prime minister. Hundreds of minor war criminals were tried, some given prison sentences, and many prohibited from holding public office, thereby paving the way for the introduction of democracy in Japan. Retained as a symbol, the emperor renounced his own divinity. The constitution was radically amended to place power in the Diet, a two-chamber legislative body of representatives elected by the people. A Supreme Court and lesser courts were created, following the American principle of separation of powers. Local governments with elected officials were also created. Women were given the vote, and thirteen million of them went to the polls in 1946 to help approve the new constitution and reject an overwhelming percentage of the prewar politicians standing for election in favor of a younger and more diverse group of candidates. Thirty-eight women were elected to the 466-member Diet in an election in which over 75 percent of the eligible voters turned out. Democracy was beginning to work.

The constitution provided for a bill of rights. American educators were brought to Japan to replace the centralized and propagandized educational system with a decentralized, modernized system. American tax experts were flown in to devise a taxing and budgeting system that provided fairness, stimulated productivity, and promoted a balanced budget. Stock in major corporations taken at fair market value from the handful of families who controlled it was sold to the public to create a free-enterprise economy. Labor unions were encouraged so workers would have an independent voice. Giant estates were purchased from their landlords and sold to tenant farmers to create an agricultural middle class. In the first three years of occupation, seventy million Japanese were vaccinated for smallpox, twenty-three million for tuberculosis. Diphtheria cases were reduced by 86 percent, dysentery was almost eliminated, and cholera stamped out. U.S. medical officers estimated that the health measures saved two million lives.

America and her statesman-general had granted the gifts of compassion and democracy to a defeated nation. While the symbol of the emperor, in the form of Hirohito, gave new Japan a continuity with its past, the symbol of America, in the form of MacArthur, provided a vision for the future. In defeat, the Japanese found a future more fertile than its fondest victory could have produced. America saved Japan from victory. America gave Japan a future.

As fifteen million American war veterans headed for home and jobs that might not materialize, some economists predicted a depression. Plants were suddenly idled by canceled war contracts. Returning GIs discovered that their 1945 dollars bought about 36 cents less than those of 1940. But as America braced for a return to the unemployment lines of 1939, people starved for consumer goods began to buy. Plants converted from tanks to cars, from GI boots to dress shoes, from walkie-talkies to radios, from fatigues to fashionable clothing, from mosquito netting to lingerie. Pent-up demand was not limited to products. Clergymen worked overtime tying couples together. Women walked out of factories and back into their homes. Older workers belatedly retired. Many GIs started their own businesses, or took advantage of the GI Bill to enroll in higher education. Banks expanded loans by 50 percent. Price and rent controls were lifted. Housing starts shot up. Postwar America boomed.

Europe was a different story. Bombed-out cities and burnt-out people struggled to survive. Millions faced starvation. One of the first, most humane acts of the United Nations after its San Francisco formation of April 25, 1945, was the creation of the United Nations Relief and Rehabilitation Administration (UNRRA). Within a year UNRRA had distributed over six million tons of food throughout Western Europe. Most of it came from America. When UNRRA was disbanded in 1947, many individual countries tried to take up the slack. None did more than America, where the CARE program was created, featuring voluntary, standardized packages of army surplus rations and customized packages of food and clothing for specific recipients.

Hundreds of thousands of such packages flowed to Europe in what became the largest single voluntary charitable effort in the history of the world. Never before had a victorious people, who had been savagely attacked, responded with such magnanimity, proving anew that America was special, America was different.

One of the CARE packages was received by sixteen year old Helmut Kohl and his family. Thirty-five years later he related how much it had meant: "We had nothing to eat and America put food on our table. The first suit I ever owned was a used American suit that came out of that CARE package. I shall never forget what America did for me and my family. And throughout Germany, there are probably six million Germans who feel as I do, because America helped us when we had nothing." As he related it, in 1980, Helmut Kohl was the chairman of the Christian Democratic Union, the largest political party in West Germany, and within two years he would be elected chancellor of the Federal Republic of Germany. But he never forgot that his first suit came from America.

Despite the massive voluntary efforts by Americans to help the people of a ravaged Europe, the continent lacked the strength to lift itself up off its knees.

Once again, guided by both heart and head, America dug into her pockets. Speaking at Harvard on June 5, 1947, Secretary of State George C. Marshall called for aid to help rebuild Europe—not only to feed and clothe it, but to provide it with the tools to become a self-sufficient contributor to the economy of the Free World. Later that year, Congress approved, and President Truman signed into law, the so-called Marshall Plan, a program for the expenditure of $13 billion to help Europe help itself. Over those next four years, the money was divided among Austria, Belgium, Greece, Iceland, Ireland, Norway, Portugal, Sweden, Denmark, France, Germany, Italy, Luxembourg, the Netherlands, Turkey, and Britain. The aid was provided in the form of commodities: raw materials and semifinished products, 33 percent; food, feed and fertilizer, 29 percent; machinery and vehicles, 17 percent; fuel, 16 percent; other, 5 percent. Approximately 70 percent of the goods were purchased in the United States, giving further impetus to American prosperity. Within a few years Europe was again producing, wobbling to its feet with the support of America.

Lest any nation doubt the prodigious economic strength of America, she proceeded to achieve in the skies what no other country could accomplish even on the ground. When on April 1, 1948, the Soviet Union threw up a land blockade around West Berlin, America, aided by Britain, began an incredible airlift operation in which 2.3 million tons of food, coal, and other vital products were flown into the city to keep it alive. For eighteen dramatic months, over 277,000 flights landed, often at sixty-second intervals, day and night, to unlock the Soviet stranglehold on two million West Berliners. On September 30, 1949, the frustrated Russian Bear grudgingly released his grip on the city and Western Europe sighed in relief. America, once again, had proved her ability to meet an awesome challenge.

America's former enemies had learned that they, too, could believe in America.

At dawn on the morning of June 25, 1950, two hundred thousand North Korean Communist troops swarmed southward across the 38th parallel dividing North from South Korea, armed with heavy artillery and Soviet tanks. South Korea's fewer than one hundred thousand troops, armed only with light weapons, were quickly routed. The United Nations Security Council urged its member states to assist South Korea, and on June 27, President Truman committed the United States to a major land war in Asia. The U.S. Constitution which states in Section 8 that "The Congress shall have power to . . . declare war" was circumvented by calling the effort a UN police action, even though American men were doing 98 percent of the fighting, bleeding, and dying, while American taxpayers at home were bearing 98 percent of the financial burden of the war.

Some claimed the war was unconstitutional, and although most Americans accepted the decision of their government and men drafted into service grudgingly complied, the seeds of doubt and distrust had been planted.

Few noted that on the same day Truman ordered U.S. forces into Korea, the first thirty-five U.S. military advisers were ordered to South Vietnam.

MacArthur devised a daring strategy to attack behind enemy lines at Inchon, despite treacherous tides which made such a feat seem impossible. American troops landed without a single fatality and quickly retook Seoul, the capital of South Korea. By early fall, American forces, numbering 140,000, along with 3,073 assorted United Nations troops, turned northward and drove across the 38th parallel into North Korea. On October 20, Pyongyang, the capital of North Korea, fell, MacArthur's brilliant strategy had worked. America had done it again. Only mopping up was left, or so it seemed.

As intelligence reports indicated a buildup of Red Chinese forces north of the Yalu River which formed the boundary between North Korea and Red China, General MacArthur received orders from Washington not to follow enemy planes in hot pursuit across the Yalu. He was also directed not to bomb hydroelectric power plants on the North Korean side of the Yalu, North Korea's major supply center at Najin, twenty miles from the border, or the Yalu bridges over which the Chinese Army could enter North Korea. In early November the Chinese quietly moved their troops across the bridges into North Korea, and on November 27, two Chinese armies of almost a million men struck in force. America may have won the first war in Korea against the North Koreans, but a new and different war, against Red China, had begun.

MacArthur clashed with the Truman administration over

the conduct of the expanded war. In a letter to Joseph Martin, Republican Leader of the House of Representatives, MacArthur advocated use of Generalissimo Chiang Kai-shek's Nationalist forces against Communist China, and closed with a politically inflammatory sentence: "There is no substitute for victory."

For the President, it was the last straw. On April 11, 1951, he relieved the general of his command. His right to do so was unquestionable. But the administration's restrained prosecution of a questionable war would ultimately extract a crushing price from America. While a military stalemate bled both sides for another twenty-seven months, negotiators at Panmunjom droned on toward an inconclusive truce. It was deep irony that after MacArthur was relieved, in August 1951, Washington lifted the ban against bombing Najin, the vital supply center in North Korea. By July 27, 1953, when the truce was signed, 33,629 Americans had been killed and 105,785 wounded.

Almost two thirds of the U.S. casualties occurred after MacArthur was relieved of command. His view that the war could have been brought to a speedy, successful conclusion by unleashing American and Chinese Nationalist forces is still being debated, but what cannot be debated are the hard historical events that followed the Korean War: America and the United Nations capitulated on their commitment for a united Korea. Armed aggression bought Communism half a loaf. For the first time, America was unwilling to use its muscle to win. General Mark Clark, the commander who signed the truce, later wrote: "I gained the unenviable distinction of being the first U.S. Army Commander in history to sign an armistice without victory." The lesson was not lost on the Communist world. Stalemate today may produce capitulation tomorrow.

At home, the American people, disturbed by a war whose legality was questionable and purpose unclear, were perplexed and dismayed at the outcome. America was not invincible. America could be stopped on the battlefield. America could be toyed with at the bargaining table. And American prisoners of war, for the first time, could be persuaded to remain with their captors rather than return home at the end of the war. Something was going wrong in America. A new wave of doubt and disbelief slowly settled in across the land.

Early in 1950, Alger Hiss, former director of special political affairs in the State Department and a protégé of Secretary of State Dean Acheson, was convicted of perjury for telling a federal grand jury that he never passed secret State Department documents to Whittaker Chambers in 1938 for a Soviet spy ring. When, following Hiss's conviction, Acheson announced, "I do not intend to turn my back on Alger Hiss," Senator Joseph McCarthy (R-Wis.) sprang to the attack. Speaking before a woman's Republican club in Wheeling, West Virginia, he waved papers on which he said he had the names of fifty-seven Communists or sympathizers working in Acheson's State Department.

Failing to produce evidence to back his claims, by the spring of 1954 Joe McCarthy was thoroughly discredited. Nevertheless, he opened televised hearings into alleged Communist influence in the army, publicly accusing a teletype operator at Fort Monmouth of being a Communist. When she denied it, the only evidence he could produce was her own testimony that a friend had given her a copy of the *Daily Worker*, the Communist newspaper.

McCarthy, by his reckless, unsubstantiated charges, had twisted a serious national security problem into a sad caricature. He became the issue.

Senator Ralph Flanders (R-Vt.) introduced a Resolution of Censure against McCarthy, the committee investigating the charges, under Chairman Arthur Watkins (R-Utah), recommended "condemnation," and on December 2, 1954, the U. S. Senate voted to condemn Joseph McCarthy. The vote was sixty-seven to twenty-two with twenty-two Republicans, forty-four Democrats, and one Independent for, and twenty-two Republicans and no Democrats against. For only the sixth time in the history of the Republic, the U. S. Senate had condemned or censured one of its own. McCarthy, ill and alcoholic, faded from view. Within a few years he would be dead, but the bitter legacy he left America cast doubt on the credibility of the U. S. Congress and injured the legitimate efforts of those who sought to protect the nation against subversion.

Although Eisenhower's election as President brought a soothing calm to the nation, it was jolted in the early evening of June 19, 1953, when 3,000 volts of electricity shot through the bodies of Julius and Ethel Rosenberg, convicted of giving atomic secrets to the Soviet Union. A mythology of innocence enveloped the Rosenbergs, even though incriminating testimony was given against them by several witnesses, including Ethel's brother and sister-in-law.

After conviction, the Rosenbergs had twenty-seven months of legal review, including seven hearings before the Supreme Court, and were offered commutation of their sentences if they would cooperate in exposing Soviet espionage operations in the United States. They refused.

Defeated on the ground in Korea, America was also defeated in its efforts to protect its most sensitive scientific knowledge. Americans shook their heads in disbelief. Soon the Soviets would be boasting openly of their presumed superiority.

At a reception at the Polish Embassy in Moscow in November 1956, Soviet Communist Party Chairman Nikita Khrushchev announced to the Americans present: "Whether you like it or not, history is on our side. We will bury you." His braggadocio was scoffed at as the puffery of an ignorant peasant dictator. Within the year, however, he got America's attention. On October 4, 1957, the Soviet Union rocked the world with its announcement of having launched the first spacecraft. While America slept, the Soviets had captured space. They named their vehicle *Sputnik Zemli*, Little Travel Companion of the Earth. The 21-inch-diameter sphere, weighing 184 pounds, rocketed 587 miles into space and then sped, 18,000 miles per hour, around the globe. Sputnik continued to orbit the earth until January 4, 1958, when it reentered the earth's atmosphere and burned up according to plan. The ninety-day space feat chilled the world. The Soviet missile and space achievement put the USSR ahead of America and suggested that manned bombers might be obsolete. An atomic-bomb-shelter craze hit the nation. America was shaken. America had been defeated on the ground in Korea. America had been defeated in protecting its vital secrets at home. Now America was being defeated in space. Doubts sank deeper into the American psyche.

While the Communist world toasted its triumph in space, a troubled America watched federal troops march into Little Rock, Arkansas, to enforce school integration. Black citizens were calling in the American promise of equal opportunity, and the nation was squirming. Sit-ins and civil-rights marches filled the television screens in the months and years ahead. Every legitimate demand to perfect the American dream exposed America's imperfections. What was right was taken for granted and what was wrong was magnified. Decent Americans recoiled when Emmett Louis Till, a thirteen-year-old black youth, was lynched in Mississippi on the accusation that he had whistled at a white woman. Protest rallies were organized across the country, many by bona fide civil-rights groups, and some by Communist-front organizations to fan the hatreds of both blacks and whites. At the Soldiers and Sailors Memorial Hall in Pittsburgh, Pennsylvania, three thousand people jammed the auditorium on a Sunday afternoon to call for justice. Known Communists and sympathizers marched outside carrying signs fomenting hatred; inside, their counterparts sprinkled through the crowd and initiated applause at each inflammatory phrase. A legitimate cause was being manipulated to divide the country. Sandpaper was being rubbed on an American sore.

As a counterintelligence agent assigned to cover domestic intelligence and, specifically, District Five of the Communist Party, U.S.A., I was present at the Pittsburgh rally and was familiar with known and suspected Communists and sympathizers in the area. I witnessed responsible protest being contorted to weaken, rather than strengthen the country.

The next day I exercised my right as an American citizen and mailed my check to join the moderate NAACP. White America had to care, or the sting of radicals would poison the nation.

Within a few months, Rosa Parks, a black woman in Montgomery, Alabama, refused to give her seat on a bus to a white man, and out of the ensuing bus boycott rose the voice of Martin Luther King, Jr., sweeping across America in a call for equality. Bus segregation was declared unconstitutional, followed by the passage by Congress of the first civil-rights bill in this century. Each gain brightened the glare on other wrongs and encouraged further action.

When John and Jackie Kennedy and their presidential entourage swept into the White House on January 20, 1961, the nation glittered. The seemingly stodgy blandness of the Eisenhower era was replaced with looks and grace and style. JFK flashed into the American mind like a meteor's blip on a screen of discontent. Fresh and bright, he carried the solutions to the nation's problems in his smile and walk. He would "get America moving again." But on this Inauguration Day, nothing moved. A bitter snowstorm had hit the nation's capital and when the D.C. government made an emergency requisition for hundreds of snow shovels and offered temporary jobs to clear the streets and sidewalks, there were few takers. The snow seemed to melt as a warm euphoria enveloped the capital, as it was overrun by a new generation of what author David Halberstam was to mockingly call "the best and the brightest." The nation's pulse picked up as the frenetic action of "new frontiersmen" energized even the sleepiest old bureaucracies with new programs, new solutions, new people—and new problems.

Washington's society swirled in elegance, unaware of the fateful judgments that were setting in motion the first major decision of their glamorous new President. As the cherry trees blossomed around the Tidal Basin, JFK grudgingly approved a plan for a non-U.S. military invasion of Castro's Cuba. A brigade of Cuban exiles, supported by the CIA, was to land on a deserted beach, drive inland, rallying the Cuban people, and overthrow Castro. They landed on April 17, and as the cherry blossoms around the Washington Tidal Basin, fragile and exposed, were being blown to the winds, the brigade was being scattered with equal ease by Castro's forces.

The Kennedy administration had given halfhearted approval to an ill-conceived plan. No one was fooled by Cuban exiles or unmarked planes. The world knew America had supported an invasion of Cuba and failed. Once again, America was humiliated. A banana-republic dictator ninety miles off the U.S. shore had won. The principle of limited commitment, tested and found wanting in Korea, had been further diluted and applied to Cuba. The result was consistent: another U.S. failure. The new President took the blame and America supported him, but the mantle of invincibility that once cloaked America was torn, if not tattered, in the eyes of its citizens, and its friends and enemies around the world.

Emboldened by its own success and America's lack of will, the Soviet Union, in the autumn of 1962, commenced the installation of missiles in Cuba, posed to shower nuclear warheads upon the United States. On October 22, President Kennedy announced that he had definitive photographic evidence of that condition, ordered an air and naval blockade of Cuba, and made clear that if Soviet ships or planes tried to run the blockade they would be destroyed. For six days the world held its breath until Khrushchev backed down. The missiles were removed and their bases were dismantled. Firmness worked. American prestige rose and Kennedy, basking in the glow of successful gunboat diplomacy, was able to negotiate a nuclear test-ban treaty with Khrushchev the following July.

On August 28, 1963, Martin Luther King, Jr., captivated two hundred thousand people in front of Washington's Lincoln Memorial and two hundred million people in front of television throughout America and around the world: "I have a dream that this nation will rise up and live out the true meaning of its creed, 'We hold these truths to be self-evident that all men are created equal.'"

The President would not live out another three months. The promise of the New Frontier died in Dallas on November 22. Kennedy's legislative program had been enthusiastically applauded, then conspicuously ignored, even though his own party comfortably controlled both Houses of Congress.

During his three-year presidency, JFK submitted 1,054

proposals to Congress, but only 414, or 39 percent, became law. The authoritative publication, *Congressional Quarterly,* commented on his 1963 record: "The final approval score was the lowest in the last ten years." Rhetoric had set off fireworks in the sky, while reality had fizzled on the ground. Shortly, Lyndon Johnson would achieve the legislative victories that Kennedy had sought.

When Lyndon Johnson became President there were 15,000 U.S. troops in South Vietnam and 3.9 million Americans out of work; the unemployment rate was 5.4 percent; the inflation rate was 1.6 percent. Johnson bullied and begged, cajoled and promised, to push a flurry of his Great Society programs through Congress. His Omnibus Civil Rights Bill banned discrimination. His War on Poverty was designed to wipe out privation. His new Voting Rights Act aimed at opening the doors to the political process for minorities. His Water Quality Act was targeted to eliminate pollution from the nation's rivers, lakes, and drinking-water supplies while also eliminating water shortages. His Medicare program tried to provide better medical care for senior citizens. They were all his programs, and he would take care of everyone. Johnson seemed driven, compulsively, to be everyone's protector; to outdo the eastern establishment with whom he reciprocated a barely disguised hatred. He promised and produced major civil rights legislation and within a year, almost perversely, Watts, the black ghetto district of Los Angeles, burned.

While Johnson fought his social war at home, a real war waged in Southeast Asia. On the night of August 2, 1964, North Vietnamese boats attacked the U.S. destroyer *Maddox* in international waters in the Gulf of Tonkin, off the coast of North Vietnam. This ship sustained minor damage and one of the projectiles that hit it remains in U.S. Navy custody. North Vietnam acknowledged the attack. Two nights later, a sister destroyer, the U.S.S. *Turner Joy,* also in international waters near the *Maddox,* picked up sonar signals of similar boats nearby. Both ships physically sighted torpedoes passing nearby and returned the fire. No hits were witnessed. Johnson rushed to the Congress a resolution that "approves and supports the determination of the President, as Commander-in-Chief, to take all necessary measures to repel any armed attack against the forces of the United States and prevent further aggression."

On August 7, the House approved the resolution 416 to 0, and the Senate approved it 88 to 2. Only Senators Wayne Morse (D-Ore.) and Ernest Gruening (D-Alaska) voted against it. Both were defeated in the next election, although other unrelated issues also worked against them.

The Gulf of Tonkin Resolution became Johnson's legal justification for committing the United States to the war. Scores of members of Congress would later plead that it was not their intention to thrust America into the Vietnamese War, but only to approve defending U.S. forces against unprovoked attack. But the words were clearly open-ended. They not only approved "necessary measures to repel any armed attack . . . ," they also gave Johnson their blessing to "prevent further aggression." That could mean whatever Johnson wanted it to mean. Never mind that the Constitution still said that only Congress had the power to declare war. Korea had already set the precedent. America, having already lost its national virginity to an allegedly illegal war, would accept another one more easily. Or so Johnson thought.

By 1965, 184,300 American troops were in Vietnam. The number swelled to 475,000 in 1967.

On January 30, 1968, with American troop strength at almost half a million, but with half of South Vietnam's troops on leave to celebrate Tet, the lunar new year, North Vietnam violated the holiday cease-fire and launched a major attack into South Vietnam. The Communists shocked the U.S. forces and, more importantly, the news media covering the war, by penetrating into Saigon with attacks upon the Presidential Palace and the U.S. Embassy. Although the Communists were driven back, and although subsequent records clearly showed that, for the Communists, their Tet offensive was a military defeat, it was turned into a psychological victory. Throughout South Vietnam, the Communists lost over three hundred thousand soldiers during the Tet offensive and during the following spring campaign.

The Communists had in fact lost the Tet offensive so badly that it took them two years to rebuild their armies.

But America was told a different story. News stories coming out of Saigon portrayed the Tet offensive as a Communist victory.

On February 8, Senator Robert Kennedy assailed President Johnson's Vietnam War policy as a failure.

On February 27, Walter Cronkite presented a half-hour CBS special on the war, announcing: "It seems now more certain than ever that the bloody experience in Vietnam is to end in a stalemate. . . ."

On March 10, NBC's Frank McGee presented an hour-long special report entitled *Vietnam: A New Year—A New War* in which he proclaimed that the United States was losing the war.

Peter Braestrup, who wrote what was perhaps the definitive work on the U.S. media's coverage of the Vietnam war, observed that "most of the media's 1968 'message' was DISASTER! . . . The first reports made it seem that the foe had succeeded, not failed, in seizing his objective. . . . Newsmen . . . were eager to believe the worst."

In the early 1970's, a Brookings Institution study analyzed CBS coverage of the Vietnam War and found that in 521 evening news reports, CBS was "strongly and persistently critical of U.S. policy and our South Vietnam allies, and was mildly favorable to North Vietnam."

As the media tom-toms in the United States drummed out their message against the war, other voices tried to break the will of American soldiers in the field. Jane Fonda came close to treason when she broadcast a series of propaganda messages while in North Vietnam during July 1972. On July 20, she spoke over Radio Hanoi to the Communist North Vietnamese, and beyond them, to the world:

> I am Jane Fonda. I am in Hanoi. All of us know that you, Vietnamese friends, are fighting for the just cause and the truth. . . . Melvin Laird . . . said that bombing of the dikes may be taking place, but that it is accidental, and it only happens where there is a military target on top of the dikes. . . . The Nixon administration has no right

to bomb the Democratic Republic of Vietnam for any reason whatsoever.

Later that day she broadcast to American troops:

This is Jane Fonda. . . . There is an invasion taking place. It's taking place from the Seventh Fleet, from the aircraft carriers, from Thailand, from Guam, but essentially from the Pentagon and from the White House. You men, it is not your fault. It is in fact tragic to think how you are being so cynically used because the time is coming very soon, it is already halfway there, when people are admitting openly that this is one of the most horrible crimes ever committed by one nation against another. . . .

The next day she broadcast a "Tokyo Rose" type of message to the GI's:

Tonight when you are alone, ask yourselves: What are you doing? Accept no ready answers fed to you by rote from basic training on up, but as men, as human beings, can you justify what you are doing? Do you know why you are flying these missions, collecting extra combat pay on Sunday? The people beneath your planes have done us no harm. They want to live in peace; they want to rebuild their country. They cannot understand what kind of people would fly over their heads and drop bombs on them.*

On March 12, on the heels of the media barrage against the war came the New Hampshire presidential primary in which antiwar Senator Eugene McCarthy surprised the nation by winning 42 percent of the Democratic party's vote.

---

*Miss Fonda did not limit her activities to propagandizing American soldiers in the field. She spoke at rallies to raise bail money for jailed Black Panther leaders. She visited convicted Communist Angela Davis in jail. At a 1971 San Francisco campus rally supporting a group accused of plotting to kidnap the Secretary of State, she raised a clenched fist and announced: "I'm not a do-gooder. I'm a revolutionary woman."

Four days later, Robert Kennedy officially announced his presidential candidacy. By March 30, a Gallup poll reported that Johnson's approval rating had reached an all-time low. The next day Johnson gave a nationwide TV speech in which he announced a partial U.S. bombing pause, repeated his willingness to negotiate a peace settlement, and then dropped his blockbuster: He would not seek reelection. Americans had clearly signaled at the polls and in the polls that they did not believe in their President nor in the war policies he pursued.

Distrusting the government, doubtful of its capacity to win, and soured by racial violence, the nation wanted change. But not the kind that came. Within two weeks, Martin Luther King's message of nonviolence was violently silenced in Memphis, and Robert Kennedy's quest for a new Camelot ended in a pool of blood on a kitchen floor of the Ambassador Hotel in Los Angeles. Vice President Hubert Humphrey won the Democratic presidential nomination but could not bring himself to break completely with his President. Standing not far enough apart from Lyndon Johnson, Hubert Humphrey suffered from the political stoning that a bitter nation inflicted, not only upon its President, but also upon those around him.

So it was that, in January 1969, Richard Milhous Nixon became the thirty-seventh President of the United States. By the time he and Lyndon Johnson rode up Pennsylvania Avenue together for the Nixon inauguration, Johnson's guns and butter policies had fed 30,490 American lives into the Vietnam inferno and tripled the inflation rate to 4.7 percent, a figure considered shockingly high at the time, but nostalgically low compared to what was to come. The false prosperity, caused by spending for war abroad and for the so-called Great Society at home, kept unemployment down around 2.8 million, or 3.7 percent. During Johnson's four-year term federal spending rose from $118.4 billion to $178.8 billion, up 51 percent. Deficits of $40 billion accumulated. The economic pain caused by Johnson's policies had not yet been fully felt, but the social wrenching of a half-fought war in Southeast Asia was shredding the nation.

America's discontent softened into pride when, on July 20, 1969, Colonel Neil Armstrong proved America could compete in space as, on the edge of the moon's Sea of Tranquility, 238,000 miles from home, he took "one small step for a man, one giant leap for mankind."

Four months later, on November 16, America's newfound luster was suddenly tarnished when news broke that some ten thousand miles from home in a South Vietnamese village called My Lai, Lieutenant William Calley took one large step backward for mankind by showing that Americans also could massacre women and children.

Announcing his Vietnamization plan to turn the fighting over to the South Vietnamese, President Nixon started withdrawing U.S. troops in April. U.S. fatalities dropped by two thirds, from 3,184 in the first quarter to 1,164 in the fourth quarter. By November, 68,200 Americans had been shipped home, but that did not stop a quarter-million demonstrators from marching on Washington on the sixteenth of that month. The following year, protests spilled over into antipollution demonstrations. By April 22, 1970, when the first Earth Day occurred, it seemed as if all of America was marching against something. Universities became protest factories against America. Doubt hardened into passionate disbelief. America was rotting. Student chants reflected the disintegrating mood. "Hey, hey, LBJ, how many boys did you kill today," gave way to "Hell no, we won't go."

Although American forces in Vietnam were reduced from 497,000 to 365,000 in 1970, some youths continued to flee to Canada and elsewhere to escape the draft. By year's end it was estimated that 30,000 American deserters and evaders had left the country. In the third quarter of 1970, U.S. deaths dropped to less than one thousand for the first time since 1965. They continued to decline in each quarter of 1971, with sixty-six deaths in the final quarter. By that time, American forces in Vietnam had been reduced to 171,000 and federal spending had increased to $211.4 billion with a 1971 deficit of $23 billion to rekindle the fires of inflation.

The Democratic-controlled Congress demanded action to put out the flames even as it poured on more gasoline in the form of still higher spending. Feeling the political prod to do something, knowing that, historically, wage and price controls did not work, Richard Nixon, nevertheless, imposed them. Republicans in Congress acquiesced. With the 1972 elections looming, a political fix seemed better than an economic cure. Unless America felt good on November 7, 1972, the people held accountable for the nation's economic health would suffer at the polls.

III

FROM DOUBT
TO DISBELIEF

If America forgets where she came from, if the
people lose sight of what brought them along, if
she listens to the deniers and the mockers, then
will begin the rot and the dissolution.
                                    —CARL SANDBURG

RICHARD NIXON'S reelection campaign began effectively with his substantive and impressively orchestrated "Journey for Peace" to Peking in February 1972. That search continued when, three months later, he became the first U.S. President in history to set foot in Moscow. After the signing of a Strategic Arms Limitation Agreement (SALT I), Nixon returned triumphantly to America.

Meanwhile, federal spending spigots were gushing. For the fiscal year which ended June 20, 1972, spending increased by another $15 billion with total spending topping $200 billion for the first time in the nation's history.

President Nixon was winding down a war he didn't start while pouring billions of federal dollars into the economy. Never mind that America would soon suffer its first complete military defeat in history and pay dearly for the profligate election-year spending with the currency of inflation and recession.

When James McCord put the tape, horizontally instead of vertically, across the locks on the stairwell doors leading to the sixth floor of the Watergate Hotel in the early morning hours of June 17, 1972, he unwittingly sealed the doom of the Nixon presidency he was trying to protect. Exposed on both sides of the doors, the horizontally placed tape at the basement level was discovered and removed by Frank Wills, an alert young Watergate security guard. When, about ten minutes later, he discovered that the same door had been reopened and another piece of tape similarly applied, he called Washington's Metropolitan Police and the rest is bitter history.

For Republican members of Congress, Watergate was a nightmare; they had no role in its creation, yet all were affected, and some politically destroyed. "Vinegar Bend" Mizell, for instance, was no dumb jock. He was as effective on Capitol Hill as he had been on the pitcher's mound for the St. Louis Cardinals and Pittsburgh Pirates. Elected to Congress as a Republican from North Carolina in 1968, he earned the respect of his Washington colleagues and was reelected by increasing margins at home. His seat seemed safe. Then the Watergate dike burst, and Republican voters sat out the 1974 elections in disgust. "Vinegar Bend" Mizell and forty-seven of his fellow Republican congressmen were defeated. Even Republicans who survived did so by margins around 10 percentage points below their previous victories. Republicans lost 674 seats in state legislatures as well as nine governorships.

Perhaps no group of elected officials was more vulnerable to the Watergate backlash than the forty-six freshmen Republican members of Congress, many of whom had been swept into office by the 1972 Nixon landslide. Fourteen of them, almost one third of the Freshman Class, were wiped out.

Ironically, it was the GOP Freshman Class upon which the White House had counted as one of its most crucial elements in its battle to preserve the Nixon presidency.

As impeachment proceedings progressed, the White House asked me, as GOP Freshman Class president, if I would help hold the group together in support of the President. My response was that I would try to accurately apprise them of the aggregate attitude, but would protect individual confidentiality.

As the courting process began, I was invited to dine with the President on the presidential yacht *Sequoia* on July 10, 1974. At the dinner table, Mr. Nixon staged a virtuoso performance, with emphasis on his grasp of foreign affairs. So captivating was his detailed understanding of the world's leaders and their countries, his discourses on nuclear arms control and on the causes of inflation that momentarily his guests almost forgot about Watergate—virtually the only national topic not mentioned.

Other members of Congress were courted assiduously at the White House and on Capitol Hill by members of the President's staff.

As the impeachment proceedings approached, White House people were in daily contact with me, sometimes several times a day. On July 17, I advised them that thirty-seven of our forty-six GOP freshmen were leaning toward supporting the President, with nine undecided. I warned them that if the President were to disobey an anticipated Supreme Court ruling to surrender the tapes of presidential conversations to the Judiciary Committee, his support would evaporate—he would be impeached overwhelmingly.

From my dealings with the President and, more significantly, from my discussions with senior colleagues who had known him for many years, it was clear that the moment I might criticize him, publicly or privately, I would be considered an enemy and would become totally ineffectual in recommending any course of action. My advice would count only if I remained a friend at court. I tried to be both sympathetic and factual in my evaluations of the mood of the forty-six Republican freshmen.

In late July, I reached the painful conclusion that, for the good of the country, efforts should be made to persuade the President to resign. Realizing that to offer the recommendation directly would only render me persona non grata at the White House, I decided to let the numbers do the talking. In daily discussions with the White House, generally with William Timmons, the President's assistant for legislative affairs, I reported the freshman count and let the numbers lead to the painful conclusion that the President had no chance of survival. I had no illusions, of course, that my counsel would make or break any decision, but I believed that it would be one of many pieces of intelligence that would contribute to the necessary decision for resignation.

After a meeting of the GOP Freshman Class on July 30, I informed the White House that the President's position was eroding badly, that of the forty-six GOP freshmen, twenty-six would vote to impeach and eleven would vote against it, with nine undecided. I warned, further, that the entire House would probably vote by about 320 to 115 for impeachment, including a majority of Republicans.

When Vice President Gerald Ford asked a group of us for advice, I responded on August 2 with a letter expressing my position and judgment:

> I have made my personal decision to vote for impeachment. I believe the President will be overwhelmingly impeached in the House. Conviction or resignation become real possibilities. . . . Our Party is tainted—wrongfully, but nevertheless, tainted. Should you become President, an unparalleled opportunity exists for a "new beginning." The American people will give you their hearts. . . .

On August 5, 1974, President Nixon released a statement and transcripts covering three recorded conversations between his chief of staff, H. R. Haldeman, and himself. The statement conceded, and the transcripts documented, that on June 23, 1972, six days after the Watergate break-in, the President instructed Haldeman to tell the FBI, "Don't go any further into this case, period." The revelation provided the smoking gun needed to prove that the President had obstructed justice. Some of the most thoughtful, highly respected Republican members of the House saw the revelation as a compelling cause to vote for his impeachment. What had remained of the President's support evaporated almost immediately. I informed the White House that, along with most members of the GOP Freshman Class, I would vote for impeachment, and that in the best interests of the country, the President should resign. Similar advice was flowing in from other longstanding supporters of the President.

Late in the afternoon of August 5, I received a telephone call from Vice President Ford's office saying the Vice President would like to have breakfast with me the following morning. Along with a small group of my Republican colleagues, I joined the Vice President at 8 A.M., August 6, in H-139 of the Capitol, for a breakfast that few of us felt like eating. With tears in his eyes, Gerald Ford softly informed us: "It's all over. The President may resign today." Then he asked for our suggestions. Although I referred briefly to my letter of August 2, it was apparent that, at that moment, he did not need our advice, he needed our reassurance. Clustering around him to shake his hand, grip his arm, or pat his back, we pledged support in the quiet, reverent tones usually reserved for churches or funeral homes. As we dispersed, it seemed as if we were gliding through a terrible dream, awaiting the inevitable. For three days we hung, numbly suspended. Then it was over. On August 9, 1974, Richard Nixon became the first President in American history to resign from office, and Gerald Ford became the first Vice President to become President under such circumstances. The nation had been spared the greater agony of impeachment, and the government could begin to run again.

Later, William Timmons would answer an inquiry about my participation in the efforts leading to the President's resignation by writing:

> To his credit, Mr. Shuster did not exploit his position as a leader of the new Members to gain media attention, as he could have during those explosive days. Because his counsel remained private, reasoned and candid, I feel he was one who played a significant role in that ultimate outcome when the President resigned for what he felt was best for the country.*

While Timmons's words were very kind, as a legislative novice who found himself immersed in a constitutional crisis, I had felt anything but comfortable during those excruciating days.

America had been traumatized by the worst scandal in its history. A President had resigned in disgrace. Within thirty

*Full text in the Appendix.

days he would be granted an unconditional pardon for all crimes that he "committed or may have committed," as Gerald Ford sought to spare the nation from another year or more of terrible drama involving the criminal trial of a former President. He argued, unconvincingly to many, that a nation that had survived three major wars and a great depression, and had just purged itself of its most sordid scandal, could not stand the prosecution of the principal player in the tragedy. By blocking further Watergate bloodletting, however, Gerald Ford damaged his own political future. While the pardon may have helped heal the nation, the giver of the gift paid the price. Two years hence, after America had denied him a presidential term of his own, even he would admit that the pardon had probably made the difference.

Gerald Ford was a rock of integrity, weathered and tested for a quarter of a century in the Congress without ever cracking, or even chipping. He was the Minority Leader when I entered Congress in 1973, and a particular experience I had with him during my first year stands out as a measure of the man.

President Nixon had vetoed the War Powers Bill. For the first time in our nation's history, Congress had passed legislation specifically limiting the war-making powers of a President. No President would be able to send American troops into battle without justifying the action to Congress within forty-eight hours and obtaining congressional approval within sixty days. Like most Presidents before him, Richard Nixon almost instinctively opposed any limitation on his presidential prerogatives. The White House mounted an all-out effort to round up the votes to sustain the President's veto.

I believed deeply that a great constitutional issue was involved: No one but the Congress had the right to commit America to war, and Vietnam had taught us that minor actions had a way of escalating. While I recognized that it may be in the nation's interest for a President to use a small force, such as a marine unit, to restore order to a destabilized area, I believed that there was a vast ethical gap between committing volunteers and committing draftees to battle.

Even a limited commitment should be able to stand the prompt scrutiny of the Congress.

I informed the White House that I would not only vote to override the President's veto but would lobby my forty-five GOP freshmen colleagues and would speak in opposition to the veto. (As it turned out, I was the only freshman to actually participate in the floor debate.)

The House chamber was full and the galleries were packed for the historic vote in the early evening of November 7, 1973. Everyone knew it was too close to call. White House lobbyists had been working members for several days, and were clustered in the hallways around the doors leading to the chamber.

As the debate began, the heavy artillery moved in on me. Gerald Ford was not only our Republican Leader in the House, he was the man who had flown into my district to campaign for me, who had helped me get the committee appointment I wanted. I owed him. And I prided myself on paying my debts. He smiled and nodded for me to sit down beside him. He told me how important it was for us to sustain the President's veto, and how he hoped that Republicans would stick together and give a President of their own party the benefit of the doubt. I replied, painfully, that I knew he needed every vote he could muster. I told him that, if in my mind it was a close call, I would give the President the benefit of the doubt and vote to sustain his veto. I also told him that I had struggled with the issue for several days and that I believed deeply that the War Powers Bill should become law. I grimaced, shook my head, and said: "Jerry, this one is a matter of conscience for me." Gerald Ford put his arm around my shoulder, nodded, and responded: "Bud, you vote your conscience."

The debate moved on as I moved through the chamber working my freshmen colleagues. Later, when it was my turn to speak, I concluded my speech by saying: "I shall vote to override this veto as a matter of conscience, and I only wish that this bill were even stronger in protecting the American people from future wars."

Minutes later, when the vote came, the President's veto was overridden by one vote: twenty-two Republican freshmen had voted to override. The War Powers Bill became the law of the land, but Gerald Ford had demonstrated that, for him, some things were more important than winning.

Despite the cloud cast by the Nixon pardon, Jerry Ford's openness, decency, and simple honesty served to start the mending process for a bitter nation. The wounds, however, were hardly sutured when new blows tore at them. As the October frost was stripping the trees bordering the Tidal Basin, a scantily clad Fanne Foxe leaped from a car into the icy waters, deep-sixing the career of one of the most powerful members of Congress. As the police pulled her out, they discovered, drunk, in the nearby car, the not-so-honorable Wilbur Mills, chairman of the Ways and Means Committee, his face scratched and bleeding. America shook its head in disgust.

Although he won reelection back in Arkansas the following month, Wilbur Mills had already become a political corpse waiting to be buried. As most Americans found comfort in the bosoms of their families for the Thanksgiving weekend, Mills hastened his own political funeral by stumbling onto a Boston burlesque stage to congratulate Fanne Foxe on her latest striptease performance. Four days later, the House Democratic Caucus ousted him from his Ways and Means chairmanship and he entered Bethesda Naval Hospital to be treated for alcoholism and eventually fade from public view.

As America's opinion of her elected officials sank even lower, revelations burst across the nation that the Central Intelligence Agency had engaged in massive illegal domestic spying operations against American citizens. In the spring of 1975, during the Senate hearings into alleged CIA abuses, Senator Frank Church called the CIA a "rogue elephant," but what the American people saw was a pack of rogues in Washington riding the nation into the ground.

Cord Meyer, the highly respected author and intelligence expert, wrote:

"In this case as in so many other instances, the specific findings of the Church Committee were in glaring and direct contrast to the ominous warning of its Chairman, Senator Frank Church (D-Idaho)."

The committee's final report indicated that "the Central Intelligence Agency, in broad terms, is not 'out of control.' " That reassuring conclusion, however, received virtually no coverage compared to the sensational headlines and network news reports which earlier had portrayed America's top intelligence agency as a monster bent on destroying the Bill of Rights. Although most of the charges would eventually fizzle out, another body blow had been delivered to American confidence. It seemed as if there was no one left to trust.

While the Church Committee was neutering America's intelligence agencies, army helicopters, on March 29, 1975, were lifting the last Americans from the roof of the U.S. Embassy in South Vietnam, graphically culminating America's first full military retreat and defeat. Communist jungle fighters hardly out of the nineteenth century had defeated what was supposed to be the world's most powerful nation. All of America was bitter, and half of America seemed pleased at the outcome.

Meanwhile, the nation sank into its worst recession since the 1930's with unemployment hitting 9.2 percent by May. Over presidential vetoes, the Democratic Congress, with its overwhelming two-thirds majority in both Houses, responded with skyrocketing spending—from $324.6 to $365.6 billion, pushing the national debt from $533 to $620 billion—$2,883 for every American.

As 1976 opened, America was reminded that corruption was not confined to Washington. Lockheed Aircraft Corporation was accused of paying $22 million in bribes to sell its planes abroad. Under pressure, Lockheed finally admitted making the skies friendlier over Holland, Japan, and Turkey by bribing high officials of those countries. In the Senate hearing room where the story unfolded, an everybody-does-it attitude made it seem almost respectable; but for most Americans it was just another tale of greed—one more measure of corruption in high places.

Just as Wilbur Mills was demonstrating that not all politicians were totally bad by immersing himself in pro bono Alcoholics Anonymous activities, Congressman Wayne Hays (D-Ohio) was proving that some came pretty close. While his colleagues might have argued over whether he, as chairman of both the House Administration Committee and the Democratic Campaign Committee, was the second or third most powerful member of Congress, few disagreed that he stood in a class by himself as the meanest man in the House.

A faint smile probably came to the faces of many members on both sides of the aisle when, on May 23, 1976, they unfolded their morning papers to read a front-page story that Elizabeth Ray was telling all, that it was all over for the feared and ferocious Mr. Hays. Over the next several days, Elizabeth Ray described in explicit detail how she had been on his government payroll to provide him with sexual favors; that there had been no need for her to have a typewriter, since everyone knew she couldn't type.

Despite the surface atmosphere of sardonic humor in which "I can type" buttons began appearing on female employees on both sides of Capitol Hill, hardworking Hill women seethed at the sexist jokes which unfairly lumped all of Washington's working women with Liz Ray. Yet, to America, Fanne Foxe, Elizabeth Ray, Wilbur Mills, and Wayne Hays made it appear that bacchanalian orgies were played out nightly along the banks of the Potomac. Some members of Congress became reluctant to hire attractive women, regardless of their competence, while America's opinion of her leaders became even further corroded.

Sandwiched between scandals, America took time out to celebrate her two-hundredth birthday. As the tall ships sailed into view of the Statue of Liberty, and as President Ford touched down at Valley Forge for the trip to Independence Hall, people again felt good about America. Unfortunately, the feeling didn't last long.

To avoid a Justice Department investigation, Wayne Hays resigned from Congress on September 1, 1976. But Justice Department investigators looking into congressional wrongdoing would not long be idle. On October 24, Koreagate erupted. *The Washington Post* labeled it "the most sweeping allegations of congressional corruption ever investigated by the federal government." Members of Congress were accused of taking up to $1 million a year in cash and gifts in exchange for voting aid to South Korea. Numbed by a torrent of misdeeds, America shrugged her shoulders and believed the worst.

Tongsun Park was indentified as the central operator who spread his gifts across the city, and Suzi Thompson, an employee in Speaker Carl Albert's office, purportedly linked the Democratic leadership to the scandal. As the Justice Department pressed its own investigation, the House Ethics Committee appointed famed Watergate prosecutor Leon Jaworski to investigate the new charges, and in a burst of sleeve-wearing ethics, the House passed unanimously a meaningless resolution urging South Korea to cooperate with the investigation. Eventually, only Tongsun Park and Richard Hanna, a former member of Congress, were indicted. With no sitting member indicted, what began as "the most sweeping allegations of congressional corruption ever" ended with a few slaps on a few wrists: Two years after the scandal broke, the House finally got around to reprimanding three California Democrats: McFall, Roybal, and C. Wilson.

Although a cloak of disrepute blanketed the House during the Korean scandal, the integrity of one of the newly appointed members of the Foreign Relations Committee, having been tested, shone brightly through the seamy mess. According to sworn testimony, Congressman Larry Winn (R-Kan.) had been handed an envelope by the ambassador from South Korea. Instructed by Winn to open the envelope, a staff member discovered a stack of $100 bills. Refusing to accept the envelope and its bulging contents, Winn immediately directed that it be returned to the Asian donor and, at that moment, joined an unheralded list of public officials, who, when their integrity was directly tested, had proved their vote was not for sale.

After a seventeen-month investigation, the Senate issued a report that recommended no disciplinary action against any of its members. The American people sneered at the outcome. To them it simply proved, once again, that Congress took care of its own. Washington was beneath belief.

It was time to clean up Sodom on the Potomac, and Jimmy Carter stepped forward declaring that he was the outsider to do it. America bought the idea.

America wanted to believe, and Jimmy Carter painted the picture America wanted to see: a small-town farm boy, devoutly religious and patriotic, an outsider who was clean and tough and smart, a soft-spoken family man who cared about the poor, yet understood that budgets had to be balanced and businesses kept profitable—he was all these things and more. Through a carefully contrived prism, the Carter image makers let people see whatever they chose to see. It was a classic case of all things to all people, of something for everyone.

When Gerald Ford left office, inflation was down to 4.8 percent; unemployment, at 7.7 percent, was still declining and interest rates stood at 6 percent.

When, on Inauguration Day, 1977, Jimmy and Rosalynn Carter walked down Pennsylvania Avenue hand in hand, America felt clean again. Here was a President who seemed decent and humble. Here was a leader who acted like an ordinary citizen.

America had wanted to believe in Jimmy Carter, but he let the country down.

Jimmy Carter ran as an outsider and, once elected, never came inside to use the levers of power to strengthen America. As a campaigner, he promised: "I would never increase taxes for the working people of our country. . . ." As President, however, he engineered the largest tax-burden increase in the history of the Republic: up 45 percent—from $357.7 billion in fiscal 1977 to $520 billion in fiscal 1980. As a campaigner, he pledged to "reduce both unemployment and inflation to 4 percent, and balance the federal budget by 1979." As President, however, he gave America 7.4 percent unemployment, 18 percent inflation, and a $59.6 million deficit. With such off-budget items as guaranteed loans by the Federal Financing Bank, the real deficit was $73.8 billion.

As a campaigner, he branded it a "disgrace" that prices had increased 59 percent for bread and hamburger and 13 percent for milk during the eight years in which a Republican was in the White House. He ignored the influence of a Democratic-controlled Congress throughout that period. As President, however, Jimmy Carter, in only four years in office, presided over increases of 100 percent for bread and hamburger, and 22 percent for milk. He invented the Misery Index, the sum of inflation and unemployment, and used its 12 percent figure to castigate Gerald Ford. Four years later, his own Misery Index hit almost 20 percent.

As a campaigner, Jimmy Carter promised to make America proud again. As President he entertained illegal aliens at the White House while his Attorney General prepared indictments against FBI law-enforcement officers accused of warrantless searches against members of the radical Weather Underground.*

As a campaigner, he promised, "I would never give up complete control or practical control of the Panama Canal Zone." As President, he gave it away.

By one count, he made 667 promises and fulfilled fewer than 133, some of which would have been better left unkept.

On January 27, 1977, he made good on his first campaign promise: He pardoned ten thousand draft dodgers. He pleased the left and poured salt into the still festering wounds of those who had obeyed the law.

To symbolize his dedication to energy conservation, he donned a cardigan sweater for a nationally televised fireside chat, inspiring former Secretary of State Henry Kissinger to drolly twit that Carter was the first President to begin his presidency by pulling the wool over his own eyes.

In the cloakrooms, members chortled as they heard the story of how Speaker Thomas P. "Tip" O'Neill was forced to undergo his first private dinner with the President without benefit of his predinner manhattan—a ritual he did not lightly forgo. As, later, the Speaker confided to his friends that things were surely different at the White House, it was obvious that the gregarious, backslapping Irishman from Massachusetts and the born-again farmer-sailor-engineer from Georgia were on different wavelengths.

When the President's right-hand man, Hamilton Jordan,

---

*On April 15, 1982, the two FBI senior officers convicted, Mark Felt and Edward Miller, were granted "full and unconditional pardons" by President Ronald Reagan who stated that they had served the nation and the FBI with "great distinction," adding that "their actions were necessary to preserve the security interests of our country. The record demonstrates that they acted not with criminal intent but in the belief that they had grants of authority reaching to the highest level of government."

refused to give the Speaker satisfactory seats for the Carter inauguration and did not return the Speaker's telephone calls, O'Neill reciprocated by referring to him as "Hannibal Jerkin." In March, the President further endeared himself to Democratic congressional Pooh-Bahs by canceling nineteen water projects without bothering to consult those whose districts would be directly affected. Meanwhile, little slights were magnified, and real affronts were deplored by members who owed nothing to, and felt little for, Jimmy Carter the outsider. By spring 1977, Democrats were wryly complaining to Republican colleagues that they had enjoyed a better shake under Republican presidents.

While Carter preached Chamber of Commerce economics, he peopled his administration with left-wing ideologues. Analyzing his subcabinet and sub-subcabinet appointments, political analysts Richard Scammon and Ben Wattenberg observed: "Ideologues live there—ideologues from every one of the activist movements of the last decade . . . have moved en masse from their ginger groups to large federal offices, controlling massive budgets and armies of bureaucrats."

Shortly after Labor Day, Jody Powell, Carter press secretary and member of the Georgia mafia's inner circle, telephoned Chicago papers with a tip that Illinois Senator Charles Percy, a critic of the financial escapades of Bert Lance, had accepted illegal plane rides in a Bell & Howell corporate plane. Like the gang that couldn't shoot straight, Carter's White House pals hadn't checked, or they would have discovered that Bell & Howell didn't own a plane. The piety pedestal on which Carter had placed himself was beginning to crack. When the Comptroller of the Currency released a report whitewashing the Bert Lance scandal, Carter beamed: "Bert, I'm proud of you." The American people weren't buying it, however, and on September 21, 1977, Bert Lance was forced to resign.

In his first year in office, Jimmy Carter proved that no one worked harder than he. But fourteen-hour days did not guarantee good decisions. Immersion in a sea of details sometimes causes intellectual drowning rather than wisdom. Illustrating this, one of Jimmy Carter's top fund-raisers told how, visiting the White House during the first Carter year, he was escorted into the President's small private office adjacent to the Oval Office, where he found the President behind stacks of papers which covered his desk. Pointing to a massive document containing the Defense budget, the President boasted that he had read it from cover to cover.

Leaving the President, the friend stepped down the hall where Hamilton Jordan, sitting in an uncluttered office behind a clean desk, philosophized about the strategy to be used in the SALT II negotiations. Later, the visitor commented: "On my way back home it hit me. The problem with the Carter presidency was that Jimmy and Ham should trade places. Jimmy was immersed in detail, thinking like an aide, and Ham was focused on strategy, reflecting like a President!"

Carter labeled the federal tax system "a disgrace to the human race," but sent Congress no substantive tax-reform legislation. Rather, he settled for an $18 billion tax cut that only helped offset the massive Social Security tax increase he had pushed through in 1977.

The President made ratification of the Panama Canal Treaties the centerpiece of his foreign policy, and on April 18, the Senate, by one vote, gave him his giveaway. His Senate supporters, however, would pay dearly. Sixteen Democratic senators and three Republican senators who voted for the giveaway were defeated in the elections of 1978, 1979, and 1980.

Andrew Young, Carter's political supporter and UN ambassador, dismayed the nation and damaged his patron when, in July 1978, he told the world there were "hundreds, perhaps even thousands, of political prisoners in the U.S."

On December 15 of that year, Carter handed the Communist world a Christmas gift by canceling America's defense treaty and diplomatic relations with her long-standing Chinese Nationalist ally on Taiwan in favor of recognizing Red China. Selling out that old U.S. friend sent shudders through the Free World. Could any small country count on the United States? In a Harris poll, the American people indicated overwhelmingly that they favored relations with

Mainland China, but not at the expense of withdrawing relations from Taiwan. Carter dangled promises of trade with Red China while, imperiously, he struck down the treaty without consulting Congress. Previously, America had terminated thirty treaties, but always by joint action of the President and the Congress.

With Carter halfway though his presidency, America was getting queasy. In the fall of 1978, the congressional elections sent a message the Democrats didn't want to hear, as Republicans gained fifteen seats in the House and three in the Senate.

Clearly, there was no reservoir of respect for Congress from which they could draw. The antics of Wilbur Mills and Wayne Hays had been followed by even more serious charges. Although Congressman Charles Diggs (D-Mich.) was convicted of twenty-six felonies, the Democratic leadership refused even to permit debate on a motion to expel him. A motion was made to censure him, which, if adopted, would have been little more than a slap on the wrist: He would have had to stand in the well of the House while the Speaker intoned a brief rebuke. Joined by forty fellow Republicans, Representatives Dan Lungren and Bill Dannemeyer, both of California, sent Speaker O'Neill a letter in which they asked that the procedure be changed to permit a vote on Diggs's expulsion. When the letter was rejected, Mr. Lungren offered a resolution for expulsion. Using a procedure that permitted no debate and required immediate action, the Democratic leadership moved to table the resolution, and 193 Democrats (75 percent of the House Democratic total) supported it while 134 Republicans (92 percent of the House Republican total) opposed the debate-muzzling maneuver.

As it developed, members accused of wrongdoing during the year could have constituted a committee quorum: In addition to Diggs, former Representative Richard Hanna (D-Calif.) was convicted of a felony; Representative Daniel Flood (D-Pa.) was indicted, got off the hook with a hung jury, and resigned; former Representative Frank Clark (D-Pa.) was indicted and convicted; former Representative Otto Passman (D-La.) was indicted, found not guilty, but later defeated, and Representative Joshua Eilberg (D-Pa.) was indicted and convicted. Representatives McFall, Roybal, and C. Wilson, all California Democrats, were reprimanded for involvement in Koreagate, and Senator Herman Talmadge (D-Ga.), investigated for financial misconduct, was eventually "denounced" by the Senate. It was not a good year for the people's choices.

When the new Congress convened in January 1979, words such as frugality and austerity were quickly woven into the rhetorical fabric of Capitol Hill. By their words, it seemed as if America's representatives had got the message from back home. But brave resolve soon melted under the relentless pressure for more spending. By year's end, the highly respected *Congressional Quarterly* reported that the year would be remembered as "a session where Members voted for massive new spending efforts and laid the groundwork for significant new federal involvement in the lives of American businesses and citizens."

Despite a large Democratic majority, House Speaker O'Neill lamented: "Everything fell apart." While the Speaker complained that Democratic members thought Carter was weak, Senator Adlai Stevenson (D-Ill.) publicly denounced the President as "embarrassingly weak" and incapable of halting the nation's decline.

Republicans, still in the minority, stuck together to give nearly unanimous votes to efforts to restrain spending, reduce taxes, and curb regulations. Although usually outvoted, Republicans were etching records upon which the American people could make their judgments when they took their next trip to the polls.

Everywhere things seemed to be falling apart. In March 1979, radioactive gases escaping from the nuclear reactor at Three Mile Island, Pennsylvania, clouded the future of increased energy production and damaged America's belief in its own competence. In Detroit, Chrysler, America's sixth-largest company, further wounded the country's pride as it headed for bankruptcy.

In July 1979, Jimmy Carter complained that the country was suffering from "malaise," while Cuban troops marched through Africa, and Soviet troops landed in Cuba. Carter fired Secretaries Califano of Health, Blumenthal of Treasury, and Adams of Transportation, causing Representative Charles Wilson (D-Texas) to quip: "They're cutting down the biggest trees and keeping the monkeys."

Shortly thereafter, a special prosecutor was appointed to investigate charges that Hamilton Jordan had used cocaine, and although Jordan eventually was cleared, the allegation further contributed to the image of an inept presidency. Andrew Young, who had asserted that Cuban troops in Angola provided "a certain stability and order," was forced to resign as Carter's UN ambassador after first denying, then admitting, that he had met with representatives of the terrorist Palestine Liberation Organization.

Signaling utter contempt for America, the Khomeini government of Iran smiled as terrorists seized the American Embassy on November 4, 1979, and took fifty-three American hostages. Jimmy Carter became the fifty-fourth hostage, as his presidency became enmeshed and dependent upon the whims of the Ayatollah Khomeini.

On Christmas Day, 1979, the Soviet Union gave the back of its hand to America and the Free World by invading Afghanistan with the first five thousand of some one hundred thousand troops who would soon pour into that country. It marked the first time since World War II that the Soviet Union had invaded a country outside its orbit of Warsaw Pact Communist states. It also marked the further decline of America's position around the world.

On New Year's Eve, 1980, Jimmy Carter told the nation: "The action of the Soviets has made a dramatic change in my opinion of the Soviets' ultimate goals." Foreign-policy observers around the world shook their heads in wonderment. There had never been any question about Soviet strategic goals. From Lenin to Stalin to Brezhnev, the Soviet objective had been explicit: world domination. The President's naïveté troubled even his friends, and for America, his incredible confession ended the year as glumly as it had begun. Meanwhile, as inflation passed 13 percent and the prime interest rate topped 15 percent, America's expectations continued to fall.

In Third World salons, America's low prestige became a

laughing matter when Pakistan refused to accept a Carter offer of $400 million in foreign aid with the claim that it was "peanuts," and would weaken Pakistani security. Shocking though they were, stories of American anemia were soon pushed off the front pages by still another scorching scandal: ABSCAM!

It broke on February 3, 1980. The thirty-one public officials accused included seven congressmen and a U.S. senator. The basic allegations: accepting bribes from an FBI undercover agent posing as a rich Arab sheik. Senator Harrison Williams (D-N.J.) and the seven representatives, six Democrats and one Republican, all were convicted. When the only Republican involved, Richard Kelly of Florida, admitted on network television a few days after the scandal broke that he had pocketed $25,000 as part of what he claimed was his own investigation, Congressman Charlie Rangel, a black Democrat from New York, quipped: "With a story like that, Kelly has destroyed the myth of white supremacy."

Republicans moved swiftly to clean their own house. Just seventeen calendar days after the ABSCAM scandal hit the headlines, the House Republican Policy Committee had examined House Rules to determine what action might be taken with regard to Congressman Kelly, and had asked the House Republican Leadership for a recommendation based on its findings.

On the evening of February 29, the answer came back: removal from the House Republican Conference and denial of all financial support from the Republican National Congressional Committee. Immediately following the issuance of that recommendation, the House Republican Policy Committee met in emergency session and unanimously endorsed the leadership recommendation.

The following morning, in an emergency session of the Republican Conference, Congressman Kelly, confronted with that resolution, resigned from the conference rather than face expulsion.

The action taken by the House Republican Leadership, Policy Committee, and Conference to remove even a shadow of scandal or doubt of integrity on its side of the aisle contrasted sharply with the fact that, nearly two years after the Diggs conviction, Congressman Diggs remained a member in good standing of the Democratic Caucus—the Democratic counterpart of the Republican Conference.

Eight months later, with the election only thirty-three days away, the Democratic Leadership moved with sudden alacrity to expel Representative Michael Myers (D-Pa.) following his ABSCAM conviction. Unlike Representative Diggs, who was permitted to remain in Congress nearly two years after his felony conviction, Michael Myers was ejected within days of his conviction.

As chairman of the Republican Policy Committee, it was my duty to preside over the committee deliberations and the drafting of the motion to expel Representative Kelly from the Republican Conference. Once the resolution was adopted by the committee, it then fell to me to present it to the entire Republican Conference. Although the decision to act swiftly was made by the entire Republican Leadership, as the point man in a sad endeavor, I was criticized by some of my colleagues for moving too quickly. It was argued that, even though Kelly was seen on videotape taking the money, and later admitted taking it, he should be given the same presumption of innocence afforded a defendant in a criminal trial. Most Republicans disagreed, pointing out that it was a privilege, not a constitutional right, to participate in conference deliberations, and that Republicans should show the nation that, although in the minority, they could act quickly and forcefully against wrongdoing by one of their own.

A few argued that the action would further weaken Kelly politically in his district and hand the seat to the Democrats.

Double vindication eventually came when Kelly was convicted in criminal court on five felony counts, and a Republican was handily elected to the seat.

Lost in the stories of Congressional corruption were examples of public integrity: Congressmen James Howard (D-N.J.) and James Florio (D-N.J.) both refused to meet with the phony sheiks, and Senator Larry Pressler (R-S.D.) turned down an offer of a campaign contribution in exchange for political favors.

The honesty, dedication, and sacrifice of most people in public life went largely unnoticed. What America saw was public servants on the take while the country careened out of control into recession, inflation, and international impotence.

By spring, Jimmy Carter got his so-called Windfall Profits Tax through Congress—a scheme which would siphon $227 billion in new taxes out of the pockets of the American people over the coming decade.

Three weeks later, eight American servicemen lay dead on the sands above an ocean of Iranian oil, and several others were injured and badly burned in an abortive effort to free the American hostages in Iran. Three of the eight U.S. helicopters had broken down. Not leaving the decision to the military commander on the ground, President Carter personally canceled the mission from the White House, twelve thousand miles away. After a helicopter crashed into a C-130 cargo plane during the getaway, all the helicopters were left behind. In them was the hostage rescue plan, sensitive intelligence equipment, and information identifying friendly Iranians who were ready to assist in the mission.

No satisfactory answers were ever provided by the President to the Congress as to how he had expected to rescue the hostages alive had the rescue team made it to the U.S. Embassy, two hundred miles from the desert rendezvous point. Spread among several of the ten buildings in the twenty-seven-acre embassy compound, the hostages most likely would have come out in body bags. Carter called the mission an "incomplete success," a phrase worthy of Orwellian double-speak, as Cyrus Vance resigned as Secretary of State in protest over the mission.

Two weeks later, on May 5, 1980, British commandos, inadvertently highlighting American incompetence, successfully stormed the Iranian Embassy in London to free nineteen hostages seized by terrorists. As America struggled to come to terms with its own ineptitude, blacks stormed through Miami, killing eighteen and injuring more than three hundred. The dead were hardly buried when black leader Vernon Jordan was gunned down in a motel parking lot in Fort Wayne, Indiana. In the west, Mount St. Helens, with the force of five hundred atomic bombs, blasted its own peak sixty thousand feet into the sky, devastating a 120-mile area. In the east, contamination of the Love Canal brought the declaration of a state of emergency, and area families were whisked away to safer surroundings. For America, nothing seemed to be going right.

Daniel Yankelovich, the public-opinion specialist, observed: "This country's mood and its prospects are bleak."

Inflation hit 18 percent, the prime interest rate soared above 20 percent, and unemployment topped 7.4 percent. With the average worker's buying power declining by more than 5 percent, real economic growth stagnated.

Embarrassed by the Ayatollah Khomeini, whose Iranian nation America had helped lift out of the dark ages; ignored by the world's other superpower, the Soviet Union, which spread its tentacles virtually at will; given only lip service by allies who had received billions in American aid and lived under America's umbrella of security; economically sinking, and morally decaying, America's self-doubt turned into disbelief. Many no longer questioned whether the country had passed its peak—they concluded that it had.

But that new breed called "American," that colossus which in the twentieth century had twice strode the globe, ridding it of tyrants, and which had fashioned a prosperity unmatched in bygone dreams, would not lie down upon command.

Asserting that America could be great again, Americans went to the polls on November 4, 1980, and handed Ronald Reagan a victory in forty-six of the fifty states, saying by their actions, "We choose to believe in America, in her strengths, in her future."

Are we whistling in the dark? Has the American eclipse begun? Are our best days behind us? How can a country, battered by public corruption, economically stagnating at home and vacillating weakly around the world, lay claim to the future?

The answers lie, perhaps, in taking stock. By measuring, then marshaling assets, tangible and unseen, we can glimpse a shining tomorrow if we are but willing to scrub our way through today.

America, prodigious, is once again waiting to be tapped by those with spirit, skill, and dedication. America the Beautiful—not a song of the past, but a dream of the future—waits to be made more fully true.

IV

ENGINE OF PLENTY

To understand is to construct.
—LEONARDO DA VINCI

WITH THE WAGON MASTER'S shout of "Wagons Ho-o," and a hot June sun rising in our faces, I swung astride my Palomino, Pitt, to join the Bicentennial Celebration's wagon train atop the Allegheny Mountains as it slogged its way through Pennsylvania to Philadelphia from the Pacific Northwest: a grueling 2,700 mile reenactment of American history achieved in 391 tiring days.

Riding point with Elam Bender, a Mennonite farmer and part-time preacher dressed in trapper's clothes of coonskin hat and homespun woolsey, we led the eighteen Conestogas, assorted outriders, and frontier-garbed families striding briskly beside their rolling homes, toward the birthplace of a nation.

Hoping to cover twenty miles that day on a journey that averaged less than seven, the drivers urged on the huge beasts pulling the twenty-two-foot-long Conestoga wagons with their six-foot-wide oaken bodies creaking and straining beneath their hooped canvas toppings.

Red-spoked and iron-rimmed, their great wooden wheels pulverized the pebbles in their path. Each time the wagons ascended or descended a grade, their cargoes gravitated to the wagons' centers down the curved, basket-shaped floors—designed that way to stabilize their loads. These sturdy prairie schooners bore the name of Pennsylvania's Conestoga River Valley where, south of Lancaster, they had been created to haul farm produce to Philadelphia and return home with supplies. It took a carpenter two months to build one wagon, and another 240 hours to fashion its five-foot rear and four-foot front wheels.

From within the wagons came the muted clanging of pots and pans, suspended by hemp cord from the tops of the hoops. In each Conestoga, a trunk of personal possessions, a small table and chairs, blankets, and foodstuffs were neatly stowed for quick unpacking each night. Tied to the outside was a wooden water barrel, two different-sized spare wheels, an ax, and a shovel. Swinging underneath from a leather thong, a "schmutz" pot held the pine tar and lard used each night to plaster the axles with a heavy coat of grease to keep the wagons rolling.

Stopping hourly to rest, the wagon train would be surrounded by well-wishers offering cold drinks and baked goods.

Finally, when nothing was left on the western horizon but the sun's crimson afterglow, the tired travelers, their day's twenty miles behind them, clucked their lathered horses onto a grassy field and unhitched for the night. After walking, currying, watering, and feeding the stock, unpacking the necessities with which to cook the evening meal, and savoring both the taste of hot food and the comfort of sitting still, they set the lanterns aglow, and fiddles and harmonicas appeared around the main campfire. The locals enjoyed listening to the stories of the trail, especially of how the travellers had managed to load river barges with their teams and wagons for the crossings of the great Mississippi and Ohio rivers. Then the community reciprocated with a show of their own, featuring popular songs, dances, and a vignette woven from their town's early history. Finally, as the campfire flickered out, families wandered back to their wagons and spread their bedrolls under the stars for a good night's sleep in preparation for the next day's journey that would eventually take them to Independence Hall for the Fourth of July celebration.

The trip from Washington, D.C., to join the wagon train vividly portrayed how America had changed between 1776 and 1976.

We flew the 168 miles from Washington to Altoona, Pennsylvania, in less than an hour, at a cruising speed of 206 miles per hour in a twin-engine Piper Aztec produced in Lockhaven, Pennsylvania, at a cost of $156,000. The engine was manufactured in Williamsport, Pennsylvania, the brakes in Cleveland, Ohio, and the body's aluminum in Davenport, Iowa. Our flight burned 22.8 gallons of aviation fuel refined at a $375 million East Coast refinery after being transported on a $35 million ocean tanker that hauled its 300,000 barrel cargo of "black gold" from the oil fields of Saudi Arabia, 12,000 nautical miles away. Those fields were opened by Americans who invested over $2 billion in the hope that each dollar might return about six cents a year to the investor, with another six cents for new exploration.

We drove a car assembled in Wilmington, Delaware. Its engine was built in Michigan, its transmission in Indiana, its axles and carburetor in New York, its radio and alternator in Indiana, its tires, trim, and shock absorbers in Ohio; its carpets were loomed in the Carolinas. The roof's material originated as iron ore in Minnesota's Mesabi Range, whence it was moved, via water, to Lake Erie ports in northern Ohio and, via rail cars rebuilt in the Altoona shops fifteen miles from where we landed, to Western Pennsylvania steel mills which processed the ore into sheet and coil steel.

Our car was one of millions assembled from over fifteen thousand parts, fabricated in over a hundred facilities across America, and assembled in over twenty-five major plants. The make we used was distributed nationwide by over thirteen thousand dealers who relied on fifty railroads and hundreds of trucking firms to deliver cars to their far-flung showrooms.

The energy used to smelt the ore into steel for our car came primarily from two sources: by-product gas pumped through privately owned pipelines from coke ovens in Clairton, Pennsylvania, and coal from mines in West Virginia.

The West Virginia coal was moved by rail seventy miles from its mine mouth to Huntington, West Virginia. There it was loaded on barges, each carrying over a thousand tons. The barge trip up the Ohio and Monongahela rivers to Clairton was approximately three hundred miles. Because, between Huntington and Pittsburgh, the Ohio River's elevation dropped two hundred feet, the barges navigated through ten separate locks and dams, built at taxpayers' expense, by the U.S. Army Corps of Engineers.

The steel was then moved by truck to another area plant which stamped it into a roof and then sent it by rail to the assembly plant at Wilmington. The transmission included components produced from ore and processed into molten aluminum or ingots at smelting plants in Kentucky. Then, by truck, the molten aluminum was shipped, at 1,700 degrees, in specially designed pots to an Indiana foundry for processing into castings, then trucked to the transmissions plant.

We traveled over roads first laid out in the 1800's at a cost of $200 per mile. Later, they were widened, upgraded to macadam, then to asphalt, and eventually to concrete, as more Americans wanted to travel farther and faster.

In an hour, we arrived at the campground. The night before, a friend had trucked my horse over Interstate 76, the Pennsylvania Turnpike, the Dream Highway of the 1940's, built at a cost of $1.1 million per mile, from Bedford to Westmoreland County where I joined the wagon train.

Had it not been for those forefathers who had the courage and the taste for freedom that drew them to an untamed land, we knew that we would not have been there on that Bicentennial Day. They were settlers willing to make the arduous trip westward, taking enormous risks to plant a new and better civilization.

Nor would we have been there on that Bicentennial summer's day but for the concrete and steel, rubber and electronics, oil and coal, managerial expertise and capital investment and economic and governmental systems—all brought together to let us be a people prospering.

In two centuries, a mere speck on the tablets of recorded history, America had become the world's premier economic engine. By virtually every economic measure, America excelled.

America, with just 5 percent of the world's population and 6.2 percent of the land surface, produces one-fourth of the entire gross world product (Table 1).

TABLE 1. Selected Gross National Products—Per Capita

	Country	Population (000) mid-1980	GNP at market prices (U.S.$ millions) 1980	GNP per capita (U.S.$) 1980
Africa	Nigeria	84,732	85,510	1,010
Asia	China	981,812	283,250	290
	India	673,207	159,430	240
	Japan	116,551	1,152,910	9,890
	Bangladesh	90,199	11,170	120
	Burma	33,313	5,910	180
	Afghanistan	15,940	na	na
	Nepal	14,288	1,980	140
	Kuwait	1,353	30,900	22,840
	United Arab Emirates	893	26,850	30,070
	Qatar	231	6,020	26,080
Europe	USSR	266,674	1,212,030	4,550
	Germany, West	60,931	827,790	13,590
	Italy	56,940	368,860	6,480
	United Kingdom	55,886	442,820	7,920
	France	53,508	627,700	11,730
	Poland	35,805	139,780	3,900
	Germany, East	16,854	120,940	7,180
	Czechoslovakia	15,336	89,260	5,820
	Switzerland	6,466	106,300	16,440
	Albania	2,732	na	na
North and Central America	United States	223,631	2,582,480	11,360
	Mexico	67,458	144,000	2,130
	Canada	23,937	242,530	10,130
	Cuba	9,859	na	na
	Haiti	5,009	1,340	270
	Nicaragua	2,679	1,930	720
	Virgin Islands	106	630	5,980
South America	Brazil	118,667	243,240	2,050
	Venezuela	14,930	54,220	3,630
	Bolivia	5,570	3,190	570
	Guyana	793	550	690

GNP at market prices rounded to U.S.$ tens of millions. GNP per capita rounded to nearest U.S. $10.

(FROM: *1981 World Bank Atlas*)

America, with her $3 trillion-plus economy, annually produces almost two and one half times the gross national product (GNP)—goods and services—produced by either Japan or the Soviet Union. Output per person in America is 20 percent greater than Japan's, and 160 percent greater than the Soviet Union's. Only West Germany and a few small, highly developed countries exceed America's GNP per person.

Over the thirty years between 1950 and 1980, GNP per person in industrialized countries increased from $3,841 to $9,684, up 152 percent. In the same time the gross national product of the low-income, underdeveloped countries increased from $164 to $245, up only 50 percent. Starting from such a pitifully low income per person, and growing at only one third the rate of the industrialized countries, the plight of the world's poor countries remains excruciatingly painful. America's prosperity is a blessing too easily taken for granted.

A child born in Nigeria shares in a per-person GNP of $1,010, only slightly above the average for all African countries, even though Nigeria's GNP is $85 billion, the largest on the continent. Among African countries, GNP per person is topped by oil-rich Libya at $8,640, but it hovers below $400 for most of these sorely underdeveloped countries.

In Asia, GNP per person ranges from over $22,000 in oil-rich Kuwait, the United Arab Emirates, and Qatar, to under $200 in Bangladesh, Burma, and Nepal.

Exposing the absurdity of Communist charges of American colonialism, the U.S. Virgin Islands, at $5,580, enjoys the highest GNP per person in Central America, with Haiti's the lowest, at $270.

Brazil's $206 billion GNP dwarfs that of the other countries of South America, although its $2,050 GNP per person is nearly doubled by Venezuela's $3,630, with Bolivia and Guyana on the bottom at under $700.

All too often, the cold economic statistics of gross national product translate into empty stomachs and diseased bodies for millions around the world. For America, however, the statistics are only the beginning of a tale of untold wealth.

*   *   *

Overall, Americans enjoy a better standard of living than any other people on Earth. Starting with the basics, Americans have available the most nutritious, balanced, tasteful, and diverse diet at the lowest relative cost. That some do not avail themselves of proper nutrition is another story. Based on a shopping basket of thirty-nine basic food items including bread, milk, meat, fish, vegetables, and fruit, the United States continues to lead the world in purchasing power and affluence. Even high-priced foods in America are bargains compared to their cost in other countries. For example, 2.2 pounds of medium-quality steak cost $7 in America, as compared to $24 in Western Europe and $41 in Japan. As a percentage of the average American family's cost of living, food has dropped from 23 percent in 1950 to 18 percent in 1981.

Contrary to a widely held view that starvation in underdeveloped countries is caused mainly by an unbalanced diet, it is in fact caused by an inadequate number of calories in the daily diet. On the average, people in India consume only 90 percent of the calories essential to the maintenance of their bodies, meaning that about half the population—325 million people—are undernourished. For 14 million people in Ethiopia, the picture is even worse, since they consume only 74 percent of the minimum daily calories required. Americans, embarrassingly, consume 135 percent of their daily caloric requirements.

Breaking an early-morning crust of ice in a water bucket, shivering while starting a fire, bundling up for a dash to the privy, chilling milk in a cellar cistern, feeling the warmth of an oil lamp on the palm of the hand cupped to blow out its flame remain everyday experiences for millions around the world; but they are only dim memories, or strange stories of distant days, for that most privileged of all people—the Americans. Virtually every American home now enjoys indoor plumbing, central heating, and electricity, although at the turn of the century, fewer than 10 percent could claim such luxuries. The typical American family lives in a home with 5.1 rooms, and almost 20 percent of those homes consist of seven or more rooms. About a million new homes are built annually, averaging 1,600 square feet, with two bathrooms, three bedrooms, a fireplace, and a garage. In 1966, 25 percent of new U.S. housing construction included central air conditioning; by 1979, that figure had increased to 60 percent.

Although inflation has driven the average U.S. house price from $23,400 in 1970 to a seemingly devastating $62,900 in 1979, the problem has been worldwide, and America has actually fared better than most other countries. America's 8.5 percent rate of annual increase in the cost of new housing was low compared to that of most other countries, including France at 10.3 percent and Sweden at 10.6 percent. The rate of increase in rents in the United States was even lower, averaging only 4.9 percent compared to around 10 percent for most other industrialized countries.

Typical of millions in underdeveloped countries, almost half the homes in India have only one room, and almost all are without indoor plumbing. Even in prosperous Japan, the average housing unit is only 3.8 rooms, with no central heating, and general-purpose rooms convert into bedrooms at night, with mats rolled out for sleeping on the floor. Kuwait, with the world's highest per-person GNP, has 3.5 rooms per housing unit, but 82 percent of the homes are without running water.

American homes are filled with appliances unavailable in many parts of the world, and at costs lower than those in other areas in which they are available. Combined, an electric or gas oven, refrigerator, washing machine, color TV set, vacuum cleaner, and electric iron cost about $2,500 in America, while averaging $3,200 in Western Europe and $5,200 in the Middle East.

Americans enjoy a level of personal mobility unmatched anywhere. Americans can go where they choose, conveniently and economically. Over 114 million automobiles are registered in the United States: one car for every two people, or 1.8 vehicles for every household. Compared to Japan, America has three times as many cars per person, twice as many as Britain, and twenty times as many as the Soviet Union. Typically, a car in America is driven ten thousand miles a year, a distance greater than that traveled by millions on Earth during an entire lifetime. A highway system of almost four billion center-lane miles ties the nation together, both for human travel and for movement of goods. Public transit systems, which once decayed as an increasingly prosperous America preferred the personal mobility of the automobile, are rebounding to meet modern transportation needs as energy costs rise. Carrying over 6 billion passengers annually, transit systems are helping Americans move about conveniently and economically. Intercity buses, carrying 330 million passengers annually—coupled with Amtrak, hauling 20 million—provide public transportation between virtually all American communities with a population of 5,000 or more.

Over 300 million passengers fill the U.S. skies each year, served by over 13,000 flights daily. Additionally, over 185,000 private aircraft are in operation. The enormity of America's wealth is vividly portrayed by the staggering level of intercity travel. Combining ground and air, Americans engage in long-distance travel amounting to 1.4 trillion miles a year—7,000 miles per person. That averages 2.5 hours of intercity travel each week for every person in the country in addition to the time spent in local daily travel. Americans are on the move as are no other people on Earth, and the enormous mobility enjoyed by the average American is a fundamental measurement of prosperity, as well as of individual freedom.

There are 742 telephones for every thousand Americans. That's nearly twice as many as in Japan, Britain, or France, nearly three times as many as in Italy, and over nine times as many as in the Soviet Union.

The various elements of personal prosperity combine to provide Americans with the overall highest standard of living the world has ever known. Certainly, when compared to the pre-Depression "good old days" of the high-flying 1920's, the average American is better off economically in virtually every respect. Compared to those earlier days, known firsthand only by senior citizens, today's average American has to work only half as many hours to pay for a new car, a child's education at a state university, a gas range, an electric washing machine, a lady's wool skirt, a dozen oranges, ten pounds of potatoes, or a half gallon of milk; he need work only one-fifth the time to purchase a vacuum cleaner, an electric sewing machine, or a ticket for public transportation.

Within two decades, the real purchasing power of the average American family has increased 40 percent, and the number classified as poor has declined 35 percent.

Despite the recurring problems, the fact remains that compared to earlier generations, Americans are vastly better off. Economic prosperity surely is not shared equally by all, nor will it ever be, so long as talents and ambitions differ. While opportunities abound, they fall imperfectly and unevenly on a heterogeneous people separated by climate, class, and culture, but joined in freedom to pursue their own enlightened ends.

Economic prosperity provides the base, the material bedrock from which noneconomic values may most securely be pursued, but it carries with it no warranty, neither written nor implied, for happiness or peace of mind.

When the car payment and mortgage are due, when the supermarket cash register slip ratchets upward every week, when children's flimsy summer sneakers cost more than sturdy winter shoes did a few years back, the indisputable fact that one is really better off may be hard to swallow, even though it's true.

Life always loses when compared with what it ought to be. The great Utopia one subconsciously seeks but never finds debases the reality in which one must live. Measured against the ideal, America falls far short, but against the humanly attainable, here or anywhere around the globe, America soars.

For Americans, the average life expectancy has surpassed the biblical three score and ten, reaching 70.5 years. Life expectancy in the underdeveloped world is twenty years less, and that stark statistic does not begin to measure the suffering experienced by almost one billion of the world's population who do not have adequate food, shelter, or sanitation. For example, infant deaths in America average 13 per 1,000 born, while in most underdeveloped countries they exceed ten times that rate, topping 162 in Ethiopia. While virtually all Americans enjoy access to a safe water supply, less than one third of the people in the under-developed world have such access, and only 6 percent of the Ethiopians enjoy such a basic necessity, taken for granted by Americans.

A comparison of the standard of living between the United States and the Soviet Union is particularly instructive. On November 7, 1977, the ruling Communist Party of the USSR celebrated the sixtieth anniversary of its Bolshevik takeover of Russia. Sixty years in which the "dictatorship of the proletariat" had absolute power to remake the society it ruled; sixty years in which it could have capitalized (pardon the expression) on such natural advantages over America as more land, more tillable acreage, more minerals, and more people; sixty years in which Russia's rich heritage of literature and music could have been further cultivated, rather than destroyed, debased, or driven westward. After sixty years of iron control, and despite its superiority of natural resources, the Soviet Union lags far behind the United States by virtually every measure.

When, in 1960, the Soviet government published its twenty-year plan, it announced that upon its completion in 1980 the "building of Communist society will be completed . . . the U.S. will be far behind . . . [Soviet] citizens will be guaranteed a Standard of Living higher than any Capitalist country." The time has come and gone, and the USSR surpasses America in almost nothing, except military buildup, brutality, and aggression. Compared to an American worker, a Soviet worker must put in many more days or months of effort to earn the money necessary to purchase goods routinely available in the United States: four times as long for a suit, five times as long for a small car, three times as long for a steak or for ten liters of gasoline. America has twice the space in housing units for a population 20 percent smaller, twice the number of refrigerators per person, and ten times the number of telephones per person. Even in Moscow, where living standards are better than in the rest of the Soviet Union, one out of every four families must live in a dormitory and share a kitchen and bath with other families. The Soviet Union produces less than two-thirds the grain, and less than one-half the meat needed for a good diet.

In his *Communist Manifesto* of 1848, Karl Marx preached that Communism laid down his presumably golden rule of dialectical materialism. By practicing "From each according to his abilities, to each according to his needs," a classless society would emerge, and government would wither away. But it didn't. It is the ultimate irony that Communists, who are the materialists, have failed to deliver economic prosperity while Americans, who are idealists, have produced material abundance. The Communist system, which preached dissolution of government, used government to subjugate its people, while the American system, which preached freedom from government, used government to unleash freedom and prosperity for its citizens.

Marx had it backward when he said that capitalism* would be replaced by Communism, claiming that Communism was more advanced in the evolutionary development of socioeconomic systems. The reverse is true. Economically, Communism preaches prosperity and produces scarcity. Politically, Communism promises equality and delivers subjugation. Communism's brutality repeatedly has been demonstrated: in Czechoslovakia in 1948 and 1968, in East Germany in 1953, in Hungary in 1956, and in Afghanistan in 1979. Such brute force shows itself only after the failure of the more constant Soviet policy of rule by intimidation— as demonstrated in Poland and elsewhere behind the Iron Curtain, and to some extent even in some countries of Western Europe and the Middle East.

Perhaps the clearest comparison between the Free World and Communism can be experienced by visiting West Berlin, then traveling as I did through the ugly wall at Checkpoint Charlie into East Berlin.†

Leaving West Berlin, with its bustle, busy streets, and

---

*Capitalism is a term invented by Marx to describe an economic system he despised, and the free world falls into an early trap when it lets its enemies define the semantics by which ideas will be developed and debated. "Free market system" is a more accurate and descriptive term by which the economic system of the free world might be defined. While the reality of the economic system in the free world is not so pure as the term, it provides an accurate theoretical basis for describing the thrust of the system.

†I toured East Berlin as a member of a congressional team inspecting NATO forces in Europe in April 1979.

prosperity, we entered a different world of empty streets, drab buildings, and blank faces, with machine-gun-toting Communist soldiers patrolling everywhere. We passed a special jail where only political prisoners were kept. A pervasive somber grayness seemed to seep inside us. The dirty air had the smell of the soft, low-grade coal used to heat homes and run factories in Pennsylvania steel-mill towns forty years earlier. As our vehicle crawled through unkept streets, we felt as if we were watching a faded black and white film moving silently in slow motion. The one million people of East Berlin had no traffic problems—their once busy thoroughfares, including the famous Unter den Linden, were almost empty—old 1940-vintage streetcars clanged about sluggishly.

At the dreary city's single department store, people queued up for hours, hoping to be able to purchase basic necessities. They knew that in West Berlin, a stone's throw over the wall, they could easily acquire any merchandise they wanted, but they also knew that if they attempted to get over the 110-mile-long wall, they would be attacked by Communist guard dogs and shot on sight. They had seen grisly pictures of over a hundred of their neighbors who had suffered such a fate. They knew that when a Communist border guard killed someone attempting to escape, he was rewarded with extra pay and a three week's furlough. The Communist machine-gun installations, barbed-wire barricades, guard towers, and dog runs formed a no-man's-land between the people of East Berlin and the wall that kept them from freedom.

Our driver stopped the van in front of the building in which, on August 8, 1945, Hitler Germany's unconditional surrender was ratified. We were prohibited from going inside to see the room where Marshal Wilhelm Keitel, Admiral Hans von Friedeburg and General Hans-Jürgen Stumpff had signed the document, and where Soviet Marshal Georgi Zhukov and British Air Marshal Arthur Tedder had accepted it for the Allies. Under rigid Soviet control, with guards stationed throughout the grounds, the building was open only to Communist dignitaries, but we were permitted on the grounds. Walking around the building to the window of the historic room, we paused and on tiptoe we tried to see the table and chairs at which the event had taken place.

Our driver, an American army sergeant in civilian clothes who regularly made the tour, indicated that we should stay put, and he would see what he could do to get us inside. Then, strolling casually over to the Soviet captain in charge, he started chatting with him and offered him a cigarette, which he readily accepted. A few minutes later, our driver walked to the van, opened the back door, removed a large brown shopping bag, then walked briskly back toward the Soviet captain who had moved in front of the empty guardhouse at the entrance to the grounds. Without stopping or saying a word, the driver handed the bag to the captain and kept on walking toward us. The captain must have given a signal to the sentry in front of the building's door, because he opened it as the driver motioned for us to join him and go in. Following his instructions, we were thrilled to visit the room where the German surrender had been ratified.

After we had passed through Checkpoint Charlie and were back in West Berlin, I leaned forward from my seat behind the driver and put the question on everyone's mind: "Sergeant, what did you give that Soviet officer?"

"Four cartons of Pepsi-Cola, sir. It works every time, if he's on duty. He loves Pepsi, and they can't buy it in East Berlin!"

Incredibly, East Berlin is considered the showcase for the rest of the Communist world because, bad as it is, its standard of living is still far above that of its Communist neighbors.

It is unfortunate that U.S. citizens who harbor doubts about the American economic and political system cannot readily visit East Berlin. The quality of life in America would suddenly seem idyllic, and such patriotic phrases as the pursuit of happiness would assume new meaning.

Even from an economic perspective, the Pursuit of Happiness must mean more than the production and distribution of goods and services. A nation might wallow in consumption while drowning in pollution, not only of the body, but of the mind and spirit as well.

The World Bank has attempted to measure the "quality of life" by comparing data about the economic and social development of countries around the world, including such measurements as GNP per person, energy consumption per person, inflation rate, labor force in agriculture, life expectancy, physicians, education, and literacy (Table 2). While the United States is among the top few nations in every category, most striking is America's vast lead in higher education and agricultural productivity. Compared to other highly developed countries, America has more than twice the percentage of young people enrolled in higher education, and is achieving more than twice the agricultural productivity.

Dr. Ben-Chieh Liu, while principal economist at the Midwest Research Institute in Kansas City, Missouri, analyzed the quality of life in thirty-three developed countries using such measurements as: social, economic, health and education, environment, and vitality and security (a misnomer that will be defined later) (Table 3).

Overall, he ranked America first, with a wide gap between the United States and Australia and Canada, which he ranked second and third, respectively. His analysis placed America economically second to Canada, but overwhelmingly first in the social quality of life. His definition of the social component, as noted in Table 3, was essentially the sum of economic factors relating to personal prosperity, i.e., standard of living.

The Soviet Union ranked poorly in every measure except the so-called national vitality and security category, a misnomer which, according to the report Appendix, actually measured the percentage of the population that worked, the acres of arable land per person, and the stability of prices. That a dictatorship can control prices is no surprise. Indeed, the Soviet experience has proved that stable prices do not guarantee prosperity. That so many must work to produce the dismal Soviet standard of living, especially in a land with vast agricultural potential, is but another measure of that system's failure.

The developed countries, representing about 25 percent

of the world's population, might be measured in terms of relative prosperity, but for most of mankind, life remains a daily struggle for food and warmth and health.

For Victor Hugo, the poverty of Paris at the end of the eighteenth century, as described in *Les Misérables,* meant starvation, literally, with no food to eat. The punishment for stealing a loaf of bread to feed one's family was a minimum of five years' imprisonment at hard labor and being branded a thief for life by the searing of a five-digit number into the skin of the left arm.

For Ernest Hemingway, 120 years later, the same Paris was *A Moveable Feast,* a city of infinite charm, a place where "we were very poor and very happy." Yet, according to him, it was also a city where the "squat toilets of the old apartment houses . . . emptied into cesspools which were emptied by pumping into horse drawn tank wagons at night . . . and the odor was very strong."

Both Hugo and Hemingway wrote of poverty in Paris, yet one had the bitter smell of burnt skin in his nostrils, and the other a sweet nostalgic longing for happy days gone by.

If Hugo and Hemingway could meet today for a glass of *eau-de-vie* at the Café des Amateurs on the Rue Mouffetard, and a tank wagon rolled up in front of them to begin pumping out the nearby cesspool, their pens would surely burn, excoriating both the city and the poverty of its inhabitants. Then, crossing the Atlantic to America, should they discover similar conditions, they would rightly condemn them. But, of course, no such circumstances would be found. Yet poverty does persist. By official definition, poverty in America is: one person with an income of less than $4,190; a four-person family with less than $8,410; a seven-person family with less than $13,940. Not to be counted in the calculations are noncash benefits such as food stamps, public housing, and medical care.

The typical poverty family in today's America lives in a rental unit of 3.7 rooms—1.7 bedrooms, one bath, a complete kitchen, and modern plumbing. The unit is located in a forty-year-old structure of two to four units, and rents for

TABLE 2. Quality of Life (Selected National Development Statistics)

Country	GNP per capita 1976 (in U.S. dollars)	Energy consumption per capita 1975 (in kg of coal equivalent)	Average annual inflation rate 1970-76 (percent)	Labor force in agriculture 1970 (percent)	Life expectancy at birth 1975	Infant mortality 1975 (per thousand)	Population per physician 1974	Persons enrolled primary school, 1975 (percent of age group)	Persons enrolled higher education 1975, (percent population aged 20-24)
Afghanistan	160	52	3.1	82	35	269	26,100	23	1
Albania	540	741	n.a.	66	69	n.a.	1,200	106	17
Bangladesh	110	28	20.7	86	42	140	9,350	73	3
Bolivia	390	303	25.9	56	47	n.a.	2,120	72	10
Brazil	1,140	670	26.1	46	61	n.a.	1,660	90	10
Burma	120	51	16.1	67	50	56	6,910	85	2
Canada	7,510	9,880	9.2	8	72	15	600	104	35
China, People's Rep.	410	693	n.a.	68	62	n.a.	n.a.	n.a.	n.a.
Cuba	860	1,157	n.a.	31	70	n.a.	n.a.	126	9
Czechoslovakia	3,840	7,151	n.a.	17	70	n.a.	430	96	11

France	6,550	3,944	9.3	14	73	14	680	109	18
Germany, East	4,220	6,835	n.a.	13	73	n.a.	560	95	23
Germany, West	7,380	5,345	6.4	8	71	20	520	129	20
Haiti	200	30	13.5	74	50	150	8,510	50	n.a.
India	150	221	9.2	69	50	122	4,160	65	5
Italy	3,050	3,012	12.9	19	72	21	500	107	24
Japan	4,910	3,622	10.1	20	73	10	810	100	25
Kuwait	15,480	8,718	35.6	2	67	44	1,140	90	7
Nepal	120	10	8.4	94	44	n.a.	36,450	27	2
Nicaragua	750	479	10.8	51	53	46	1,720	85	6
Nigeria	380	90	16.1	62	41	163	25,440	49	1
Poland	2,860	5,007	n.a.	39	70	n.a.	590	100	16
Switzerland	8,880	3,642	7.4	8	72	11	590	92	8
USSR	2,760	5,546	n.a.	26	70	n.a.	340	99	22
U.K.	4,020	5,265	13.3	3	72	16	750	116	16
U.S.A.	7,890	10,999	6.8	4	71	16	610	104	54
Venezuela	2,570	2,639	13.4	26	65	46	870	96	19

(Table extracted from the World Bank's *World Development Report, 1978*)

TABLE 3. QOL Indicators and Rankings by Country, 1975

Nation	Social ranking	Economic ranking	Health and education ranking	Environment ranking	National vitality and security	Overall Index	Overall Ranking
U.S.A.	1	2	7	6	6	.93	1
China (Taiwan)	20	32	28	28	5	-.36	30
Argentina	29	30	30	3	30	-.41	31
Australia	15	8	10	1	2	.78	2
Austria	17	14	23	21	19	-.02	14
Belgium	10	9	22	33	20	-.10	22
Bulgaria	18	28	16	14	4	-.05	18
Canada	4	1	6	2	8	.77	3
Chile	33	33	33	5	33	-.91	33
Czechoslovakia	12	22	21	24	3	.03	13
Denmark	5	7	8	15	18	.29	6
Finland	19	17	13	8	23	.05	11
France	13	11	14	23	24	.04	12
Germany, East	7	12	19	26	7	.11	9
Germany, West	11	6	17	29	15	.07	10
Greece	21	19	27	7	14	-.06	19
Hungary	14	24	25	20	10	-.09	20
Ireland	22	16	12	11	31	-.04	16
Italy	25	15	15	25	27	-.15	24
Japan	9	23	4	30	26	-.09	21

Netherlands	23	13	5	32	29	-.10	23
New Zealand	8	5	9	18	28	.22	7
Norway	16	3	2	19	9	.40	5
Poland	31	20	20	22	22	-.20	25
Portugal	30	26	29	12	11	-.28	28
Romania	26	29	26	16	12	-.26	27
Spain	32	21	24	10	25	-.23	26
Sweden	2	4	1	17	13	.46	4
Switzerland	3	10	3	27	21	.18	8
USSR	24	31	18	4	1	-.04	15
U.K.	6	18	11	31	17	-.04	17
Uruguay	28	25	32	9	32	-.54	32
Yugoslavia	27	27	31	13	16	-.35	29
Mean						.00	
Std. Dev.						.3749	

(From: *The Pursuit of Happiness: A Comparison of Quality of Life Indicators in China, U.S.A. and Other Developed Countries* by Ben-Chieh Liu, Institute of American Culture, Nankang, Taipei, December 1979) about $170, part of which is subsidized. The family's personal belongings include a television set, radio, and motor vehicle. Adequate clothing is taken for granted, for even the poorest have shoes, shirts, dresses, and pants. Free health care is provided through Medicaid in modern medical facilities located within a dozen miles of most homes; food stamps and free school lunches provide for a balanced nutritional diet, if used properly. In setting up the Food Stamp Program, the federal government established a scientifically based formula for a family of two adults and two teenagers to ensure that poverty-level families could enjoy a nutritious diet. Entitled the Thrifty Food Plan, it spelled out the quantities of food to be consumed weekly in various groups including: milk, meat, vegetables and fruit, and bread and cereals. The problem was, however, that the plan's promoters never bothered to distribute the Thrifty Food Plan to food-stamp recipients, realizing that few would have adhered to it since, under the law, recipients can buy any kind of food they want. The Thrifty Food Plan established Recommended Dietary Allowances as set by the National Academy of Sciences for protein, calcium, iron, magnesium, vitamin A, thiamine, riboflavin, niacin, vitamin B_6, vitamin B_{12}, and vitamin C. Dr. Robert Rizek, director of the Consumer Nutrition Center for the U.S. Department of Agriculture, told a congressional committee that "the plan provides twenty-three pounds of red meat and seven pounds of poultry (monthly), despite the fact that chicken is a more economical source of protein than most types of red meat." He added: "Many households, whether or not they are eligible for food stamps, do not select nutritious assortments of food."

That many Americans do not avail themselves of good nutrition is one of the many choices that they are free to make. But even the poorest of the poor seldom goes to bed hungry for want of food or the wherewithal to get it.

Compared with most of the world, poverty in America loses much of its sting. For nearly a billion human beings elsewhere, poverty, American style, would seem like unleashed luxury. Yet, to the extent that people in America who have the capacity and desire to participate in the production and consumption of America's wealth cannot do so, they are, indeed, disadvantaged. Their plight is a festering sore on the most productive and prosperous national body the world has ever seen, and must be healed in order for that body to be entirely healthy.

In centuries past, kings lived neither so well nor so long as the poor in America today. Yet, for those at the bottom of the U.S. economic ladder, the bottom is still the bottom —and the genius of America has been that it has held out real opportunity for people to better themselves—to bootstrap themselves out of poverty, however officially defined. Should that opportunity no longer exist, a vital part of the American soul would surely die. But the good news is that, while still imperfect, the opportunity shines as bright as ever, and the desire to achieve it burns fiercely in the hearts of millions. The substantial decline in the number of Americans defined as poor, the doubling of the average American's standard of living every twenty years, the explosion of young people enrolled in higher education, and the increasing numbers of college graduates and professionals among the minorities, are but a few of the measurements which confirm the continuing health, vigor, and viability of the American dream.

The opportunities for growth and upward mobility are no better exemplified than by the electronic-computer industry, in which I worked for seventeen years, from the early days of vacuum-tube computers through the explosion of the software revolution and introduction of microprocessors. During that exciting period, thousands of young men and women were introduced to new technologies, as they entered exotic worlds of bits and bites, of microseconds and logic boards, of binary arithmetic and excess-three codes, of machine language and COBOL, of high-speed printers and random-storage devices, of display terminals and acoustic couplers. As young people just out of college learned to electronically manage data to tell factories how to run, planes where to fly, and investors what to buy, they participated in a technological revolution that rocketed America ahead. The sons and daughters of steel-mill workers and gas-truck drivers, electronically redesigning blast furnaces and calculating where to dig for oil, were doing so at salaries four times the earnings of their parents.

Aristotle had said mockingly: "When looms weave by themselves, man's slavery will end," to make the point that slaves would always be necessary, because looms would never weave alone. America proved him wrong. Today, a whole nation "weaves" by itself, building products and scheduling events automatically, at the touch of a button. But behind the button is the ingenuity and effort of people making machines to do the work for them, faster, better, and more productively than ever before.

Hundreds of new companies have been spawned by the high technology explosion, creating thousands of new, exciting jobs, and making poor men rich. Bittersweet for some, as life most always is, and mixing failure with success, American high-technology engineers and entrepreneurs tried whole new ways of doing things and, in the process, changed the world. Not content, now they reach for worlds beyond, with *Columbia* shuttling between Earth and space, and deep probes peering into Mars and Venus. But while Americans try to touch the stars, others around the globe still scratch for food.

For much of the world, poverty is still poverty. Over eight hundred million people live in absolute poverty, meaning they go to bed malnourished and hungry, and live a quarter-century less than people in industrialized areas. Meanwhile, three out of every four can expect to die without ever having learned to read or write.

Poverty, then, has different faces for different people. For millions in Africa, Asia, and South America, it means total despair and resignation. It is existing, rather than living, while waiting to die. It is life without hope, relief only through death. It is Edwin Markham's "Man With the Hoe," only painted brown or yellow and having even less: "The emptiness of ages in his face, and on his back the burden of the world. . . . a thing that grieves not and never hopes, stolid and stunned . . ."

For Americans, it is a condition to be changed. Not stopping to note how well-off even poor Americans are compared to well-to-do citizens of underdeveloped countries,

Americans dream of better days. They hope because they have been taught to hope. It is part of the great American dream, of a better tomorrow, however good today. Surrounded by prosperity, what they see so widely spread about them, they know they too can touch and have.

V

PRODUCERS
UNDER FIRE

We rail at trade, but the historians of the world
will see that it insured the principle of liberty,
that it settled America, and destroyed feudalism,
and made peace and keeps peace. . . .
—RALPH WALDO EMERSON

AYN RAND may not have been thinking about this century when she wrote: "The Producers have been the forgotten men of history." Surely, such names as Carnegie, Edison, Ford, Rockefeller, and others like them who fashioned America's industrial might and economic wealth will be remembered long after many politicians and statesmen have been forgotten.

Attention swirls around supply-side economics as if it were a newly minted coin when, in fact, the great economist John Stuart Mill taught in the 1830's that the basic economic laws apply primarily to production, not distribution nor consumption; that society may decide how to distribute its wealth, but there will be no wealth to distribute if the basic economic laws of production are not followed.

For America, the plenty has existed because of the economic engine that produced it—an engine made to work by millions of Americans free to strive, to lend their energies to a system from which they can rightfully expect a just return. For every generation, that return, in the form of disposable income, has provided for the doubling of the average American's standard of living. Such prosperity has been possible only because productivity, the output per man-hour, has doubled since the end of World War II and quadrupled since the end of World War I.

At the time he was president of the United Steel Workers, I. W. Abel observed: "Increased productivity is the only real basis for prosperity and security." Productivity is at

maximum efficiency only when well-trained, highly motivated workers are given the best possible tools and competent managerial direction. To produce the goods and
services that create American abundance, men and women,
machines and management, must perform in harmony like
a great symphony orchestra. The most highly motivated
workers in the world will not work productively if they lack
modern plants and equipment. That, of course, requires
billions of investment dollars each year to keep the American economic system humming. A capital investment of
between $50,000 and $75,000 is required for each job
created. It can come only from the savings of individuals or
profits of businesses willing to part with funds in anticipation
of a reasonable return. In 1980, the U.S. economic system
generated $430 billion in domestic investment, almost
$4,000 for every American. The U.S. economic system cre-
ates twice the capital of West Germany, three times that of
France, and five times that of Britain, but only 1.2 times that
of Japan. While America's present economic strength remains unmatched by any other nation, storm warnings signal trouble ahead if America does not further increase its
annual capital investment in new plants and equipment.

On a per capita basis, Japan's and West Germany's capital
investments are substantially ahead of the United States.
The impact is vividly portrayed in a comparison of productivity increase over the past decade: United States up 27
percent, West Germany up 70 percent, Japan up 107 percent. Another measure indicating the need for increased
capital investment to modernize American facilities is the
average age of her industrial plants: twenty years in America, twelve in West Germany,· and ten in Japan.

Recognizing the problem is, of course, the first step toward correcting it, and the signs are encouraging that reme-
dial action is on the way. A change in the federal tax code
to provide more realistic depreciation of plants and equipment, easing of the regulatory burdens on business, and a
decrease of marginal tax rates for individuals are steps which
will generate increased capital for investment.

Yet, despite her problems, America remains prodigiously
productive. Even a partial recitation of categories in which
America is the world's top producer is breathtaking: energy,

copper, aluminum, cars, natural gas, coal, petroleum refin-
ing, locomotives, airplanes, corn, eggs, soybeans, and
cheese. America is also first in value added per worker, gold
holdings, pipelines, cargo handled by ports, graduate population, university professors, scientific authorship, and book
production.

The Book of World Rankings notes: "America's domi-
nance in agriculture is so great that it could be called the
bread basket of the world. America produces 42 percent of
the world's corn, 52 percent of the soybeans and sorghum,
55 percent of the tallows and grease, 13 percent of the
wheat, 17 percent of the tobacco, and 20 percent of the
cotton, meat and barley. U. S. agricultural exports account
for more than one-fifth of the total U.S. exports and about
one-fifth of the total world trade in agricultural products."

Conspicuously ranking behind the Soviet Union in steel
production, and with Japan rapidly gaining, America's steel
industry is in trouble. But there is reason to believe that the
steel industry will share in gains brought about by moderni-
zation made possible through an improved investment climate.

America has repeatedly demonstrated its capacity to ad-
just, and its ability to grapple successfully with vexing problems. The story of America is one of challenge and response.
To sell short this generation's ability to meet its test is to
ignore the enormous capacity and the mountain of economic strength upon which this generation stands. From
the steel valley of Western Pennsylvania, across the rolling
wheat fields of Kansas, to the silicon valley* of Northern
California, America produces.

U.S. economic strength lies not only in its annual productivity but also in the cumulative effect of that productivity
over many years. Even Japan or West Germany, which
today are world-class producers, cannot match the American wealth accumulated through decades of productivity
and prosperity. In this, America still stands alone.

Annual gross national product, which to a nation is what
an annual income statement is to a business, does, of course,

*The Santa Clara area south of San Francisco where hundreds of high technol-
ogy companies have sprung up in the past two decades

deserve great emphasis. It is the measurement of a nation's economic activity for a given year. Inadequate attention has, however, been given to what might be called "gross national wealth," which to a nation is what a balance sheet is to a business: the sum of assets and liabilities.

From many different sources, one is able to construct a comprehensive, if not totally complete, picture of America's physical wealth, private and public, as indicated in Table 4. ("Paper" wealth is excluded because each asset of such wealth is offset by a liability.)

TABLE 4. Physical Wealth of the United States 1980 (Dollars in billions)

Corporate plant and equipment (Manufacturing and commercial)		$1,382.9
Business inventories		342.2
Farm land and buildings		659.4
Other farm assets		200.4
Household durable assets		
a. Autos and parts		1,218.5
b. Housing stock		3,710.3
c. Nonprofit plant and equipment		118.8
d. Other consumer durables		1,567.7
Household nondurable assets		
a. Food		9.4
b. Clothing		286.7
	Private Subtotal	$8,251.7
Federal Government		
Gold and silver		163.1
Land		200.0
Buildings and facilities		110.2
Equipment		45.9
Building in progress		22.8
Military hardware		152.3
Other assets		24.4
	Federal Government Subtotal	718.7
State and Local Governments		
Fixed capital other than roads		1,802.1
Roads		3,500.0
Buildings		52.1
	State and Local Government Subtotal	5,354.2
	Grand Total	$14,324.6

TABLE 4. *continued*

SOURCES FOR WEALTH ESTIMATES

1. *Plant and equipment:* Calculated by Data Resources, Inc., based on depreciation rates in a 1973 study for the Office of Emergency Preparedness, *Development of Capital Stock Series by Industry Sector.*

2. *Business inventories:* U.S. Department of Commerce, Bureau of Economic Analysis, *National Income and Product Accounts of the U.S.,* Table 5.10.

3. *Farm land, buildings and other assets:* Estimated by the Department of Agriculture, 1979. Adjusted for inflation through 1980.

4. *Household durable assets:* Calculated by Data Resources, Inc. The 1980 values for autos, nonprofit plant and equipment, and other consumer durables are arrived at by taking the 1979 values and adding to them the 1980 value-added in these categories from the national income accounts, less inventory accumulation. Unsold current output in these categories appears in the business inventory component explained above.

The 1980 *housing stock* component of household durable assets is computed by multiplying the physical stock of housing (in millions of units) in 1980 by the average dwelling price during the year. Unfortunately, this series includes only single-family houses and townhouses because there exists no reliable *price* series for multiple-family dwellings.

5. *Household nondurable assets:*
(a) *Food.* A ten-day supply of food on hand was estimated. Thus, the dollar figure arrived at was computed by taking one tenth of the 1980 production of food and beverages for home use.
(b) *Clothing.* It was assumed that clothes depreciate linearly over five years. Therefore, at the end of 1980 the stock of clothing is assumed to be the sum of 1980 clothing sales plus four fifths of 1979 sales plus four fifths of 1979 sales plus one fifth of 1976 sales.

6. *Roads and highways:* Provided by the Federal Highway Administration. It is essentially the replacement cost of the road and highway system.

7. *Official gold stock:* U.S. government holdings of gold valued at the December 1980 average price. These figures appear monthly in the *Federal Reserve Bulletin.*

8. *State and local governments:* "Fixed Capital Stock in the United States," revised by John Musgrave, Department of Commerce, *Survey of Current Business,* February 1981.

9. *Population base:*

U.S. population, 1980	:	224 million
Families		57.8 million
Average size of family		3.31

Total private wealth in America is almost $9.5 trillion, averaging $43,165 for every American, and $142,000 for each family. This, of course, does not mean that the average family has net assets in that amount, since the figures include business and farm assets as well as personal. It does mean, however, that, directly or indirectly, about $43,000 is employed in the private sector for every man, woman, and child, or $142,000 for every family, as wealth available for consumption, use, or production.

Almost $2.6 trillion, or $11,750 per person, is employed by manufacturing, commercial, and farming enterprises to help produce the nation's annual gross national product.

Americans own over $3.7 trillion in housing, or $16,865 per person. The average American owns $1,303 in clothing, $7,125 in durable goods such as furniture and appliances, $43 worth of food in the house, and $4,438 in motor vehicles.

Assets held by the federal government total $718.7 billion, or $3,200 per person. (The federal debt exceeds $1 trillion. If the federal government had to be liquidated to pay off that debt, the assets, theoretically, would be transferred to the holders of government securities, and hence the physical values would remain the same, although ownership would change hands.)

The physical assets of state and local governments exceed $5.3 trillion, most of them in the nation's highway system.

Not counting natural resources, America's total physical wealth exceeds $14.3 trillion, or $64,000 per person.

Not counting natural resources, the physical assets of Japan approximate $5.3 trillion, or $45,000 per person (Table 5). By comparison with the world's second-largest economy, America, then, possesses 2.7 times the gross national wealth of Japan and 42 percent more wealth per person. The gap between America and the world's second-wealthiest nation would widen even further were natural resources considered, since they are abundant in America and scarce in Japan.

Thus America is far ahead of any other country—not only in its annual gross national product but also dramatically ahead in gross national wealth.

With such an awesome superiority of national wealth, Americans accept their prosperity as a natural state, foreordained and always present. Americans have come not only to believe in America but also to believe in their right to

TABLE 5. Capital Stock, Japan, 1979 ($ in billions)

I. *Nonfinancial incorporated enterprises*

(1) Inventories		$ 239.5
(2) Net fixed assets		916.2
(3) Land		697.5
(4) Forests		34.9
(5) Minerals		2.4
	TOTAL	$1,890.5

II. *Financial institutions*

(1) Net fixed assets		$25.7
(2) Land		41.0
	TOTAL	$66.7

III. *General government*

(1) Net fixed assets		$548.6
(2) Land		151.7
(3) Forests		19.1
	TOTAL	$719.4

IV. *Households*

(1) Inventories		$ 39.3
(2) Net fixed assets		662.1
(3) Land		1,825.8
(4) Forests		112.8
(5) Other		3.6
	TOTAL	$2,643.6
	Grand Total	$5,320.2

Population: 115,835,000

(Source: Japanese Embassy, June 1981)

prosperity. Sometimes forgetting that the nation's base of wealth exists only because it was produced by those who came before, too many reach into the national storehouse, more willing to take than to replenish.

Rousseau wrote that the word *economy* was derived from the Greek words for *house* and *law,* that the original meaning was a "wise government of the house for the good of the whole family." He stated further that political economy is wise government of the state for the good of the whole people. Few would doubt that the explosive growth of the U.S. economy over the past fifty years has vastly improved life for virtually all Americans. The extent to which government can claim credit for the gains is, however, highly debatable, and many doubt how wisely government itself has been managed for the good of all the people, particularly in the past two decades.

In an earlier time, Henry David Thoreau observed: "Government never of itself furthered any enterprise, but by the alacrity with which it got out of its way. . . . The character inherent in the American people has done all that has been accomplished; and it would have done more, if the government had not sometimes got in the way."

Whatever government's contribution might have been in the past, it seems in recent years to have lubricated the nation's economic engine more with sawdust than with oil.

It took 173 years, from 1789 to 1962, for the federal government's annual spending to reach $100 billion. It took only another nine years, to 1971, to hit $200 billion; just four years, to 1975, to top $300 billion; two years, to 1977, to pass $400 billion; two years, to 1979, to reach almost $500 billion; and two years, to 1981, to shoot past $600 billion. By fiscal 1983, federal budget outlays, even with the newly imposed Reagan restraints, will reach nearly $800 billion. That represents over 23 percent of the nation's gross national product. When state and local government spending is added, total government spending, at all levels, consumes over 42 percent of the nation's output.

Twenty years ago government consumed approximately 20 percent of the GNP. Half a century ago, just before the crash of 1929, government consumed only 8 percent of the national economy. In 1950, the federal government spent $23 billion in social programs; in 1960, $26 billion; in 1970, $75 billion; and in 1980, $300 billion—an explosion of 1,300 percent in thirty years. During the past two decades, expenditures for social programs as a share of the total federal spending have increased from 25 to 41 percent, and the share for national defense has declined from 44 to 32 percent.

All that government spends out of the nation's annual output is, of course, not available to be spent by the working people and businesses who have earned the income. What is siphoned out of their pockets into Washington, state capitals, city halls, and county courthouses is more than money taken—it is a slice of economic freedom—personal decision-making—transferred from private citizens who have labored to earn the income, to public bodies which, theoretically, exercise the decision-making function on their behalf. It cannot be denied that government must spend to fulfill its duties, to "establish Justice, insure domestic Tranquility, provide for the common defense, promote the general Welfare . . ." What must be challenged, however, is the extent to which government injects itself into the lives and pockets of supposedly free people. If government spends 42 percent of the gross national product, government is making 42 percent of the economic decisions, and the people have given up 42 percent of their economic freedom.

Two hundred years ago Adam Smith observed:

> The statesman who should attempt to direct private people in what manner they ought to employ their capital, assumes an authority which could safely be trusted to no body, and which would nowhere be so dangerous as in the hands of a man who had the folly and presumption enough to fancy himself fit to exercise it.

Substitute government for statesman, and his words have particular relevance to the pernicious growth of government in America over the past half century.

Struggling to work its way out from under the dead weight of socialism, Smith's own country, Great Britain, is paying a dear price for nearly four decades of cancerous government growth and control. It is of historic significance that in 1976 even James Callaghan, then British Prime Minister and leader of the Labor Party, acknowledged the futility of excessive government spending, saying, "We used to think that you could spend your way out of a recession. . . . I tell you, in all candor, that that option no longer exists, and that insofar as it ever did exist, it only worked by injecting bigger doses of inflation into the economy followed by higher levels of unemployment as the next step. That is the history of the past twenty years." An analysis by the National Westminister Bank of England confirmed Callaghan's complaint: "Each 5 percent increase in national income spent by Government eventually causes a 1 percent decline in economic growth. . . . The problem stems from an environment in which politicians have tended to see a larger state consumption sector as one useful means of buying votes while at the same time concealing the fact that such largesse needs to be paid for by a diversion of economic sources from productive ends."

The experience of Sweden shows that when government spends more, people work less. As a percent of GNP, the Swedish government increased spending from 24 percent in 1950 to 64 percent in 1980, one of the highest governmental takes in the free, industrialized world. Compared to 1960, Swedes are working 24 percent fewer hours, absenteeism is up 63 percent, and overtime is down 70 percent. The Swedes are making rational decisions: If the government chooses to take and spend most of what they earn, the Swedes will choose to earn less. They are opting for more leisure time, to do their own home repairs, to barter their services (albeit inefficiently compared to their output at their jobs) outside their country's confiscatory tax system, and they are devising schemes to cheat the government out of at least a portion of its 64 percent tax take.

America has not yet reached the tax burden of Sweden, but if present trends continue, the 1980's could be the decade in which the U.S. tax burden exceeds 50 percent of GNP. Should that occur, Americans would be working more for their governments—federal, state, and local—than for themselves and their families.

Direct spending is at least measurable, but spending inflicted upon Americans by government regulations, while massive, is not so measureable. Annual budgets of federal regulatory agencies amount to $4.8 billion, but that represents only the top of the tip of the iceberg. The Joint Economic Committee sees the cost to the American people of complying with government regulations as a hidden hemorrhage.

In short, government costs, direct and indirect, have inflicted the dual pain of massive taxation and runaway inflation. The engine of plenty pings and knocks with overload, as signs of stress emerge.

If Chief Justice John Marshall's observation is true, that "the power to tax involves the power to destroy," then destruction in recent years has been an unrelenting visitor to America. Between 1972 and 1977, federal taxes increased 72 percent, state taxes 69 percent, and local taxes 56 percent: a combined increase of 68 percent. When the increased government take is compared to the increased total national income, an even more ominous pattern emerges. For fiscal 1981, total national income increased approximately $162 billion; federal government tax collections increased $96 billion; state and local collections increased $30 billion. Hence, the $126 billion increase to all government take represents 74 percent of the total increase in national income. Thus government, per se, makes itself the biggest beneficiary of any increase in national income, leaving less than a quarter of the increase in the hands of those who have produced the increase.

The nineteenth century economist Henry George observed: "Taxation . . . operates upon energy, and industry, and skill, and thrift, like a fine upon these qualities. . . . We punish with a tax the man who covers barren fields with ripened grain; we fine him who puts up machinery, and him who drains a swamp."

Contrary to what some would like to believe, it is neither the rich nor the poor who pay most of the income tax extracted by the federal government. While the rich pay a higher percentage of their income in tax than any other economic class, there simply are not that many of them, and the poor are mostly excused by law from paying income taxes. So it is that the great American middle class carries most of the federal income tax burden.

People with incomes under $10,000 pay only 2.2 percent of the total federal income tax collected. About half of the people with incomes under $10,000 pay no federal income tax at all. Persons in the $10,000 to $50,000 range pay 65 percent of the taxes. Persons in the $50,000 to $100,000 range pay 18 percent of the taxes.

Contrary to the widespread view that the wealthy get away with paying no taxes, those with incomes above $100,000, representing only 1 percent of the taxpayers, pay 15 percent of the tax collected. There are 700,000 such returns, of which only eight tenths of 1 percent produce no tax.

In the U.S. adult population of 158.5 million, 40.3 million people, one quarter of the population, pay no federal income tax, virtually all of them at the low end of the income scale.

John Stuart Mill wisely noted: "Those who pay no taxes, disposing by their votes of other people's money, have every motive to be lavish, and none to economize." In his time, that argument was used against giving the vote to those who did not pay taxes, but today it can more appropriately be used to bolster the case for policies that stimulate economic growth. For it is with growth that jobs are created, standards of living elevated, and more Americans become taxpayers. With their tax payments, their stake in America grows, as does their interest in an efficient and frugal government.

The case for personal tax cuts has been much debated, but what seems obvious is this: If a person is able to keep more of his income, he will be more highly motivated to work harder to earn more. If something is subsidized, more of it is produced, and if something is taxed, less of it is produced. For example, American milk-price supports have caused an overproduction of milk, while in Sweden, high tax rates have caused the Swedes to work less, as noted earlier. The Kennedy tax cut, finally pushed through Congress by Lyndon Johnson in February 1964, is a classic case in point. The average personal tax rate schedule was reduced by 20 percent. Even though the tax rates were reduced, the actual income to the Treasury increased for every income group except those with incomes under $10,000. The income group between $10,000 to $20,000 paid 15 percent more in taxes; those over $50,000 paid 28 percent more. The explanation for the flow of more taxes into the Treasury, created by reducing the tax rate, is fundamental, simple, rational, and based on human nature: People work more so they can earn more, when they can keep more; people invest in productive tax-producing ventures, rather than tax shelters, when they can keep more of the profits they earn.

The case for lowering marginal tax rates* need not, and should not, however, be based on the premise that they will generate more taxes. The case for lower tax rates should be based on the premise that they will generate taxes more efficiently while increasing economic activity, thus increasing productivity, creating jobs, and raising the average standard of living. Taxation in America is already too high, so marginal tax rates should be set at levels necessary to raise only those taxes required to pay for a more streamlined government.

Unfortunately, the debate on taxing and spending policy has focused mainly on whether or not reduced marginal tax rates can increase government revenue rather than on the relationship of reduced marginal tax rates to reduced spending. Indeed, the federal government's tax appetite, voracious as it is, remains inadequate to meet the needs of the federal spending machine.

Other solutions, even worse than increased taxes, have been relied upon to keep Washington in the manner to which it has become accustomed.

The most pernicious form of federal fiscal policy is deficit spending: spending, year in and year out, more money than the government takes in.

The political motivation behind this is obvious: Politicians can hand out benefits without having to raise taxes to pay for them. David Hume, the eighteenth-century philoso-

*The marginal tax rate is the tax rate that applies to each additional dollar of income. For example, at $20,000 of taxable income, an additional dollar of ordinary income, such as cash wages or interest income, is taxed at a marginal rate of 24 percent. At $30,000 of taxable income, the rate is 37 percent. (Taxable income is generally equal to adjusted gross income, less exemptions, less itemized deductions.)

pher, noted how enticing it was for public figures to engage in great spending programs without increasing the tax burden: "The practice therefore of contracting debt will almost infallibly be abused in every government. It would scarcely be more imprudent to give a prodigal son a credit in every banker's shop in London, than to empower a statesman to draw bills, in this manner, upon posterity."

For America, the federal government's power to borrow, and to spend beyond its means, has inflicted a rapidly escalating burden upon future generations of Americans. It took 154 years, from 1789 to 1943, for the federal government's debt to pass the $100 billion mark. The following year, at the peak of World War II, it hit $201 billion. It took another twenty years, until 1962, for it to reach $303 billion. Then the dike against deficit spending burst: In ten years, 1971, it hit $409 billion; in another five years, 1975, it hit $544 billion; it hit $651 billion in 1976, $727 billion in 1977, $802 billion in 1978, $914 billion in 1980, and on October 22, 1981, the federal debt of the United States of America passed the $1 trillion mark, a burden of about $4,500 for every living American. The interest on the national debt exceeds $100 billion annually, more than it cost to run the entire federal government in 1961.

Deficit spending, at bottom, is not a fiscal issue only. It is a profoundly moral matter. When one generation spends at the expense of a future generation, it must justify its actions to itself and to posterity. It is one thing for an individual or a family to borrow to enjoy a present comfort—a home, a car, a vacation—knowing that in the months or years ahead it must repay the loan, with interest, from future earnings. It is quite a different matter for one group of people to borrow so they may enjoy a present benefit and pass along the responsibility for repayment of the debt and its recurring interest to another group of people: a future generation.

While a case can be made for deficit spending during an extreme emergency, or during the low point of an economic cycle, the deficit should be covered by a surplus, within a few years, during the high point of the economic cycle. Otherwise, one generation is benefiting immorally by imposing an economic burden on children, some of whom are yet to be born. Surely, history cannot be kind with such a people. Surely, good people eventually will lose confidence in elected representatives who use public debt to buy present popularity by mortgaging future generations.

Just as, two centuries ago, "No taxation without representation" became the battle cry of the colonists who freed America from British chains, so should it be today. Deficit spending is taxation without representation. It is the imposition of a fiscal burden upon millions of future Americans who can have no voice in the matter. They cannot vote, for they are either too young or yet unborn. The issue is clear: The present population benefits at the expense of the future population; one receives, the other pays; one gains, the other loses.

Beyond the burden of debt and interest, the injustice is compounded by the relationship of deficit spending to inflation. Deficit spending is the father of inflation.

There is no great mystery to inflation, even though some would like Americans to believe that it is esoterically complex, pervasively uncontrollable, possibly even made in Heaven. Scapegoats for inflation range from businessmen accused of setting prices too high to labor unions charged with pushing wages too high. Energy companies have become favorite whipping boys. Many politicians, including Jimmy Carter, lashed out at them during the 1980 elections, knowing full well that the administration's own Bureau of Labor Statistics had advised the Congress that energy price increases accounted for only 1.9 percent of the 12.4 percent inflation in 1980.

Rising prices can siphon spending away from some products and into others, thereby limiting demand and distorting investment, but only government can cause inflation.

Just as surely as cars are made in Detroit, rubber in Akron, and steel in Pittsburgh, inflation is produced in Washington, D.C. Almost invariably, when government expands, the value of the dollar declines. Government growth in the past thirty years has meant deficit spending, and with it, a related increase in the money supply.

When Congress passes spending bills, the sum of which

exceed the revenues to be collected by the Treasury in taxes, the difference must be found somewhere to pay the government's bills. The Treasury Department tries to borrow the needed funds by offering government securities for sale: savings bonds, Treasury notes, etc. When the deficit is so large that the Treasury Department finds it difficult to raise the funds in the private financial markets without driving interest rates to unacceptable levels, or drying up the private markets as a source of capital for industry, it turns to a mechanism available only to the federal government. The department transfers its notes to the Federal Reserve System, the arm of the federal government that controls the money supply. The Federal Reserve, in effect, prints up more money on the government printing presses and pays it to the Treasury Department in exchange for the notes which Treasury printed. Treasury then uses the new money to pay the government's bills.

There is, of course, one rub. If the government continues to flood more newly printed dollars into the economy in excess of the annual increase in goods and services produced by the economy, then the increased number of dollars in the economy will represent the same amount of goods and services that the smaller number of dollars previously represented. When it takes more dollars to represent the same amount of goods and services—that's inflation.

Suppose America awakened one morning to find that nothing of economic value was left in the world except ten apple pies. Suppose, further, that there was no money in the world, and that the government decided to print ten one-dollar bills to represent the total money supply. Each pie would be worth one dollar. If the government then proceeded to print an additional ten one-dollar bills, the total money supply would be doubled. Each pie would be worth two dollars. The pies would not be any bigger nor any better, nor would there be any more of them. They would just cost twice as much.

Obviously, this is oversimplification. It is, nonetheless, essentially the way the national money supply works. When the government presses print more paper money to pay for deficit spending, the real value of the dollar goes down,

since it takes more dollars to buy the same product or service. Paper money is valuable only to the extent that it
represents something of value: that is, all the paper dollars
in the economy stand only for all the things of real economic
value within the economy. If the total number of paper
dollars is increased without increasing the goods and services which represent real economic value, then each dollar
stands for a smaller amount of real economic value. The
proof of the pudding lies in the economic statistics of the
past two decades. According to the Treasury Department,
the money supply (M1: currency and demand deposits) increased at the average rate of 3.3 percent from 1957 to
1967. Inflation (according to the Consumer Price Index) averaged 1.7 percent during that period. From 1967 to 1977,
the money supply increased an average of 7.3 percent, and
inflation averaged 6.1 percent. From 1978 through 1980,
the money supply increased an average of almost 8 percent,
and inflation averaged 11.5 percent.*

The foregoing can be represented by a simple economic
law: If, over the long run, the money supply is increased at
a rate greater than the increase in productivity, inflation will
occur.

People don't like this economic law. When adding up
their income, they wish that two plus two equaled five.
When adding up their bills, they wish that two plus two
equaled three. Regardless of their wishes, the sum always
equals four, and until they squarely face that fact, their lives
will be on shaky fiscal ground. Over the past thirty years, a
majority of U.S. congressmen and senators, as well as several
Presidents, have refused to face squarely this economic fact
of life.

When Lyndon Johnson decided that the American people could finance a "guns and butter" policy—that is, pay for
a war in Southeast Asia as well as for his so-called Great
Society programs without raising taxes—he sowed the seeds
of inflation. But it took at least 218 congressmen and 51
senators to vote the funds for these misadventures. No Presi-

*In February 1980, the definitions of the money supply were changed so that
M1-A represented currency and demand deposits, and M1-B included M1-A plus
negotiable orders of withdrawals (NOW accounts).

dent can spend a penny unless Congress appropriates it, and few congresses can spend money over presidential vetoes. Whatever the rate of spending and pileup of national debt, the members of the House and Senate who vote to spend the funds must be held accountable.

John Maynard Keynes, the father of "Keynesian" economics, is credited (or blamed) for providing the economic theory upon which deficit spending is based. Many politicians remember that he argued for priming the pump with increased federal spending in bad times, but those politicians prefer to ignore that he also argued for generating fiscal surpluses in good times so that the debt created by the deficits could be repaid. Keynes, who clearly saw the folly of unremitting deficit spending and the debilitating effect of the inflation which it created, warned: "There is no subtler, no surer means of overturning the existing basis of society than to debauch the currency. The process engages all the hidden forces of economic law on the side of destruction, and does it in a manner which not one man in a million is able to diagnose."

When American politicians stop debauching the currency, stop voting to spend more than the government takes in, stop monetizing the debt by forcing government printing presses to provide the dollars to pay the public bills, then, and only then, will inflation be brought to an end.

Elimination of inflation, by itself, will not guarantee economic prosperity; it must be accompanied by increased economic productivity. That is a fundamental prerequisite.

In 1948, West Germany, under the leadership of Chancellor Konrad Adenauer, stopped its ruinous postwar inflation and achieved economic growth in one year's time by cutting the budget and removing wage and price controls. In 1953, America, under the leadership of President Eisenhower, reduced inflation to under 1 percent and stimulated economic growth by cutting the budget and removing wage and price controls. In 1958, France cut spending and devalued the franc, and within three years inflation and unemployment were down, and the economy growing.

In all three experiences, the common denominators are clear: Reduce artificial economic controls, reduce deficit spending, and thereby control the money supply. The short-term pain of contracting public spending and the money supply produces long-term gain. Inflation can be controlled. Productivity can be stimulated. Prosperity can be produced. It requires the will to make it happen. Right decisions by government can create the climate in which Americans can be freed to unclog the nation's economic engine and make it hum again.

That America will opt for work and thrift, and for investing a piece of today's prosperity so tomorrow may be strengthened, is not a certainty. But if the past is any measure, the smart money will bet on America. The land of prosperity personified is not willing to slide into decay. Compared to what America is, Al Jolson's line should aptly describe what America can be: "You ain't seen nothin' yet!"

If America embraces the no-growth policies of those who want to lock up the wilderness and make the world safe for the snail darter, then the smart money will lose, and Al Jolson will be proved wrong. The future, indeed, will be bleak.

For the past decade, it has been fashionable in some circles to preach the coming of gloom and doom, starting with the 1969 assessment of U Thant, then Secretary General of the United Nations: "Members of the United Nations have perhaps ten years left in which to subordinate their ancient quarrels and launch a global partnership to curb the arms race, to improve the human environment, to defuse the population explosion, and to supply the required momentum to development efforts. If such a global partnership is not forged within the next decade, then I fear that the problems I have mentioned will have reached such staggering proportions that they will be beyond our capacity to control."

In 1972, the Club of Rome, a collection of thirty intellectuals from ten countries, published its prophecy in *The Limits of Growth,* claiming ". . . the length of life of the biosphere as an inhabitable region for organisms is to be measured in decades rather than in hundreds of millions of years. This is entirely the fault of our own species."

The final sentence of the Commentary on the report, signed by the club's Executive Committee, left little question: "The crux of the matter is not only whether the human species will survive, but even more, whether it can survive without falling into a state of worthless existence." They seemed to be expanding upon the theme of the first U.S. Commissioner of Patents, Henry L. Ellsworth, who in his annual report to the Congress in 1843 advised: "The advancement of the arts from year to year, taxes our credulity and seems to presage the arrival of that period when human improvement must end."

The no-growth advocates in America and around the world, in and out of government, have painted a nightmare picture of the future: a hideous world, spilling over with hungry people shivering as forests are denuded and oil deposits sucked dry, choked by pollution, and ravaged by disease. They have America's cities smothered under toxic wastes and automobile exhaust fumes. For them, the car has become a symbol of what is wrong in America. Seeing phallic symbols in pointed grills and irrational macho satisfactions in high-horsepower engines, they have condemned the car for clogging roads, fouling air, consuming energy, taking lives, encouraging urban sprawl, and spawning dull, unfulfilling assembly-line jobs.

The car has become their devil, and the so-called Highway Lobby his consortium of fallen souls, mesmerized under his spell, and pursuing his dictate to rape the earth. Never mind that over 80 percent of adult Americans have chosen to get driver's licenses, that virtually every sixteen-year-old has rushed to take his driver's test, that people have wanted the personal mobility and freedom offered by owning a car, that families have yearned for living space in suburbs, that cars and roads have made distances shrink, have brought families and friends closer together and products within the reach of the average person, nor that healthy paychecks have poured out of the plants, firms, and garages that have helped America move.

For the elitists who have needed no growth, because they or their families before them had already banked their stake, the matter of spreading jobs and expanding freedom of mobility across the country has been unimportant. They had theirs. Disturbing their environment to create economic growth was not in their selfish interest. Setting balanced national goals to improve both the environment and the economy was beneath their sense of self-righteousness. Spending $100 million to eliminate 90 percent of the pollution from the coke ovens at U.S. Steel's Clairton mill wasn't good enough if $500 million could eliminate the last 10 percent, even though it meant closing other facilities for lack of capital investment. Failing to see that the worst environment of all is the one in which people are cold, hungry, and without jobs, they have gone after business with a vengeance—using government to block the production of energy, increase the costs of industrial production, and slow the growth of America's productive capacity. Slowing America's economic engine might make the skies clearer, and the fields greener, for those who could bask in the sun, but for most Americans, dependent upon a weekly paycheck, it would mean fewer jobs to go around.

In 1976, the elitists and their cousins, the negativists, found a friend in Jimmy Carter. He peopled the subcabinet levels of his administration with those who emerged from the trendy no-growth subculture. They told him what they wanted to hear. They crafted their vision for America in the summum bonum of their works, *The Global 2000 Report to the President,* prepared by Jimmy Carter's Council on Environmental Quality and Department of State. In their major findings and conclusions, they scolded America for her wasteful habits, and made dire predictions for the future unless America mended her ways. For example:

> ". . . the world in 2000 will be more crowded, more polluted, less stable ecologically, and more vulnerable to disruption . . . the world's people will be poorer . . . the world's finite fuel resources . . . pose difficult economic and environmental problems. . . . Regional water shortages will become more severe. . . . Significant losses of world forests will continue over the next 20 years. . . . Serious deterioriation of agricultural soils will occur worldwide. . . . Atmospheric concentrations

of carbon dioxide and ozone-depleting chemicals . . . could alter the world's climate. . . . Extinctions of plant and animal species will increase dramatically."

Congressman Henry Reuss (D-Wis.), chairman of the Joint Economic Committee, said the report projected "a world a bare twenty years from now that is desolate and dying. . . ."

What cannot be denied is that the report accurately presented the opinions, the collective mind-set, of those who believe America's best days are behind her, if indeed, they believe she had any best days. To the Jeremiahs, crying in front of the factory gates and alongside the superhighways, "Repent or be destroyed," America is on the skids. But the evidence, even some of their own, tells a different story. Surely, the wealth and productive capacity of America, detailed in previous pages, are not the ebbing life signs of a dying patient. *The Global 2000 Report* acknowledged, not in its narrative, but in its accompanying data, that GNP per person for the less-developed countries will increase over 50 percent in the next twenty years. It failed to square this, however, with the assertion that the "world's people will be poorer."

Herman Kahn, the highly respected futurist and chairman of the Hudson Institute, characterized *The Global 2000 Report* as "Globaloney 2000." He pointed out:

> The bias of Global 2000 is toward pessimism on practically every issue; a perverse tendency always to see every glass as half empty rather than half full . . . The world population growth rate declined sharply to 1.7 percent . . . a 20 percent drop. . . . By assuming the opposite, the Global 2000 seems to be engaging in deliberate scare tactics. . . . The insistence of Global 2000 that the world is headed straight for disaster is intrinsically implausible. Gross World Product and Gross World Product per capita have been growing inexorably almost every year for at least a century. Life expectancy, the best single available indicator of

human health and welfare, continues to lengthen almost everywhere, year after year. Pollution levels in
the developed world are being reduced. . . . Crying
wolf . . . is the strategy of the do-good establishment
which specializes in claiming that disaster will strike—
unless we follow their advice in a big way right away.
. . . Our society pays a heavy cost in terms of low
morale when its establishment endorses the notion
that our socioeconomic system is, in effect, corrupt
and evil.

Ben Wattenberg, a demography expert and Senior Fellow at the American Enterprise Institute, confirmed the
population trend: "All around the world, birthrates have
gone down. The so-called 'population explosion' is receding
—and quite rapidly in most places. . . . A quick tour of these
poor nations shows declines in birthrates everywhere, although at very different speeds. . . . In the past twenty years
India got about a third of the way to rates that will produce
zero population growth."

So much for those who seem to have a perverse need not
only to focus on the worst of all possible future worlds but
also to invent a generalized pathology for the world, not
warranted by the evidence.

Speaking for the mainstream, who reject the gloom and
doom thesis, Austin Kiplinger, whose forecasts have helped
guide thousands of Americans in their economic planning
over the past three decades, sees an even better, more prosperous America in the years ahead:

Living standards will be better. . . . Records will topple
for production, profits, economic growth. . . . New oil
sources . . . will be tapped. . . . Many more new
households . . . a market for 22 million more housing
units . . . adds up to billions in new business. . . . Profits
. . . will be plowed back into modern machinery, new
products, expansion, research. . . . Inflation will come
down gradually. . . . More emphasis on work, output,
growth. A different mix, reflecting the adaptability of
our population. Confident, pragmatic, energetic, ready

to change as necessity dictates. This is what provides the basis for optimism about the future.

The Futures Group, in cooperation with Peat, Marwick, Mitchell & Co., has forecast an 88 percent real growth in GNP for America by the year 2000, under a medium-growth scenario. Even under a low-growth scenario a 27 percent real increase is forecast, and under a high-growth scenario, a 120 percent increase is projected. The range of annual growth in the three scenarios is from 0.8 to 4.1 percent.

In June 1981, Robey Clark, president of the American Association of Petroleum Geologists, stated that with conservation and domestic production, the United States could have all the energy she needs within five years. On the heels of that announcement came another from one of Britain's largest food producers, Ranks Hovis McDougall, Ltd.—the announcement that the company had developed, and was producing in a pilot plant, a protein equivalent to the best beefsteak at a fraction of the cost. This product can be turned into palatable imitations of meat, fish, cheese, or cake. Commercial plants could produce ten thousand pounds of meat-substitute protein a week and would be naturals for less-developed countries.

Contrary to the prophets of gloom and doom, the world isn't sitting on its hands waiting to expire. People and organizations are planning, inventing, investing, and producing.

By the year 2000, America will have grown to 260.3 million people, an increase of 32.7 million, or 15 percent. For every new mouth to feed there will also be two hands to work. America's gross national product in constant 1972 dollars is projected to increase to $2.7 trillion, an increase of $1.2 trillion, or 84 percent. GNP per person in constant dollars will grow to $10,442, an increase of $3,937, or 61 percent, over 1980. The labor force will grow to 134.2 million, an increase of 29.5 million, up 28 percent.

Nothing guarantees, however, the continued growth and affluence for America. It must be made to happen. But given the base of wealth, prosperity, technological capacity, and managerial proficiency, there is no reason why it should not come to pass. Only the will is needed because the tools are all at hand. And who dares speculate that a people who, in their past, fashioned the greatest nation on earth have somehow lost the desire to make their future shine? Casting aside the naysayers, Americans once again are turning to the producers.

That means, for America, the prognosis: Promising.

VI

PROMETHEUS UNBOUND

God grants liberty only to those who love it, and
are always ready to guard and defend it.
                    —DANIEL WEBSTER

"WE ARE FREE TODAY because of America."

Spoken with great passion, those were the words of a
bright young Lutheran minister as he stood before his
fifteenth-century stone church in the rural village of Herbitzheim, just fifteen miles from the southwest border of
Germany.

"Free," he continued, "not only because American
troops liberated our village in 1945, but also because today
America provides the umbrella of security for the entire
Western world."

Standing nearby, Herbitzheim's elderly Roman Catholic
priest and the Burgermeister nodded emphatic agreement.

The articulate, sandy-haired, freckle-faced Lutheran
clergyman insisted that we step inside the ancient church,
move to the altar, and inspect the well-thumbed Holy Bible
with the inscription of a U.S. Army chaplain far from home
on Christmas Eve, 1945.

It was the first Sunday after the first Easter in the new
decade of the 1980's. The leaders of the small rural village
along the French-German border perceived what millions
around the world believed, but what others either feared or
wanted to forget. After leading the Free World to victory in
World War II, America, with her military might, secured the
peace. From the North Sea to the South Seas, from the
lowlands of Holland to the highlands of Korea, American

commitments stemmed the tide of tyranny; and where those commitments faltered, freedom failed.*

Since World War II, America has committed herself to preserve the peace around the world through seven collective defense treaties covering forty-one countries, four executive agreements covering four additional countries, a memorandum of agreement with Egypt and Israel (the Camp David Accords), four presidential doctrines covering broad political declarations, five congressional resolutions expressing national resolve during times of foreign-policy crises, and thirty-four executive branch policy declarations and communiqués jointly issued with foreign governments. All the treaties stipulate that they are subject to the constitutional processes of all parties. Time and changing conditions have eroded the sense of shared commitment among some of the signatories. Since 1967 France has not participated in NATO military matters; however, most Western strategists believe she could be counted on in a major crisis.

The SEATO Pact was a casualty of the Vietnam War. Cuba has been excluded from the Rio Pact since 1962, and Communist revolutionary activity in Central America, along with the Falklands crisis, has put added strains on hemispheric relations.

Nevertheless, America's treaties with her allies continue to represent a collective commitment to peace through mu-

---

*In a strange twist of history, while I was being told that Herbitzheim was free because of America, I was also being informed that America was free because of Herbitzheim, at least in a round-about sort of way.

It was in the village of Herbitzheim, while tracing my own ancestral roots, that I first heard the little-known story, later confirmed by the German-American Institute at Saarbrücken, of how Benjamin Franklin's boudoir diplomacy saved the day for America at Yorktown.

While U.S. Minister to France during the American Revolution, Franklin had engaged in a liaison with the young Countess of Vorbach, spending a month with her near Herbitzheim to persuade her to help the American revolutionary cause (one assumes the good doctor could have had no other motive). As a result of Franklin's entreaties, she implored her elderly husband, the count, to send troops to help Washington. He responded by sending the Régiment du Ponts, led by French officers, hence the French name, but composed almost entirely of German soldiers from the Herbitzheim area, and it was they who held the line for Washington at the Battle of Yorktown.

The director of the German-American Institute spelled out the moral, lest it escape me: The American Revolution was really won in a boudoir near Herbitzheim by the inestimable Dr. Franklin, rather than through his high diplomacy in Paris. The director was, perhaps, not altogether wrong.

tual defense, and though they guarantee less than perfect harmony among the signatories, they convey a warning to potential aggressors around the world.

America's presidential doctrines promulgated since World War II all expressed determination to prevent aggression. The Truman Doctrine (1947), brought about by Communist efforts to gain control of Greece, indicated that America would aid subjugated peoples around the world. The Eisenhower Doctrine (1957), precipitated by the Lebanese crisis, stated America's intention to prevent aggression in the Middle East. The Nixon Doctrine (1969), developed as a strategy in the Vietnam War, stated that while America would aid her allies, the manpower for the defense of a country must be provided by that country. The Carter Doctrine (1980) claimed that "an attempt by any outside force to gain control of the Persian Gulf Region . . . will be repelled by use of any means necessary, including military force."

In addition to the various obligations entered into around the world by America since the end of World War II, the Monroe Doctrine, in the Western Hemisphere, remains officially in effect, never having been repudiated. Set down in a speech to Congress by President James Monroe, on December 2, 1823, it held these key words:

> The American continents . . . are henceforth not to be considered as subjects for future colonization by any European power. . . . We should consider any attempt on their part to extend their system to any portion of this hemisphere as dangerous to our peace and safety.

In addition to America's openly negotiated international agreements, it is not unreasonable to suspect that covert understandings and agreements may also exist. While a free society abhors secrecy, such agreements, limited and cautiously drawn, may well be in the best interests of the nation. Who could argue that circumspect support for the Afghan rebels, or support for a more moderate government in Iran, would not be in America's best interests? Indeed, if presidents do not judiciously use secret diplomacy to further

America's interests, they will be strait-jacketed by the glare of media hyperbole as they face a complex world.

But beyond America's formal obligations, open or undisclosed, lies the question of America's interests. Although no treaty nor agreement exists, would America stand idly by if the Soviet Union were to invade the southern part of Africa, with its strategic mineral deposits of chromium, iron, manganese, nickel, uranium, platinum, copper, and vanadium? Even though America's mutual-security pact with Taiwan has been terminated, would it be in the nation's interest to permit Red China to overrun that island?

Israel is, indeed, a special case. America has no mutual-defense treaty with Israel. Yet, setting aside completely the political relationship of Israel to America, no soil anywhere in the world beyond America's shores is more vital to U.S. interests. Israel is the only land bridge connecting the three continents of Africa, Asia and Europe. Europe keeps only a thirty-day supply of oil. The Soviets could cut that thread and prostrate Western Europe. Africa contains eighteen of the world's twenty strategic minerals. It is a geopolitical reality that a free Israel stands as a bulwark against the Soviet thirst for oil and minerals. Israel is the only democracy, and the only constant friend of America, in the Middle East. The existence or nonexistence of a mutual-defense treaty between America and Israel is irrelevant. Israel's freedom is vital to American interests.

Conversely, despite a mutual-security agreement with Pakistan, or a treaty with Thailand, would America send troops to protect those two countries in the event of their invasion? Despite commitments or the lack of commitments, America must act where her interests are threatened, and to the extent that a measured response matches those interests. No more, no less, and not just today but in the future, recognizing full well that America's strength is in some degree dependent upon the strength of her allies. For that reason, and for that reason alone, our concept of security must provide a decent measure of protection for America's willing and worthy allies. And for thirty-five years it has done precisely that.

Lost in the spectacular failure of Vietnam is the fact that

America's mutual-security treaties, agreements, and declarations have protected most of the world successfully from overt Communist aggression. At the turn of the century, Secretary of State Elihu Root said, "The main object of diplomacy is to keep the country out of trouble." Despite the terrible failure of Vietnam, diplomacy backed by military strength has kept America and most of her allies free. NATO, ANZUS, and SEATO countries, Japan, the Philippines, South Korea, and even Taiwan, today remain free from Communist military intervention. Ironically, certain of the Rio Pact countries of the Western Hemisphere are a different and disgraceful story, but even there, most of Central and South America is not yet irretrievably lost.

Lest there be any doubt about the significance of America's umbrella of security, one need only observe the thousands who take enormous risks to get securely under that umbrella.

Since World War II, over eight hundred thousand European refugees have been admitted to America. First, they came mainly from Germany, Austria, and Italy. Following the 1956 Hungarian Revolution against Communism, over fifty thousand Hungarians sought and received refuge in America. When Communism brutally put down protests in East Germany, Czechoslovakia, and Poland, thousands more fled to America. During the 1979–80 peak period, more than fifty thousand refugees, mostly Jewish, came to the United States from the Soviet Union. Between the imposition of martial law in Poland on December 13, 1981, and September 30, 1982, about seven thousand Poles emigrated to America.

When in mid-1982 Poland's Red martial-law regime permitted around five hundred Poles to travel to Spain for the World Cup soccer matches, about half of them sought political asylum there.

Following the Korean War, three hundred thousand Koreans emigrated to America. Since Castro seized power in Cuba in 1959, one million Cubans have landed on U.S. shores. Following the Vietnam War, about six hundred thousand Indochinese traveled halfway 'round the world to put their lives back together in America. In the past three decades, over 1.6 million Mexicans have entered the United States legally, and between five and eight million are estimated to have entered illegally. Over one million attempting to enter illegally are apprehended annually.

Altogether, since the end of World War II, over twelve million people have legally poured into America seeking new and better lives, and one can only speculate on how many additional millions wanted to immigrate. While the wisdom of America's permitting such massive immigration can be questioned seriously, there can be little doubt about the message such immigration conveys: America continues to be the world's best place to live. While Communism must build walls to keep people in, America cannot keep people out.

A modern symbol of the world's crosscurrents of hope and despair is the famous refugee camp at Traiskirchen, Austria. Since 1955, over three hundred thousand refugees en route to the Free World have been fed, clothed, counseled and consoled at the camp, most of them on their way to America. Located on the fringe of Communism within a day's ride from Poland, Czechoslovakia, East Germany, Hungary, and the Soviet Union, the Traiskirchen refugee camp has provided safe haven to those who have managed to escape from behind the Iron Curtain.

Inspecting that camp, as I did on a snowy January day in 1982, one senses, firsthand, the despair and hope commingled in the hearts and minds of those crammed into the Traiskirchen barracks—despair over the plight of friends and family left behind; hope for the new lives they seek to build in America or other free countries willing to admit them.

Poland's imposition of martial law had swamped the camp with refugees from that unhappy land. The barracks we visited, probably the best, served as a grim reminder that even the best of refugee camps is among the worst of places to live. In a nearby kitchen, refugees stirred huge kettles of soup with long-armed wooden paddles, while others scrubbed the plain gray walls and floors of the hallway.

Andrey Bobrowski was lying across an upper bunk near the door. One of the lucky few, he would leave for America within the week. A Polish journalist with a sister in Chicago, he had been cleared for immigration into the United States.

For most of the 150 Polish refugees sprawling on double-decker cots jammed tightly together in a thirty-by-eighty-foot room, the future was not so bright. Nearly all under forty, they had fled Poland because its Communist system simply didn't work. Rather than producing plenty, the economic system created scarcity. Rather than permitting them to think as they chose, the political system forced them to conform or resist in sullen silence. They wanted to be free; they wanted a chance to build their futures. Most of all, as they stressed repeatedly, they wanted to get as far away as possible from Communism and the Soviet Union. For an American, it was surprising to hear many of them say they preferred not to immigrate to one of the Western European democracies because they would still be too close to Communism for comfort. One was jarred by the intensity of their feelings against Communism in general and the Soviet Union in particular.

The young Poles crammed into the stuffy barracks at Traiskirchen spoke passionately for their thirty thousand countrymen at refugee camps scattered throughout Austria —and they spoke for countless thousands of others who remained in confinement behind the Iron Curtain. In broken English or through able interpreters, they expressed the universal language of desire for freedom and opportunity.

When I asked whether the Polish people thought the Soviet Union was behind the military takeover of Poland, they laughed incredulously, and one replied for all: "Of course. There isn't a person in Poland who doesn't know this is the work of the Soviet Union."

Katrine Tatar, a skilled Polish medical biologist, shared two upper bunks with her husband and their five-year-old daughter. Asked why she had applied for immigration to Australia rather than America she replied: "For two reasons: It is the land of the future that seems to need people, and America is so difficult to get in."

She was correct, of course: America is difficult to enter; but not because America does not accept thousands of refugees each year. Rather, it is because most refugees the

world 'round choose America first. By their choice they
confirm a belief in America. They make a mockery of those
who mock and castigate America—the freest, most prosperous, most compassionate country on earth. No numbers can
better measure a nation's quality than the numbers of people who seek to pull up their roots and transplant them to
their chosen land. They desire to become Americans, believing they will be free because America has the strength to
keep them free. Many of them know this firsthand, for they
have witnessed America using her power to help her friends
around the world.

During the past thirty years, America has provided military assistance to forty-seven countries—$53 billion in mili-
tary equipment grants, $22 billion in low-interest military
equipment loans, $6 billion in excess U.S. military supplies,
and $2 billion in military training programs. Although most
of the funds went to Europe following World War II, the
more recent major beneficiaries of the foreign military sales
program have been Israel ($12 billion), Vietnam ($15 billion), and South Korea ($5 billion). The fiscal 1982 budget
provided for $4 billion in loans and $47 million in foreign
military education and training. It is hardly arguable that
military aid buys America more security than she could have
by spending like sums on U.S. forces stationed around the
world.

In addition to the military aid America has provided
around the world since the end of World War II, ninety-one
countries have received $14.6 billion in economic aid from
America. Believing that American dollars could help build
healthy economies, thereby promoting freedom and peace,
America dug deeply into her pocket and gave away the
earnings of her people on a massive, unmatched scale.

No doubt, American dollars helped. But the effectiveness
—the cost-benefit ratio—of the torrent of dollars is extremely doubtful. Indeed, the evidence indicates overwhelmingly that billions were wasted, misdirected, and
squandered. All of Africa received U.S. economic aid, and
today most of Africa is against America. India, Iraq, Iran,
Syria, Cuba, and South Yemen received aid, and today they
are America's enemies. Red China received it, and is in line

for more, despite its support of North Korea and North Vietnam against America. Japan received it and, while prospering today, is unfairly subsidizing its exports to America and refusing to carry its share of the mutual-defense burden in Asia.

Representatives of one U.S. television network traveled to the Indian subcontinent to prepare a documentary on the impact of America's $8 billion gift to that region of the world and returned reporting: "If we did a two-hour documentary on American aid to the Indian subcontinent, you'd hate it. There's almost nothing left to show for the money."

The lessons learned from distributing economic aid around the globe for thirty-five years seem clear: Don't give U.S. economic aid unless the evidence shows that the political and economic systems of the recipient country are capable of effectively using the aid and the recipient country has demonstrated its constant friendship to America.

The spreading of America's wealth around the world clearly has been the weak link in the support system America has provided her allies. American dollars have been better spent when they have been related directly to expenditures for mutual defense. When dollars are sent to foreign countries to be spent by foreign governments, they can easily go astray, but when fighter planes are provided to defend a previously agreed-upon stretch of border as part of a larger multinational defense agreement, they can hardly fit into the palaces or pockets of foreign princes.

America's international security agreements, military grants, loans, and training programs, are only the beginnings of a global strategy to preserve peace. Only America can provide the leadership to keep the Free World free. But America cannot want for others what they do not want for themselves. America cannot protect friends who seek to embrace the lightning in the storm, hoping it will not harm them. America should not protect friends who refuse to maintain their own security. Those who enjoy the umbrella of security will not want to pay the price of its protection until they clearly see the intensity and enormity of the storm that rages all too near, until they understand what havoc past storms have wreaked upon mankind, and how frequently they have swept down upon civilization. By hoping for sunshine, free people too often are unprepared when storms descend. Facing reality, seeing the world as it is rather than as one wishes it were, becomes a vital prerequisite for dealing with an hostile world rather than being dealt with by one.

Twenty-five hundred years ago, Heraclitus observed: *Polemus pater panton*—War is the father of all things. In our time, historian Will Durant has updated and confirmed it, noting that in 3,421 years of recorded history, the world for only 268 years has been without a war somewhere.

From the days when Christopher Columbus dreamed of sailing westward, to the eve of World War II, that span of time known as "modern history," 278 wars have drained the blood and destroyed the homes of people across the earth. The total number of people killed by warfare probably exceeds 100 million. Although the slaughter of 6 million Jews and 20 million Russians hovers as a grim monument of death in this century, wars of earlier centuries were far more devastating than the popular images of combatants dying on a field of battle while the populace watched unscathed from behind castle walls. During the Thirty Years' War (1618–1648) inhabitants of entire cities were sometimes slaughtered following a siege. The population of Germany sank from 16.5 million to 4 million; the population of Bohemia from 4 million to 800,000.

In two short centuries America has endured eight wars, not counting Indian wars or foreign skirmishes. War, tragically, is a part of the human condition. While man may dream of peace, he must prepare for war, or be crushed by it. From the Roman legions to the Berlin Airlift, history teaches that peace is preserved by strength; from Munich to the Yalu River, the bitter fruit of weakness is aggression.

For that reason, America's global commitments—her promises of help—are only as good as her ability to support them with American muscle. More important, America's own security rests, ultimately, upon her ability to defend herself against all comers. American freedom is secure only to the extent that American military strength is sufficient to repel those who may seek to vitiate that freedom. To hope for freedom without such strength is tantamount to depending upon an iron lung for air: Someone else decides whether you breathe.

While one-quarter billion Americans work and play and sleep, 2 million of their countrymen stand guard around the globe. From the shores of America to the boot of Italy, from West Germany to South Korea, from the Isthmus of Panama to the islands of Japan: 774,000 soldiers, 528,000 sailors, 189,000 marines, and 555,000 airmen serve our country. And behind them there is a half century of resolve—sometimes faint, but mostly firm—to keep the Free World free. In West Germany alone, 200,000 Americans dressed in khaki face eastward, announcing by their presence America's determination to resist aggression. Another 30,000 in South Korea, backed by a marine division in Japan, convey the same silent message.

But the story of America's military strength only begins with the numbers of Americans in uniform. It is at the tips of their fingers that the real story lies.

By pushing the right buttons, American servicemen can rain megatons of death on an aggressor. With twice the conventional (nonnuclear) firepower of just thirty years ago, the army has the muscle to face any enemy in the field: 16 divisions, 11,560 tanks, 3,140 artillery pieces, 17,195 antitank missiles, 20,000 Vulcan antiaircraft guns, 8,000 helicopters.

During the same period, the U.S. Navy's conventional firepower has remained about constant with: 173 major combat surface ships, including 14 carriers, 24 cruisers, and 90 destroyers; 84 attack submarines, and 1,200 combat aircraft. The number of navy gunbarrels over five inches has actually declined from 925 to 231, but increased payloads have made them roughly equivalent. Although the number of navy and marine tactical aircraft has actually declined since Korea from 4,327 to 2,345, the superiority of today's aircraft is awesome. The U.S. Navy's F-14 Tomcat fighter plane, two of which knocked two of Libya's Soviet-supplied SU-20 jet fighters out of the sky in a one-minute dogfight over the Gulf of Sidra on August 19, 1981, flies at speeds up to four times the speed of sound. It carries four short-range Sidewinder missiles, six long-range Phoenix missiles, four medium-range Sparrow missiles, and a 20-millimeter cannon. The Tomcat is designed to intercept and destroy strategic nuclear missiles, and can track twenty-four targets simultaneously.

Air force conventional firepower, more difficult to quantify because its aircraft can carry either conventional or nuclear weapons, may at least be defined as massive: 2,665 fighter planes, 585 tactical aircraft, and 304 strategic aircraft.

In addition to America's conventional military might, and fundamental to her defense, the U.S. Strategic (Nuclear) Forces—based on the Triad concept of balanced land, sea, and air capability—have the raw capacity to level literally every large city in the world. Circling high above the earth, gliding silently beneath the sea, or resting in their silos, the Strategic Forces are capable, every minute of every day, of delivering lethal counterblows should an aggressor foolishly strike first.

Thirty-six ballistic-missile submarines, averaging 16 ballistic-missile launchers per submarine, together cradle 5,040 nuclear warheads—Trident, Poseidon, and Polaris—capable of bursting through the ocean's roof and, like shooting stars, flashing thousands of miles through the sky to explode up to 200 kilotons of destruction on targets pinpointed to within a football-stadium's size—a single warhead being capable of obliterating most of Moscow.

Meanwhile, a mix of 316 long-range bombers and sixty medium-range bombers take turns circling the globe. Together, they are capable of showering 2,534 nuclear warheads, fraternal twins of their brothers in the sea.

On land, resting in silos, are Minutemen and Titan missiles, carrying 2,152 warheads in all, ready on command to streak 7,000 miles in about 30 minutes, to strike within 200 yards of their designated targets.

By land, sea, and air, America's Strategic Forces, totaling over 9,000 warheads—some as deadly as 60 Hiroshima bombs—communicate to an hostile world essentially the same message as that rattlesnake flag, flying over frontier forts west of the Allegheny mountains when Washington was still a boy: "Don't tread on me."

Unlike George Washington, who relied on Indian runners and frontier scouts to tell him when attack was near, today's America must match her Strategic Forces with a comparably sophisticated detection capability to know when death is on the wing. The North American Defense Command (NORAD), a joint U.S.-Canadian organization headquartered in Colorado, uses a variety of highly sophisticated warning systems so Americans may rest secure that surprise attack cannot occur.

In the skies, 327 manned interceptor aircraft perpetually circle America's borders, while far above them three satellites hover—one over the Eastern Hemisphere, two over the Western Hemisphere—to detect within moments the launching of submarine- or land-based missiles from any point on earth or sea.

Meanwhile, on the ground: Six United States-based Space, Detection, and Tracking Systems identify and track satellites; three Ballistic Missile Early Warning Systems (BMEWS) in Alaska, Greenland, and England scan the skies with radar to detect and track intercontinental ballistic missiles (ICBMs); a Distant Early Warning Line (DEW) of thirty-one radar stations watches the skies along the 70° N parallel; a Pinetree Line of twenty-four stations does likewise across central Canada; a Perimeter Acquisition Radar Attack Characterization System located in North Dakota searches two thousand miles across the northern skies; a Cobra Dana Radar System in the Aleutian Islands looks for land- and submarine-launched missiles; a Semi-Automatic Ground Environment (SAGE) System with six locations in the United States and Canada, is being upgraded by a Joint Surveillance System to coordinate the tracking of objects in North American airspace; fifty Ground Radar Stations, forty-seven of them in the Federal Aviation Administration's system, also feed data into the Colorado command center. On the ground, in the air, and beneath the sea, America's electronic sentries silently survey the world, looking and listening for a potential enemy's hostile move.

*   *   *

One never knows with certainty how good a military machine is until it is called upon to perform in the real world of human clash and confrontation. For America and her military forces, no one wants that call ever to come. Short of U.S. involvement in war, however, there are actual combat conditions in which some components of the American arsenal have been tried. In that testing, U.S. weapons have been proved superior to those they faced.

The 1982 Israeli war in Lebanon provided a stunning comparison between American and Soviet weaponry. Using United States-built Hawkeye radar planes, the Israelis were able to locate Soviet built MiG-21 and MiG-23 planes taxiing on Syrian runways even before they became airborne. Then using United States-built F-15 and F-16 planes with Sidewinder and Sparrow missiles, the Israeli Air Force was able to engage and destroy the Syrian-flown, Soviet-built fighter planes. In air battles over Lebanon eighty-seven MiGs were destroyed while none of the United States-built planes were shot down.

United States-built M-60 tanks destroyed Soviet-built SAM missiles, U.S. Cobra and Defender helicopters gave the Israelis superior low air cover, and, in one encounter, Israelis firing U.S. TOW missiles destroyed eleven highly vaunted Soviet T-72 tanks.

Summing up, one highly placed Israeli general praised "the superiority and quality" of U.S. weapons over those of the Soviet Union.

Peru was so impressed by the performance of U.S. military equipment against Soviet military equipment in the Israeli Lebanon invasion that, in a major shift from dependence on Soviet weapons, it sought and received Reagan administration permission to negotiate with General Dynamics Corporation for the purchase of twenty-six F-16s. Earlier, Venezuela had sought and received such permission.

Meanwhile, on the high, cold Atlantic off the coast of South America, the British success in retaking the Falkland Islands from Argentina had clearly demonstrated the superiority of U.S. weapons, logistical support, and naval strategy.

American Sidewinder missiles fired from British Harrier fighter planes were credited with winning the air battles for the British: twenty-seven Argentine jets downed without a single British plane lost in air-to-air combat. British nuclear submarines, their designs derived from the U.S. nuclear-submarine program, kept the Argentine Navy bottled up in port, its commander knowing that to venture out to sea would be to invite certain destruction.

Operating more than ten thousand miles from home, the British acknowledged that they would not have been able to achieve their sweeping victory but for the substantial logistical support of the U.S. Navy.

While the Falklands naval engagements showed weaknesses in British naval strategy, ships, and armaments, they confirmed the soundness of America's naval doctrine. Britain's small, light, aluminum-hulled mini-carriers held but a fraction of the jet fighter planes of great U.S. carriers such as the Nimitz class. Those they could carry were vertical takeoff Harriers with a combat range of only fifty miles. Lacking airborne radar stations such as the U.S. AWACS or Hawkeye planes which, from an altitude of 30,000 feet can see ships 150 miles away, the British had to rely on ship-level radar which, limited to the horizon, can see only about 20 miles away. Consequently, the British had to put their destroyer escorts on picket duty to pick up incoming enemy raids. Thus exposed, the destroyer *Sheffield* was attacked and sunk.

Compounding the fragility of their aluminum hulls, the British ships suffered a lethal lack of U.S.-style sophisticated damage-control systems, making them vulnerable to excessive damage from fires after being hit. Nor was the British battle group equipped with U.S.-type sophisticated electronic jamming equipment with which to deter incoming enemy planes. Nor was it equipped with U.S.-type Phalanx Gatling guns which hurl up a rapid-fire barrage of hot metal, forming a deadly screen of detonation and destruction for incoming missiles before they can reach their targets.

In short, British naval strategy was designed for short-range missions, such as protecting the waters around the British Isles with the help of nearby land-based support, rather than for being a self-contained flotilla thousands of miles from home.

Conversely, U.S. naval strategy provides for highly sophisticated, flexible, self-contained, and massive offensive and defensive firepower. Deployed at sea, a U.S. Navy battle group composed of ships, planes, and submarines takes roughly the form of a series of expanding rings protecting one or more giant aircraft carriers at the core.

A U.S. Navy carrier of the nuclear-powered Nimitz class weighs ninety thousand tons—nearly five times the size of British carriers. With 5,440 personnel, it becomes a virtual moving city, carrying over ninety planes, more than a third of which are capable of delivering nuclear strikes several hundred miles away. Steel-hulled, these mighty U.S. carriers are designed with two thousand separate compartments which, with decentralized damage-control systems, greatly enhance their ability to contain and minimize the damage from a direct hit.

About twenty miles out from the carrier, Aegis destroyer escorts provide a second ring of defense with ship-to-ship and surface-to-air missiles capable of being directed by airborne and surface radar tracking stations that can identify hostile planes, ships, and missiles. Like the carrier, the destroyers are equipped with Phalanx Gatling guns, and with helicopters that can seek out submarines and release heat flares which can decoy and divert incoming missiles.

About a hundred miles out from the carrier, long-range early-warning U.S. Hawkeye radar planes circle thirty thousand feet above the fleet to pick up enemy planes, ships, or missiles and, through their advanced command-control systems, communicate with the rest of the battle group in order that it may take all measures appropriate to the conditions. (It was this capability that picked up the two Libyan jets while they were still on the ground and tracked them out over open, international waters as they approached U.S. Navy exercises in the Mediterranean, thereby enabling U.S. jets to destroy them as they attacked.)

About 150 miles out from the carrier, F-18 attack jets armed with Sidewinder and Sparrow missiles and a Gatling gun provide another ring of defense. Another fifty miles out, F-14 fighter jets armed with Phoenix missiles provide still another ring.

Also cruising with the U.S. battle group is a heavily armored battleship carrying long-range Tomahawk cruise missiles and short-range Harpoon missiles. Beneath the surface, one or more nuclear attack submarines, heavy with electronic gear, scan the depths to spot and destroy enemy submarines or ships while overhead fly several Hawkeye airborne warning and command-control planes capable of detecting and directing strikes against enemy planes, missiles, and ships.

Together, the U.S. Navy battle group has the capability of dominating a five-hundred-mile ocean radius virtually anywhere in the world. Manned by over eight thousand highly trained Navy and Marine personnel, and costing about $7 billion to put in place and another half billion annually to maintain and operate, this great offensive flotilla represents the most formidable concentration of naval power ever assembled.

Thus, the lessons of the Falklands become very clear: To be effective, a blue-water navy must contain a flexible and carefully integrated mix of massively overlapping levels of detection, warning, attack, and defense. That is the crux of U.S. naval strategy, and that is precisely what must be continued and augmented if America is to maintain its global position on the high seas.

America's military strength is wrought of many things, not the least of which are: a sailor whose microprocessor reduces his firing time from minutes to milliseconds; a soldier whose M-16 rifle is three times as fast as the old M-1; a Strategic Air Command pilot whose nuclear payload can erase a dozen Hiroshimas; a U.S. satellite that can spot an enemy warhead before the dust can settle around its launching pad; an antimissile system that can knock a warhead out of the sky a thousand miles from home, or a Marine Corps detachment that can rapidly secure a beachhead.

Like Prometheus, who gave the gift of fire to man that man might forge weapons to set himself free, the U.S. military establishment preserves freedom for Americans by standing with its weapons and its lives as both the first and last line of defense against a hostile world.

But how much is enough? Prometheus, huge Titan that he was, nevertheless was bound by the stronger Zeus.

There is a tendency to shunt aside the military as persons doing a dirty job unfit for finer minds. Yet the very core of America's freedom depends directly upon the ability to defend America. And short of war, a million minute cells grow or die each day, based on how strong or weak America seems—to herself, to her friends, and to her adversaries. No calling is higher than that of keeping people free.

America's military might is promethean and, like Prometheus, is in danger of being bound to the dead rocks of antagonism and indifference. Unless America gives her military the respect and the tools necessary to preserve the peace by being prepared for war, the day will surely come when America's Prometheus will be bound by a Soviet or Asian Zeus. Should that sad day come, the umbrella of security praised so highly by the pastor of Herbitzheim will have been destroyed, and with it, the remaining freedom in the world.

VII

PROMETHEUS THREATENED

It is seldom that Liberty of any kind is lost all at once.

—DAVID HUME

AWESOME THOUGH IT IS, America's military might stands challenged by the Soviet Union, which has been engaged in the most massive military buildup in the history of the world. Cold, hard, verifiable comparisons tell the somber story of the Soviet edge: military manpower better than two to one; ICBM warheads better than two to one; ballistic-missile submarines better than two to one; submarine-launched warheads nearly four to one; tanks better than four to one; armored personnel carriers better than four to one; artillery better than six to one; antitank missiles 1.5 to one; land-based fighter planes 1.4 to one; frigates better than two to one; attack submarines better than three to one. The American edge is limited to: strategic bombers 1.7 to one; carrier-based fighter planes eleven to one; aircraft carriers six to one; destroyers 1.4 to one. In tactical aircraft and cruisers, a virtual standoff exists (Table 6).

The Soviet Union spends 15 percent of its GNP on defense, almost three times what America spends, but those statistics do not tell the story completely: Historically, the Kremlin rulers have hidden many military items in their nonmilitary budget; also historically, these professed champions of the working class have extracted from those they rule more work for less pay. For example, the all-conscript Soviet military system pays army privates $6 a month, compared to over $500 in the U.S. all-volunteer army.

TABLE 6

John M. Collins, Senior Specialist in National Defense, Library of Congress, offers the following U.S.-Soviet military comparables, as of January 1, 1981:

Item	U.S.	USSR
Active military manpower	2,094,000	4,842,000
ICBM launchers	1,052	1,398
warheads	2,152	5,002
ballistic missile subs	36	84
SLBM launchers	576	986
SLBM warheads	5,040	1,306
strategic bombers	376	215
divisions	28	173
16 army and marines=19		(of which 82 are
reserve = 9		categories 1 and 2
		[roughly our
		"active"] with
		81 category 3
		[roughly our
		"reserve"])
medium tanks	11,560	48,000
armored personnel		
carriers (APCS)	15,975	65,750
artillery	3,140	19,300
antitank missiles	17,195	25,090
medium bombers	252	960
land-based fighter attack	2,665	3,725
carrier-based fighter		
attack	695	60
aircraft carriers (attack)	12	2
helicopter carriers	24	2
cruisers	27	27
destroyers	90	64
frigates	72	173
attack subs	84 (78 of them nuclear)	278 (98 of them nuclear)
strategic airlift	304	150
tactical aircraft	585	500

Qualitatively, American technology has provided more accurate weapons, but the Soviet Union is catching up to the point where several American experts believe the USSR will achieve parity in accuracy before the end of the decade. Meanwhile, Soviet SS-18 and SS-19 intercontinental ballistic missiles and SS-20 medium-range missiles are powerful nuclear weapons capable of destroying even missiles housed in silos dug deeply into the earth and protected by massive walls of concrete and steel. Based on Soviet soil, the SS-20s can hit Western Europe, and the SS-18s and SS-19s can hit the United States. They will not be matched by the United States until the MX system becomes operative—not until 1987 at the earliest. In the meantime, the USSR is reportedly hardening its own missile silos to the point where even a direct hit from a U.S. missile would have to be accompanied by a tremendous nuclear blast before the missiles themselves could suffer serious damage.

On the ground, meanwhile, the Soviet Union continues to build a military capability which is clearly offensive rather than defensive as Moscow continues to claim. The fact is that, for years, its military doctrine has stated that Soviet armored units should have the capability for rapid, deep penetration into Western Europe. For example, the USSR has tanks and other armored vehicles sufficient to reach the Rhine in a matter of days; it also has the ability to lay down sixty miles of pipe per day to provide the vital petroleum support for such an attack. Such capabilities are totally inconsistent with purely defensive needs. They are, however, completely consistent with the Marxist-Leninist doctrine underlying Soviet military strategy.

In his "Annual Report to the Congress for Fiscal 1982," General David C. Jones, then chairman of the Joint Chiefs of Staff, warned:

> The military balance between the United States and the Soviet Union continues to shift toward the latter. . . . The trend in military balance is having a profound and dangerous effect on world affairs. Military power is the Soviet Union's most effective instrument for advancing its interest: its economy is stagnating, its political institutions are showing increasing strain, and around the world its ideology is frequently rejected. Only its armed forces command universal attention and concern.

Few Americans are more deeply concerned about the growth of Soviet military power than Dr. Edward Teller. Perhaps no American is better qualified to harbor such concern. A member of the scientific team at Los Alamos which developed the atomic bomb, and the father of the hydrogen bomb, he suffered the excruciating effects of two world wars. Persecuted by both Communists and Nazis, and losing several members of his family to the Holocaust, this world-renowned, Hungarian-born nuclear physicist found asylum in America. No refugee contributed more to the American-led Allied victory in World War II, nor to the postwar security of his adopted country.

As associate director emeritus of the Lawrence Livermore National Laboratory, he has told me of his deep fear that the Soviet Union appears to be on the verge of developing new, highly sophisticated, defensive nuclear weapons capable of intercepting and destroying incoming nuclear missiles. If so, America's ICBMs would be useless, and the credibility of U.S. nuclear deterrence would be destroyed. Other responsible scientists have agreed with Dr. Teller's assessment of such a Soviet development.

The Soviet Union could feel relatively safe in launching a first strike once they had a defense against a nuclear response.

The strategic antidote would be an American defensive nuclear weapon capable of destroying Soviet first-strike missiles. Such a system is under development at the Livermore Laboratory and recent progress has been encouraging, but the U.S. government has not yet made the commitment to continue and complete the project.

America's, if not the world's, greatest living nuclear physicist argues that unless America moves quickly to neutralize this potential Soviet advantage by developing her own defensive weapon, American security could be seriously jeopardized within a decade. Unfortunately, the alarm he sounds is one that many prefer not to hear.

Although the question of developing such a defensive nuclear weapon is but one of many strategic decisions America must address concerning national security, it symbolizes the dangerous future facing the country. While Americans collectively weigh the risks and responses required to meet an increasingly ominous Soviet threat, they and their allies must rely on existing military capabilities to protect the great democracies of the world.

Both America's European allies and the Soviet Union's East European client states add resources to the current U.S.-Soviet military equation, but the basic pattern does not change.

The Warsaw Pact has combat manpower of 5.2 million. NATO has 4.8 million.

The Warsaw Pact has 5,795 tactical aircraft. NATO has 3,300.

The Warsaw Pact has 950 submarine-launched ballistic missiles. NATO has 784.

The Warsaw Pact has 710 intermediate-range ballistic missiles. NATO has 18.

The Warsaw Pact has 26,700 battle tanks. NATO has 11,000.

Only in numbers of nuclear warheads and strategic bombers does NATO hold the advantage: 9,200 nuclear warheads to 6,000; 448 strategic bombers to 158.

The military strength of the United States and its allies need not be inferior to the Soviet Union and the Warsaw Pact states it dominates. The productive capacities of the NATO countries, as measured by GNP, industrial base, or technological capabilities, are several times those of the Warsaw Pact. The Free World has simply chosen not to expend that portion of its resources necessary to keep up with the Russian Bear and its cubs.

President Dwight Eisenhower reminded the world in 1953 that "every gun that is made, every warship launched, every rocket fired signifies in the final sense a theft from those who hunger and are not fed, those who are cold and are not clothed." Heeding his admonition and yearning for peace, the Free World has been most reluctant to enter an arms race with the Soviet Union. However, the evidence now is clear: An arms race has been under way for the past two decades, but only one side has been running.

Only recently has America recognized the imbalance

and begun a move to redress it. Strong bipartisan support now exists for increased defense expenditures to check the Soviet threat. But Western Europe is a different story. There, the fear of war continues to stifle the defensive efforts necessary to strengthen the cause of peace.

America is on a collision course with her allies, and unless the entire Western alliance stiffens, it will eventually collapse.

Americans spend $537 per person for defense, but not a single NATO ally spends more than three-quarters that amount, and most spend less than half as much.

West Germany, America's strongest European ally, spends $404 per person on defense. A careful look at the defense policies of our strongest ally may help to indicate how weak the others really are.

During West Germany's 1980 election campaign, Chancellor Helmut Schmidt promised that if he was reelected, "no German soldier will serve on foreign soil." While his assurance placated the German people, it raised a troubling question for the American people: Why should two hundred thousand American soldiers serve on German soil if West German allies refused to let their own troops leave home?

More significantly, the West German position on troops is only one of a cluster of policies which, taken together, form a picture of a wavering ally—one who wants the benefits of an alliance with the West while simultaneously seeking advantages through a closer relationship with the Soviet Union and the Warsaw Pact countries.

In 1980, the Bonn government promised to increase defense expenditures by 3 percent in real dollars, but in January 1981, it announced a defense budget of just $21 billion, a real increase of less than 1 percent.

In 1980, the Bonn government gave what, at best, amounted to tepid support of allied sanctions against the Soviet Union for its invasion of Afghanistan. When Lech Walesa and his Polish fellow workers called for reforms in Red Poland, the Bonn government announced its support of Soviet efforts to stabilize Poland.

Following the death in December 1980 of Soviet Premier Alexei Kosygin, Willy Brandt, former West German

Chancellor and still head of Helmut Schmidt's ruling Social Democrats, lauded the career Bolshevik as "a man who served the cause of peace," choosing to ignore, among other things, the one hundred thousand Soviet troops still waging the then year-old aggression against Afghanistan, and the hundreds of thousands of other Soviet troops then massing along the Polish border.

The Socialist-led West German government is turning into a Janus-headed political economic body straddling the Iron Curtain: One head looks westward for protection against the Soviet East; the other looks eastward for whatever temporary advantages the Kremlin might choose to promise in an effort to further alienate Bonn from Washington. The West German newspaper *Frankfurter Allegemeine Zeitung* acknowledged that "the Germans want to have it both ways," with the umbrella of American security covering them while they pursue a policy of trade and self-interest with the Soviets.

Because West Germany has served as the great linchpin of the Western alliance, a continuation of Bonn's present course could easily lead all of Western Europe into the full grasp of what could become a condition of Soviet-imposed "Finlandization"—a condition in which the mere suggestion of Soviet military action would be sufficient to evince from Western Europe whatever concession the Kremlin might choose to demand.

In addition to America's policy of rebuilding her military might, a corollary policy emerges as essential: A time for toughness with our allies will be necessary if the NATO alliance is to stand as a bulwark against the Soviet Union. Rather than détente, a policy of determination is needed.

If America's allies are unwilling to increase their military preparedness, to impose trade sanctions that bite against Soviet aggression, and to defend the cause of freedom, America must be willing to reduce her troop commitment to NATO, to give a lower priority to protection of the energy supply lines to Western Europe, and to initiate bilateral trade and defense agreements with those allies who are willing to cooperate.

America's allies need America more than America needs

them. Until America adopts a new toughness in dealing with the other nations of the world, she will be taken advantage of by adversaries and allies alike. With isolationism impossible in a world tied together by jet streams and multinational flows of trade, internationalism is all too often a code word for giving away what is rightfully America's. The time is ripe for a new policy in world affairs. Isolationism and internationalism must give way to global Americanism—to seeing the world as an integrated whole but approaching it with toughness to protect America's interests; to being a good neighbor in promoting the causes of freedom and prosperity among those people willing to carry their share of the load.

As America becomes tougher in her dealings around the globe, allies who cooperate will grow in strength along with her. That, perhaps, is the best foreign aid America can give. We should demand more from them, and help those allies who rise to meet the challenge.

While Europe, among the foreign continents, has always enjoyed America's primary attention due to ties of blood and trade, the Far East, with one quarter of the world's people, and with philosophies largely alien to democracy, could, by the turn of the century, become a dragon spitting fire on the world's free nations.

Communist China alone has 4.5 million people in military service: roughly as many as the Soviet Union, and more than twice as many as America. Although Red China lacks the quantity of sophisticated weaponry available to the U.S. military, the image of poorly armed Chinese soldiers throwing mattresses over barbed wire to attack in hordes is sorely outdated. Red China's military capabilities include: ICBMs capable of delivering nuclear warheads over 2,000 miles, with 8,000-mile ranges nearing deployment; 90 medium bombers; 4,000 fighter planes; over 10,000 anti-aircraft weapons; 13,000 tanks; 16,000 artillery weapons; 38 major surface combat ships; 97 attack submarines, including 1 nuclear sub, with others to follow. In addition to the active duty military, almost 15 million Chinese serve part-time in various militia units.

North Korea has almost 700,000 in military service, including 35 infantry divisions; 2,700 tanks; over 600 combat aircraft, and 16 submarines. Vietnam has over 1 million in military service, including 38 infantry divisions; 25 surface-to-air missile (SAM) regiments; 2,500 tanks; almost 500 combat aircraft, and almost 500 coastal and river patrol boats.

With 600,000 troops, as well as over 8,000 artillery pieces, Hawk and Nike-Hercules surface-to-air missiles, 10 ex-U.S. destroyers, and 362 combat aircraft, South Korea provides a military balance against North Korea. But with Asia, the balance stops.

The armed forces of the anti-Communist island of Taiwan consist of 440,000, less than one tenth that of Red China. Taiwan has fewer than 400 combat aircraft, less than one tenth that of Red China. Taiwan also has 2 submarines and 22 ex-U.S. destroyers which, together, are less than one third the number of Red Chinese attack submarines. With 4 surface-to-air missile battalions deploying Hawk and Nike-Hercules missiles, Taiwan's forces could at best make conquest painful should Red China attack. Clearly, the threat of possible American intervention remains the only significant barrier against such an attack.

When President Jimmy Carter unilaterally abrogated America's mutual-defense treaty with Taiwan in 1978, it sent shock waves through the capitals of America's allies. When President Ronald Reagan announced in 1982 that America would reduce arms shipments to Taiwan and essentially freeze their quality at current levels, it too sent another disquieting signal, especially to America's smaller, more dependent allies: Don't count on U.S. commitments.

The change in U.S. policy toward Taiwan was made public through a communiqué issued jointly on August 17, 1982, by America and Red China. One old China hand observed: "Now the Chinese Communists need only wait. Time is on their side. Eventually they will gain air superiority over the Straits of Taiwan and be in a position to launch an amphibious landing against the island, or intimidate Taiwan into submission."

Since the Taiwan Relations Act of 1979 provides that "the United States will make available to Taiwan such defense articles and defense services in such quantity as may be necessary to enable Taiwan to maintain a sufficient self-defense capability," the issue of America's reduced commitment to Taiwan is far from settled. Taiwan could become an international hot spot at any moment, should Red China decide to test Taiwanese-American resolve.

Taiwan is particularly important to America because it is a long-standing ally in a vital part of the world where America has few allies. It provides a check against further Communist aggression in Asia. The lure of potential markets, coupled with Red China's antagonism toward the Soviet Union, enticed many Americans to forget the essential character of Chinese Communism. Amnesty International issued a 1979 report documenting the arrests and punishments without fair trials of suspected political dissenters. Thousands were sent to forced-labor camps, including more than five thousand young people from Peking alone. During the purge of Mao Tse-tung's widow in 1977, thousands of executions swept the country, according to intelligence reports. America's commitment to Taiwan must be reaffirmed and strengthened, or other allies, particularly in the Far East, may find it necessary to seek accommodation with the Communists at the expense of the Free World.

The Philippines with 100,000 troops, New Zealand with 12,000, and Australia with 71,000, couldn't last a fortnight against any one of Asia's Communist powers; only America provides the shield.

With fewer than a quarter million in uniform, and a constitution that prohibits fighting, Japan hides behind America's skirts, while channeling productivity, freed from producing for defense, into economic competition with America and the other peaceful nations of the world.

In Asia, there is no equivalency except for the dual fears of American nuclear superiority and Soviet thirst for hegemony. Asia's two dominant forces, China and Japan, both fearful of the Soviet Union, see America as both buffer and an easy mark: a buffer whose military strength keeps the Soviet Union from biting off more than it can chew; an easy mark whose willingness to sacrifice both militarily and economically gives other nations the opportunity to progress at America's expense.

Henry Kissinger, one of the chief architects of U.S.-China policy, cautioned in his memoirs: "Once China becomes strong enough to stand alone, it might discard us. A little later it might even turn against us. . . ." Any long term U.S. strategic calculation that counts Red China as a neutral or ally in the world balance of power is fraught with risk.

But America need not rely solely upon theoretical projections of what might happen, because actual events around the globe speak clearly for all who wish to hear.

Nearly 100,000 Soviet-Communist troops in Afghanistan, 45,000 Cuban-Communist troops marching through fourteen African countries, Soviet, Czech, and East German-Communist troops encircling Poland, Communist arms and subversion fomenting revolution in El Salvador, Guatemala, and other Central and South American countries, Communist genocide and imprisonment practiced on a massive scale in Cambodia and Vietnam, and the Soviet Gulag Archipelago of political prisoners and executions so vividly portrayed by Alexander Solzhenitsyn—taken together, they paint a picture of a world convulsing, up to the very boundaries of those countries that still retain their freedom.

Actions not only speak louder than words, they also show how seriously words are meant to be taken.

The actions of Communist governments verify their spoken commitment to world domination. Lenin meant it when he said: "Morality is entirely subordinate to the interests of class war. . . . Not a single problem of the class struggle has ever been solved in history except by violence." Khrushchev meant it when he said: "If anyone believes that our smiles involve abandonment of the teachings of Marx, Engels and Lenin, he deceives himself poorly. Those who wait for that must wait until a shrimp learns to whistle." And Brezhnev meant it when he said: "In the ideological field, there can be no peaceful coexistence, just as there can be no class peace between the proletariat and the bourgeoisie. . . . The revolutionary process has gained a truly worldwide scale."

From the beginning of Communism to the present, its

leaders have embraced the *Communist Manifesto* as their bible, and Karl Marx, its author, as their patron saint. Just as the moral philosophers of the Judeo-Christian tradition turn to the Bible for guidance, the amoral leaders of world Communism turn to their Manifesto for direction. Through that "bible," the words of Marx speak to young Communists around the world today with the same chilling consistency drummed into their Red forebears.

> The theory of the Communists may be summed up in the single sentence: abolition of private property.
>
> Abolition of the family! . . . On what foundation is the present family . . . based? On capital, on private gain.
>
> The working men have no country.
>
> In short, the Communists everywhere support every revolutionary movement against the existing social and political order of things.
>
> They openly declare that their ends can be attained only by the forcible overthrow of all existing social conditions.

Revolution and subversion, brutality and terrorism, are not the rhetorical flourishes of Communism; they are the essential elements of the system. Worse, the principles of Communism require not only the domination of the world but also the subjugation of their own peoples. Alexander Solzhenitsyn revealed that over 6 million political prisoners languished in Soviet jails, and 1.7 million of their countrymen were executed.

From Soviet Communism's rule by fear throughout Eastern Europe to Chinese Communism's bloodbath throughout Asia, the willingness to use force to achieve its ends has been the constant policy of the Marxist system.

Winston Churchill observed concerning the Soviets: "There is nothing they admire so much as strength and there is nothing for which they have less respect than weakness, particularly military weakness." It is as true today as when he said it thirty-five years ago. The Soviets have demonstrated, repeatedly, that where they find weakness, they rush in; where they find strength, they back away, to probe elsewhere. Their activities in the Caribbean demonstrate this policy; more important, they expose again the ultimate Soviet goal of world domination.

Nowhere is the evidence more conclusive, nor the implications more sinister, than in Communist efforts to overthrow governments just off America's shores.

From the Soviet Union, millions in military and economic aid pour daily into Cuba, Moscow's launching pad for aggression and subversion throughout the Caribbean and Latin America. Financed by Moscow, over two thousand Cuban advisers helped the leftist Sandinista regime consolidate its power in Nicaragua. A direct agreement between the Soviet Communist Party and the Sandinista Marxist Party called for Soviet "technicians" to help guide the affairs of Nicaragua.

Despite clear evidence, verified by U.S. intelligence, of the Sandinista Marxists' being financed and guided by the Moscow-Havana connection, the Carter administration nevertheless withdrew support for the pro-United States Somoza regime and watched supinely as the red tide engulfed Nicaragua. Once in power, the Sandinista regime with one hand smilingly accepted $60 million in foreign aid largesse from the Carter administration, while with the other it funneled Soviet arms from Cuba into neighboring El Salvador to foment revolution there.

Forcing Uncle Sam to play the Uncle Sap, the Carter administration fed U.S. tax dollars into the Marxist regime of Nicaragua in the hope that good relations might ensue. Meanwhile, support and guidance flowed into Nicaragua, not only from the regime's major patron, the Soviet Union, but from Communist East Germany and terrorist Libya.

The Reagan administration stopped the U.S. foreign aid and adopted a tougher stance, but the damage had already been done. With power consolidated, the Sandinista regime moved to build the largest army in Central America. The announced objective: a regular army of fifty thousand and a militia of two hundred thousand. General Anastasio Somoza, whom they overthrew and later allegedly assassinated, had, at the peak of his power, an army of only fourteen thousand.

Meanwhile, Marxist guerrillas, armed by Castro and supported by supply lines through Nicaragua, launched their attacks on neighboring El Salvador, promising prosperity but destroying crops and blowing up water and sewer systems.

To the east, Honduras continued to serve as another entry port for Communist-supplied arms into El Salvador.

Bordering Honduras and El Salvador on the west, Guatemala had become vulnerable to Marxist pressures. Military officers and other anti-Communists trying to run Guatemala expressed fear that an element within the Carter State Department actually sought establishment of a Communist government in El Salvador. While warring with Marxist rebels inside Guatemala, the government wanted to help the anti-Marxist forces in El Salvador, but feared the weak and inconsistent policies of the United States.

Meanwhile, Costa Rica, trapped between Nicaragua and Panama, was becoming destabilized by the subversion and revolution around it.

At the eastern entrance to the Caribbean, the Moscow-Havana axis was busy pumping into the strategically situated island of Grenada both military aid and Marxist propaganda with the exuberant approval of Maurice Bishop, the British-educated lawyer, who, with Castro's support, had come to power in the left-wing coup of 1979. Although the new international airport being built on the island by Castro was billed as commercial, it was large enough to accommodate the type of giant Soviet troop-transport planes that had airlifted thousands of Cuban troops into Africa.

Less than seven hundred miles from Grenada, the government of Surinam had been toppled by a coup, and northward, Mexico severed relations with Nicaragua's Somoza regime, recognizing the Sandinistas even before they completed their revolution. Communist Party representation was admitted to the Mexican Chamber of Deputies, while Mexico looked the other way as thousands of its citizens poured illegally across the border into the United States.

If further proof were needed of growing Communist influence south of the border, by the summer of 1980, it was readily available:

- About eleven thousand teenagers from Africa, Nicaragua, and other Caribbean countries were undergoing Communist indoctrination sessions on Cuba's Isle of Youth.
- Cuba was being supplied with Soviet submarines.
- Soviet submarines and surface ships routinely called at Cuban ports.
- With five thousand Soviet troops, the Cuban naval base at Cienfuegos was being expanded.
- Cuba was upgrading its Soviet-supplied SAM-2 antiaircraft missiles, believed to be 144 in number, by adding three new boosters to the single-stage rockets.
- Soviet storage and maintenance sheds were being constructed next to the Cuban naval base at Cienfuegos.
- The Soviets were digging several large holes in Cuban soil, capable of housing nuclear missiles aimed at the United States.
- Two of Cuba's airfields were expanded to accommodate Moscow's vaunted Backfire bombers.
- The Russians were building a nuclear power plant at Cuba's Punta Movida, complete with rail line to the naval base.
- Soviet pilots were flying routine patrols over Cuba and monitoring U.S. naval movements in the Atlantic.

The Caribbean had, indeed, become America's Achilles' heel, or as one military theoretician put it: "America's soft underbelly."

On Saturday, January 17, 1981, while Warren Christopher, U.S. Deputy Secretary of State, negotiated around the clock for the release of the fifty-two American hostages being held in Iran, and decent people around the globe held their breath hoping for the best, the *Pravda* news story by Pavel Demchenko, Communist propaganda specialist, was broadcast throughout Iran by Soviet-controlled radio stations, claiming that the United States was preparing for a military attack against Iran.* At that moment of historic sensitivity, instead of aiding a humanitarian effort, or at least remaining silent, the Russian Bear was displaying its basic nature, was fomenting discord and revolution in accordance with its Marxist principles.

Propaganda is one of the basic weapons used by the Soviet regime to destabilize the world, and its efforts to block release of the American hostages ranks as one of Moscow's more blatant actions of purposeful interference with the peaceful settlement of a most difficult issue—an issue centered on arranging a humane release of American citizens seized in contravention of every known international law and standard.

Given documentation of these Soviet actions, which then Secretary of State Muskie personally denounced as "scurrilous propaganda," it is difficult to blind oneself to the Soviet character, to fail to see the brutish immorality of Soviet actions. Yet not one protest, not one sympathetic word, was heard from other countries. America's supposed allies sat silently as Moscow sought to destroy the negotiations, preferring, selfishly, to focus allied energies on how normal trade relations with Iran might quickly be resumed.

---

*"Reports which arrived in the editorial office today testify to the danger posed to peace by the U.S. adventurist policy with respect to Iran.

"The threat of armed U.S. intervention has been hanging like the sword of Damocles over that country since the very outset of the Iranian revolution. It is the overthrow of the Shah and the collapse of American positions in Iran which were presented by the Pentagon as one of the 'most forcible' arguments in favor of dispatching its fleet into the Persian Gulf and hastily setting up its Rapid Deployment Force. The emergency of the hostage problem in November 1979, was used to intensify pressure on Tehran.

"Assessing the developments which have occurred since that time, many foreign observers come to the conclusion that possibilities to resolve this problem were opened on several occasions. Washington, however, did not use them, preferring to brandish arms and even undertaking the so-called 'rescue operation' in April last. That is, in fact, an aggressive incursion into Iranian territory by its Air Force, and landing units. From the military viewpoint it was, as is known, a complete failure while in the political aspect it aggravated even more the U.S.-Iranian relations.

"Washington did not stop its dishonorable game around the hostages, although the matter is not reduced only to them. Reports were made in the newspapers in many countries, including the U.S., that under the cover of negotiations on that problem, the Pentagon is preparing a new 'intimidating' operation against Iran."
—TASS, Soviet News Agency
January 17, 1981

By intruding upon the delicate hostage negotiations at their most sensitive moment, the Soviet Union demonstrated, once again, for all the world to see, its determination to dominate and destroy.

But few wish to look. The Soviet propaganda war lashes at America, while her allies search for economic gain.

Still worse, even in America the Soviet drums beat out their message, sometimes paid for by American tax dollars.

"Let it be clear, I'm for Communism . . . ," Stokely Carmichael told the students at Shippensburg State College in Pennsylvania, on October 2, 1977. Calling the American system "vicious, savage, barbaric, erratic and doomed to its own destruction," he announced himself to be a "total revolutionary" as he collected his $1,500 fee from the student activities fund, paid for by the students (or more likely their parents) at the taxpayer-supported educational institution. That Carmichael had a right to express his Communist views is undeniable. Indeed, it is a right that must be protected. But that it should be supported by taxpayer dollars—directly through the use of public facilities, and indirectly through publicly funded student loans and grants—is outrageous.

If Stokely Carmichael were a free-spirited intellectual espousing a radical point of view, and if his appearance were paid for by private individuals who shared his views, then a strong case could be made that college students should have the opportunity to hear such views as part of their overall, balanced, education.

Savaging America from such Communist capitals as Havana, Prague, and Hanoi, Stokely Carmichael called for "total revolution," urging the complete overthrow of the "imperialist, capitalist, and racialist structure of the United States." Expelled from Canada, and declared persona non grata in his native Trinidad, Carmichael set up headquarters in the West African country of Guinea from which he preached violent revolution against America.

On April 23, 1980, he appeared at Princeton University, decked out in an elegant suit, still calling for revolution against America.

Together, Carmichael and hundreds like him have spewed the anti-U.S., pro-Soviet line throughout the world.

Systematically attempting to discredit America and weaken her at home and abroad, the propaganda agents of Communism do their dirty work while millions of unsuspecting Americans, themselves decent and God-fearing, can't bring themselves to believe that they live in such a bitter world.

While propagandists sow seeds of doubt as they set the stage for the advance guard of their brave new world, terrorists destroy and kill, sapping the strength of those who would resist the siren call of Communism.

Terrorism seems to strike like a wild dog, sinking its fangs into innocents in its path. But what the shaking victim, if he survives, and the shaken world do not understand is that far from being wild, the dog attacks only on command, having been trained in academies of terror stretching from Moscow to Cuba, from South Yemen to Tripoli.

Since 1968, when the compilation of international terrorism statistics began, over 6,000 terrorist incidents have been recorded. Americans are the primary targets of international terrorism; 2 out of 5 such incidents involve U.S. citizens. In 1981, there were 258 terrorist attacks on American citizens and property, 31 of them causing casualties. Six Americans were killed: three in Guatemala, two in El Salvador, and one in Colombia. Thirty-one Americans were wounded, with diplomats the victims in 95 of the incidents which were perpetrated by 72 different groups.

During the thirteen years from 1968 through 1981, bombings accounted for 46 percent of all terrorist attacks. Also occurring, however, were over 421 kidnapping attempts, 514 assassination attempts, and 171 barricade/hostage situations. During that period, 129 events were classified as state-sponsored terrorism, with 44 such events occurring in 1981 alone.

During the more recent period, through the first half of 1982, there were 135 terrorist attacks upon American citizens and property, with diplomats the target in 60 of those incidents, American diplomats having passed American businessmen as the main targets in 1980.

The evidence clearly shows that the approximately 140

terrorist groups are neither separate nor wild; rather, they consist of controlled killers seeking blood from the ends of their leashes—which lead back to Moscow. Thousands have been trained, and are being trained, in known camps in Libya, the Soviet Union, Cuba, South Yemen, North Korea, East Germany, and other Soviet bloc countries. The point being: It is from the Soviet camp that terrorism springs.

The Soviet intelligence apparatus, the dread KGB, sent its own man, Colonel Viktor Simenov, along with five thousand Soviet technicians, to take control of Cuba in 1968. Today, Moscow-backed Havana remains the leading advocate of armed revolution throughout Latin America.

In *The Terror Network,* her stunning exposé of Soviet terrorism, Claire Sterling tells how the KGB has used Aden, the capital of South Yemen, to train thousands of terrorists, including Palestinians, Iranians, Turks, Irish Provisionals, South Americans, Dutch, Belgians, Spaniards, Scandinavians, Swiss, Japanese, Italians, and Germans.

She reports that the Irish Provisionals, the IRA, far from being a homegrown, spontaneous revolutionary force, is funded and armed, in significant measure, by the Soviet Union and its clients.

Libya alone, under the frenzied dictatorship of Colonel Kaddafi, is known to have supported terrorists, from the PLO to the IRA, in forty-five countries. Kaddafi has used Libyan oil wealth to invest over $13 billion in Soviet arms, and has threatened to use them on nations ranging from Israel and Egypt to America.

One of the world's leading experts on the subject, Dr. Hans Horchem, director of West Germany's Office of Anti-terrorism, has succinctly summed up the status of this malignancy: "The KGB is engineering international terrorism. The facts can be proven, documented, and are well known to the international Western intelligence community."

Although tanks are not rolling, planes not bombing, and soldiers not marching, the world today is in a twilight zone of war. Ten thousand assassins roam the earth, ready to kill, or maim, or kidnap upon command. Their objective—not to take a life nor steal a purse, but to sew fear deeply into the fabric of society; to show that governments cannot govern, cannot protect their own; to create anarchy as a prelude to a new world order in which the terrorists will rule supreme.

Only by exposing the roots of terrorism to sunlight can the process of drying and shriveling begin. That means information—intelligence—the gathering of evidence to show the world who pulls the strings. Surely the revulsion of public opinion against those who seek to freeze the world in fear will slowly build, eventually extracting from outlaws a price too dear to pay.

World condemnation, tough domestic laws to punish terrorists, and stern economic sanctions against governments that encourage or even wink at terrorism, will in time make the human beasts think twice. But neither the words of warning nor isolation from decent nations will curb the controlled killers. Only the presence of a club will make them back down. For the civilized world, that club must be its military might, and its cautious, careful willingness to use it whenever freedom is denied.

The price of freedom past may be roughly calculated, both in human and economic terms. For America, it has meant, directly, over 1.1 million lives.* The U.S. cost of World War II alone, which exceeded the cost of all other wars combined, was $350 billion in 1945 dollars. The uniqueness of America's sacrifice, in men and money, is that it was paid not to purchase territory but to preserve freedom. Alone among the great nations of the world, America stands on the moral high ground of not using her military might to expand her borders.

But what of the price of freedom, present and future? America spends over $200 billion annually on defense: 24 percent of her federal budget, about 5.6 percent of her gross national product. Since the pre-Vietnam War days of 1964,

---

*Americans killed in war:

Revolution	4,000
Civil War	497,000
World War I	116,000
World War II	406,000
Asia	80,000

(Korea: 26,000; Vietnam: 50,000)

U.S. defense expenditures have fallen from 42 percent to 24 percent as a percentage of the federal budget, and from 9.3 percent to 5.6 percent as a percentage of the gross national product.

About 2 percent of the U.S. labor force serves in the armed forces; they are men and women who otherwise would be available to produce goods and services for civilian consumption.

Is it worth the investment in people and money? By comparison, Americans spend $25 billion annually for tobacco, $35 billion annually for alcohol, and $100 billion on recreation.

If one accepts the Roman maxim *Salus populi suprema lex* (The people's safety is the highest law), then expenditures for defense are of the greatest priority. If one sees the world as it is—dangerous and hostile—rather than as one wishes it were, the need for a strong defense is obvious. But if one believes—despite the hard evidence of massive military buildups, coupled with propaganda, subversion, and terrorism—that the peace-loving instincts of peoples will prevail, that America need not be prepared for war, then billions are wasted on defense.

On this point, the lessons of history are clear. In his *Decline and Fall of the Roman Empire,* Gibbon showed that one of the cornerstones of Rome's greatness was its military superiority: "They preserved peace by constant preparation for war." And when they turned their backs on the need for a strong defense, when the citizens of Rome backed away from serving their country, they "introduced a slow and secret poison into the vitals of government."

Almost two thousand years later, twice in one century, the world again was taught the same lesson. In *The War Hitler Won,* Nicholas Bethell described the climate that led to World War II:

> There were tens of millions ready to fight tooth and nail against any increase in military expenditure or manpower, taking the short-sighted view that defense is a waste of money. . . . They would not accept the truism that without a valid defense policy a country's wealth

can be stolen from it, that without defense a country has nothing.

Power can corrupt, but weakness can corrode. It can sap and stop a nation from taking the actions essential to its self-preservation.

NATO Secretary General Luns has revealed that documents captured in World War II indicate that Hitler would not have invaded Czechoslovakia had France and England taken a clear and forceful stand against him.

Conversely, President John F. Kennedy's tough stand against the Soviet installation of missiles in Cuba caused Khrushchev to back down.

Toughness works. Military strength provides the muscle to demand justice. First, however, there must be the will to defend freedom, the national purpose to resist aggression. There must be a love of freedom to pave the way for paying the price.

In his 1970 Nobel lecture, Alexander Solzhenitsyn spoke of the "spirit of Munich" dominating this century:

> The intimidated civilized world has found nothing to oppose the onslaught of a suddenly resurgent fang-baring barbarism, except concessions and smiles. The spirit of Munich is a disease of the will of prosperous people. . . .

Since Solzhenitsyn uttered those words, Western Europe has demonstrated in a thousand different ways that it has not learned the lesson of Munich. From West Germany's panderings for Soviet trade concessions to the refusal of Belgium, Denmark, the Netherlands, and Norway to station U.S. Pershing II and Cruise missiles on their soil to counteract Soviet SS-20 nuclear missiles pointed at their heads, it is apparent that Western Europe hopes to smile away the Moscow menace.

On June 6, 1980, when representatives of the NATO countries met in an extraordinary session of the North Atlantic Assembly in Luxembourg to consider the Soviet invasion of Afghanistan, the spirit of Munich hovered like a shroud. A member of the Netherlands Parliament asserted that "the

Soviet Union sent military forces into Afghanistan . . . perhaps influenced by the deteriorating character of the East-West relations reflected in the deferral of SALT," thereby blaming the United States for the Soviet invasion.

During the debate, parliamentarians from NATO countries argued that the U.S. response to the invasion—the imposition of trade restrictions and the boycott of the Moscow Olympics—was too "dramatic," that it divided the alliance. Further, they castigated America for creating a Rapid Deployment Force (paper tiger though it was), claiming that it "may be used to the disadvantage" of other NATO countries. Seemingly, they were oblivious to the fact that America was only 8 percent dependent upon the Persian Gulf for its energy, while Western Europe was 32 percent dependent.

Although the assembly eventually passed a resolution criticizing the Soviet Union for invading Afghanistan, a crucial vote urging the United States to ratify SALT II regardless of the Soviet aggression was narrowly defeated, forty-seven to thirty-five, with several abstentions, thereby signaling to the world, especially to the Soviet Union, that the Western Alliance would split badly if the Russian Bear said boo.

That the NATO countries met on June 6—the anniversary of the World War II Allied invasion to free Europe—to consider a reaction to modern-day aggression, was highly appropriate. That they met in Luxembourg—the headquarters of General George S. Patton as he directed his sweep toward Hitler's Germany—also was fitting. But that the NATO countries were so badly split on the question of criticizing armed aggression showed how easy it was to forget.

Not a half-dozen miles away, on the outskirts of Luxembourg, lies an American military cemetery where Patton rests along with 5,076 American soldiers. Among them are twenty-two graves, where eleven pairs of brothers lie side by side. Standing among them, and reflecting on the strain of weakness eating at the Western Alliance, one wonders if free and prosperous people will ever learn that only strength will stop aggression, that only firmness will deter a war before it can begin.

Only when the world sees that America means to be

strong again, only when the world sees that America is willing to stand alone if she must (although she most assuredly prefers not to), will the nations of the world be willing to give for what they get. Only then will the Soviet Union be willing to sit down and negotiate, not just arms limitations, but the elimination of organized terrorism and subversion—because, for Moscow, the alternative will be too costly.

Prometheus can lie inert, threatened by enemies and ignored by friends, or he can stir to break the shackles wrapped about him. In so doing, he can rally free nations to stand against the tyrants, who will flinch only when they see steel.

VIII

ATLAS ALIVE

Who owns the earth? Did we want the earth that
we should wander on it? Did we need the earth
that we were never still upon it? Whoever needs
the earth shall have the earth: he shall be still
upon it, he shall rest within a little place. . . .
—THOMAS WOLFE
Of Time and the River

THE EIGHT-YEAR-OLD LAD and his dad lay in their
sleeping bags under the stars, high atop the Wyoming Rockies, studying the full moon with a special intensity. At precisely 10:37 P.M., the pocket radio propped between their
heads told them what they were watching but could not see:

SPACECRAFT: Okay. We just appeared to get a solid
lock for the last dash. . . . We're just
finishing up our fuel-cell purge. . . .

CONTROL: Roger, Eleven. . . . That really winds
things up as far as we're concerned on
the ground, for the evening. We're
ready to go to bed and get a little
sleep. . . .

SPACECRAFT: Yes. We're about to join you.

Apollo 11 was speeding toward the moon.
Seventeen hours later, at 3:17 P.M. EDT on July 20, 1969,
Colonel Neil Armstrong informed NASA and the world:
"Houston, Tranquility Base here. The Eagle has landed." Six
hours later, via live telecast, an electrified world watched
him step from the spacecraft onto the moon and calmly
proclaim: "That's one small step for a man, one giant leap
for mankind."
For the boy and his dad, as for millions of their thrilled

countrymen, those few steps filled them anew with justifiable pride as America reaffirmed a belief in herself. That Americans could travel 952,700 miles through space, land on the moon and then return safely to earth, proved that Americans still harbored the pioneer spirit, could still produce both the technology and the breed of men needed to begin the peaceful conquest of the universe.

But as the boy and his dad peered into that universe, seeing with their minds the American spacecraft that they could not see with their eyes, Neil Armstrong and Buzz Aldrin, his co-pilot, held in clear focus the planet Earth. And despite the prodigious efforts of American scientists and engineers, supported to the tune of $21.3 billion by the American people and their elected representatives, the mission would not have been possible but for the natural resources of planet Earth.

The sheer physical characteristics of America made possible not only the landing on the moon but also the technological and economic achievements that have provided Americans with an incredibly wide range of choice. For example: watching a television program about a sunny southern beach in the dead of winter; hopping a plane that puts one there within a few hours; backpacking in the Rockies or fly-fishing in the Appalachians; working amid the skyscrapers of New York City, Chicago, or San Francisco, or toiling on the open stretches of Kansas prairie or Texas sagebrush; living in snug apartment buildings, or stretching out in homes surrounded by grass and space and neighbors.

In significant measure, America is what she is because of her size and shape, her longitude and latitude, her altitude and amplitude; because of her soil, the products that grow above it and the minerals that lie beneath it; because of her rivers and streams, her sun and snow; because of her people, their numbers, their diversity, and where they choose to make their homes.

Through physical characteristics alone, America is an Atlas, a giant holding the world upon his back.

In size alone, America is the fourth largest country in the world. With 20 percent of her 3.6 million square miles cultivated, 27 percent used for grazing, and 32 percent forested, America's land is functioning productively. With

12,000 miles of coastline and 78,000 square miles of inland water, America has the fisheries, water resources, and transportation waterways to support her prosperous and growing population.

Compared to island England, landlocked Russia, or arid Egypt where civilization could not flourish much beyond the banks of the Nile, America has been blessed with a natural diversity that let her stretch in all directions.

The world's largest political entity, the Soviet Union, is nearly 2.5 times the size of America, but has only 10 percent of its land under cultivation. While two thirds of the Soviet Union is bordered by water, most of it is the water of the frigid, relatively useless Arctic. The Soviet climate is dominated by the polar continental air mass which extends over most of the land for much of the year. Annual rainfall is generally less then twenty inches, about ten inches less than that of the United States.

Japan, with only 143,500 square miles, an area smaller than Montana, and less than 15 percent of that sufficiently level to permit agriculture, survives and prospers on one of the world's poorest pieces of geography.

Mainland China, although thought by many to be the world's largest nation, is, in fact, no larger in size than America. Only in population is it first, with almost one quarter of the world's people. Almost 80 percent of China is desert or wasteland, and most of it is too dry, too steep, or too cold for farming.

America, by comparison, is blessed not only with the vastness of her continent, but with a climate, soil, and contour that provide the incentive and potential for productivity. More than most other nations of the planet Earth, America has within her own physical characteristics the vital prerequisites for fertility. Americans can be productive because their land lets them. Physical America is a cooperating partner in achieving the American dream of prosperity. Physical America provides the raw material from which prosperity may be fashioned.

If the land itself is one of America's most precious assets, then a crucial question must be: Who owns the land? Thanks to America's unique concern with gathering data about herself, major pieces of the answer are available: America is comprised of 2.3 billion acres. One billion acres, or about 44 percent, is owned by 2.3 million farm families, or about 7.5 million people. The average farm is about 440 acres, indicating that among farm families land is widely dispersed. While concern over foreign ownership of agricultural land is understandable, the fact is that foreigners own only 7.8 million acres of American agricultural land, less than one half of 1 percent. Neighboring Canada is the largest holder of such land, with about one one hundredth of 1 percent, followed by Britain and West Germany. About 40 percent of foreign agricultural holdings are not in farmland, but in forest land.

At the end of 1979, 2,613 U.S. companies were 10 percent or more foreign-owned with a total foreign investment of about $65.5 billion. They represented about 1 percent of the total 2.5 million U.S. corporations reporting total assets of $6.8 trillion. The Netherlands, Britain, and Canada were the three largest holders, with the OPEC countries near the bottom.

In 1980, 29.8 million Americans owned stock in U.S. businesses; by early 1982 that figure increased to 32.3 million. Beyond these direct stockholders, 133 million Americans were participants in pension funds owning stock in U.S. enterprises. Pension funds, representing the interests of America's working and retired people, held a total equity of over $140 billion in U.S. corporations, about 15 percent of America's total corporate equity. At the beginning of 1982, the market value of their holdings was over $220 billion, 14 percent of all stockholdings in publicly owned American corporations. (See Table 7.)

To the question of who owns America, it is fair, then, to conclude: America is owned by a majority of her citizens, and that ownership becomes more widespread each year.

In the Soviet Union virtually everything is owned by the state. Apartments are parceled out based on one's importance to the state, jobs are assigned by the state, and even vacation spots are allocated in accordance with the state's desires. Communist dignitaries and famous personages are sometimes awarded dachas—summer homes—as prizes for their contributions to the state, but ownership remains with the state, with possession generally reverting to the state upon the death—or fall from favor—of the beneficiary. Even former heads of state, such as Nikita Khrushchev, were not immune to such repossession. Theoretically, the Nobel physicist, Andrei Sakharov, still has possession of the dacha awarded him for his contribution to the development of the Soviet hydrogen bomb; however, having been exiled to the off-limits city of Gorki for his anti-Soviet propaganda on behalf of human rights, he has effectively been dispossessed from his prize.

In America, no landed gentry controls the arable land. Of the nonfarm population, almost fifty million families own their own homes, representing approximately 60 percent of all dwellings in America. Even that handsome statistic does not tell the whole story, since many affluent Americans choose to live in comfortable rental properties.

While Americans know that land and home ownership are widely distributed among millions of their countrymen, some are quite surprised to learn the extent of the holdings of America's largest landowner: Uncle Sam. The federal government owns 770 million acres—about one third of America. With state and local governments owning another 6 percent, total government ownership of America's land is 40 percent. Since government theoretically represents the people, it could be said that America owns America. If however, one accepts the dictum "When everybody owns something, nobody owns it," then nobody owns 40 percent of America!

At least two conclusions can be drawn from the foregoing facts:

First, private ownership of land in America is widely distributed among the American people. While it is always wise to worry about the possibility of undue concentrations of ownership in the hands of a small portion of the population, that problem appears more theoretical than real.

Second, federal-government ownership of land is massive. In some Western states, the federal government owns most of the land: Nevada, 86 percent; Alaska, 80 percent; Utah and Idaho, 64 percent; Wyoming, 49 percent; Califor-

TABLE 7. MARKET VALUE OF STOCKHOLDINGS OF INSTITUTIONAL INVESTORS AND OTHERS
(Billions of Dollars, End of Year)
January 1, 1982

	1973	1974	1975	1976	1977	1978	1979	1980
1. Private Noninsured Pension Funds	90.5	63.4	88.6	109.7	101.9	107.9	123.7	175.8
2. Open-End Investment Companies	43.3	30.3	38.7	43.0	36.2	34.1	34.8	44.5
3. Other Investment Companies	6.6	4.7	5.3	5.9	3.1	2.7	1.8	2.3
4. Life Insurance Companies	25.9	21.9	28.1	34.2	32.9	35.7	40.5	52.9
5. Property-Liability Insurance Companies[1]	19.7	12.8	14.2	16.9	17.1	19.4	24.8	32.3
6. Personal Trust Funds[2]	101.3	72.0	86.9	100.8	97.1	95.1	106.1R	132.9
7. Mutual Saving Banks	4.2	3.7	4.4	4.4	4.8	4.8	4.7	4.2
8. State and Local Retirement Funds	20.2	16.4	24.3	30.1	30.0	33.3	37.1	44.3
9. Foundations	24.5	18.4	22.7	27.1	26.1	27.0	31.2R	32.9
10. Educational Endowments	9.6	6.7	8.8	10.4	9.8	10.2	10.2	10.4
11. Subtotal	345.8	250.2	322.0	382.5	359.0	370.2	414.9	532.5
12. Less: Institutional Holdings of Investment Company Shares[3]	6.7	6.5	8.6	10.0	10.5	10.3	8.5	12.6

13. Total Institutional Investors	339.1	243.7	313.4	372.5	348.5	359.9	406.4R	519.9
14. Foreign Investors[4]	37.0	28.4	52.6	63.9	67.7R	80.0R	92.0R	114.5
15. Other Domestic Investors[5]	525.3	369.6	483.5	569.2	529.6R	548.2R	679.2R	938.9
16. Total Stock Outstanding[6]	901.4	641.7	849.5	1,005.6	945.8	988.1	1,177.6R	1,573.3

R = Revised

[1] Excludes holdings of insurance company stock.
[2] Includes Common Trust Funds.
[3] Excludes institutional holdings of money market funds.
[4] Includes estimate of stock held as direct investment.
[5] Computed as residual (line 15=16-14-13). Includes both individuals and institutional groups not listed above.
[6] Includes both common and preferred stock. Excludes investment company shares but includes foreign issues outstanding in the United States.

SOURCE: U.S. Securities and Exchange Commission

nia, 47 percent; Arizona, 44 percent; Colorado, 36 percent; and Montana, 30 percent.

Vast stretches of public lands in the West remain as vestiges of that time when territories were untapped and most of the population lived east of the Mississippi River. The U.S. Department of the Interior claims it cannot place a value on the 770 million federally owned acres, but at current market prices their value probably approaches $500 billion. Additionally, beyond the three-mile state-ownership limit of the outer continental shelf, the U.S. government owns over a billion acres where resources of oil, gas, and hard-rock minerals might be unlocked.

It is time that America seriously address the following questions: How much land should be held in the federal domain? How much should be returned to the states or made available for sale to the American people? What policy will best ensure that the public interest is best preserved, that the American people are given a fair opportunity to own land that, supposedly, is theirs?

In a nation in which mineral resources grow increasingly scarce, it is wrong to lock up such supplies behind a federal shield; it is wrong not to encourage private investment to expand the nation's domestic production of energy, timber, and other natural resources. With approximately 55 percent of all federal lands closed or restricted to mineral development, America's vast reserves count for little if they can't be used to fuel the nation's growth. It is America's natural resources that provide the sinews of the nation's muscles. The American Atlas is fed from the soil and the mines beneath. To choke off the flow of those resources in the name of preserving a pristine wilderness is to inflict deadly economic consequences, especially for the poor and disadvantaged. For them, the price of a public policy that leaves a major portion of America's natural wealth untouched must be fewer jobs, less money, food, clothes for their children, and a dark future, clouded by a veil separating them from opportunities which earlier generations of Americans were able to seize and mold.

From the minerals and renewable resources available, America has been able to fashion a high-technology, high-prosperity standard of living under which the drudgery of eking out a living has largely been replaced by automation or drudgery-saving devices which have steadily upgraded much of the work force from laborers to skilled technicians and specialists.

Nowhere have America's raw resources been more productively converted than on the nation's farms. Twenty years ago American farmers led the world, with each farmer producing enough food to feed twenty-six people. Today, American farm productivity has so skyrocketed that one farmer can now feed sixty-eight people. Only one-sixth as productive, a Soviet farmer can feed only ten people. Chronically unable to produce enough grain for its own people, the Soviet Union has become dependent upon other nations—especially America—for that most basic of all commodities: food.

In the 20-below-zero weather of January 1982, I personally witnessed Soviet women, with empty baskets, queuing up in front of food stores in Moscow and Leningrad. I was told that even in the comparatively well-stocked showcase cities of Moscow and Leningrad, a Russian housewife must plan to spend two hours a day searching for food and other necessities.

Beyond America's fecund prairies and river valleys rise 737 million acres of forests, of which 482 million acres generate one out of every eighteen dollars in the nation's economy by producing over 70 billion board feet of timber— enough to build 5 million homes every year and, from the residue, heat another 8 to 10 million homes.

Beneath the soil lie 438 billion short tons of coal, 29.8 billion barrels of proven oil reserves, and 1.99 trillion cubic feet of proven gas reserves.

Off America's shores, U.S. commercial fishermen catch 6.5 billion pounds of fish each year. Foreign fishermen pull another 3.6 billion pounds from those same waters. Together, they provide the equivalent of about 50 pounds of fish annually for every American.

From Appalachia to the Rockies, deep in the mountains, and facing jagged canyons lie the minerals that drive America's high-technology society.

America, the world's leading industrial nation, ranks first

in production of total energy—coal, natural gas, and nuclear —and of lead, sulfur, salt, and copper. America also produces almost 70 percent of the world's mica and molybdenum and nearly 50 percent of its magnesium.

Despite America's extraordinary supply of vital minerals, the absence of several minerals is ample cause for alarm.

Deputy Secretary of Commerce Joseph R. Wright, Jr., testified before a congressional committee:

> Our defense capabilities and economic well-being are critically dependent on more than twenty nonfuel minerals and we import more than 90 percent of our annual needs of seven of these minerals—including manganese, cobalt, chrome, and the platinum-group metals—and more than 50 percent of our annual needs of the other thirteen. And the continued supply of some of these minerals is dependent on imports from potentially unstable regions.

Table 8 shows the extent of American dependence on other countries for importation of critical nonfuel minerals.

When *Apollo 11* landed on the moon, it had a dry weight of about 22,000 pounds, of which about 20,000 pounds were metallic, including: 75 percent aluminum alloys, 15 percent titanium, and 8 percent stainless steel. In addition there were high-nickel-based alloys including inconel, as well as traces of columbium, molybdenum, and beryllium. About 90 percent of the bauxite for the aluminum raw material had to be obtained outside the United States from such places as Guinea, Australia, and Surinam. Chromium, which makes up most of the stainless-steel alloys, had to be obtained from the Soviet Union, South Africa, or Rhodesia. Most of the nickel-based alloys came from Canada; cobalt from Zaire, Zambia, Finland, and Belgium; and columbium exclusively from Brazil, Thailand, and Canada.

Since World War II, America has developed a strategic stockpile of sixty-one crucial raw materials valued at about $15 billion. The Federal Emergency Management Agency reports a shortfall of at least 50 percent in twenty-three of

TABLE 8. United States Import Dependency and Long-range Outlook for Imported Non-fuel Minerals

Commodity	1978 value of new materials added to the U.S. economy (dollars in millions)	Net Import reliance as a percent of apparent consumption 0 25 50 75 100	Major Import sources	Percentage of 1976 2000 demand obtainable from known reserves U.S. alone	Entire world
Chromium	600	100	So. Africa, USSR	10	950
Manganese	200	100	Brazil, So. Africa, Gabon	0	460
Cobalt	150	100	So. Africa, Zaire	0	120
Tin	700	100	Bolivia, Malaysia	10	150
Platinum	500	100	So. Africa	0	300
Nickel	750	94	Canada	10	220
Aluminum	6,400	92	Jamaica, Australia	10	580
Asbestos	170	84	Canada	20	50
Gold	1,100	56	Canada, USSR, So. Africa	60	110
Fluorine	110	82	Mexico, So. Africa	10	40
Zinc	680	69	Canada	60	80
Silver	620	67	Canada, Peru, Mexico	40	50
Tungsten	160	62	Canada, Bolivia	40	140
Potash	450	61	Canada	90	1,000
Iron	19,000	42	Canada	150	510
Lead	530	24	Canada, Mexico, Peru	100	110
Copper	2,300	23	Canada, Chile	150	160
Titanium	230	52	Canada, Australia	140	410
Sulfur	550	10	Canada, Mexico	50	90

(SOURCE: U.S. Department of the Interior, Geological Survey)

the stockpiled materials, including cobalt, bauxite, nickel, tantalum, and the platinum-group metals. Another $12 billion investment is required to fill the nation's strategic warehouse. Although America's present stockpile would keep the nation running for several months in an emergency, neither Western Europe nor Japan has a strategic stockpile. A cutoff of vital minerals could bring them to their knees within weeks. With virtually no raw materials, Japan is particularly vulnerable.

From spacecraft to toasters, from sophisticated hospital operating rooms to cans that sit in kitchen cupboards, America is dependent upon faraway countries for her vital minerals. The American Atlas will continue strong only as long as the Atlas continues to be fed the vital minerals needed—and that depends upon the continued free flow of international trade.

Fortunately, that need not forever be the case with energy. Although America depended upon foreign sources for about half her petroleum supply during the 1970's, through increased domestic production and conservation that dependence has been reduced to 30 percent. Petroleum accounts for almost half of America's energy requirements. Meanwhile, evidence grows that alternatives to such imports do, in fact, exist.

About five hundred million U.S.-government-owned acres—a quarter of the entire nation—are off limits to oil and gas development as a result of federal laws and regulations. By opening at least a portion of them to development, America can substantially reduce her remaining oil dependence. Beyond that, we have thirty-five billion barrels of heavy oil deposits in California, with thirty billion barrels embedded in tar deposits in Utah. Combined, those deposits are double the total of our proven oil reserves. Heavy oil is expensive to extract, but further improvements in the process could make it competitive with rising energy costs. Coupled with the conservation that is clearly taking hold, these developments can and should reduce substantially America's long-term dependence on foreign oil imports.

Beyond petroleum, however, coal must be a major part of the answer for America. Her coal resources are estimated at 1.5 trillion tons, enough to last over two thousand years at present production rates. Yet, while coal constitutes 93 percent of U.S. energy reserves, it is used to supply only 17 percent of the nation's total energy. By converting 138 utilities as well as 2,000 industrial and 940 commercial oil burners to coal, over 4 million barrels of oil can be saved per day —more than two-thirds the current import levels. With 1 ton of coal selling at about $30 and having the BTU equivalency of 4.3 barrels of oil, coal must be a major part of the energy solution.

Electrification of railroads and mass-transit systems represents a further opportunity to reduce the nation's oil dependency. If half of America's railroad main lines were electrified and fueled by coal, about one hundred thousand barrels of oil would be saved per day. Unfortunately, fewer than 1 percent of U.S. main lines are electrified, compared to over 75 percent in the Soviet Union. Russian transportation officials openly admit that the main reason their railroads were converted from diesel to electricity—and that the remaining 25 percent will be converted within the next decade—was to reduce oil dependency. Even though the Soviet Union is today a net exporter of oil, its rulers fear their supplies will be inadequate in the future and therefore are planning accordingly. For them, the alternatives are hydroelectric and nuclear power. For America, however, coal can play the central role. Comprising 30 percent of the world's reserves, American coal can join food as a major export product. America's current coal export capacity, slightly under one hundred million tons per year, could be tripled to meet world demand and, in the process, create thousands of new American jobs and tip the balance of payments back in America's favor.

What must be changed are federal and state environmental laws to permit coal to be mined and burned more easily, thereby stimulating the public and private investment necessary to open new mines and provide the transportation infrastructure needed to move the coal by rail, barge, truck, and ship. The total investment required could exceed $1 trillion over the next fifteen years, but the return on that investment would provide ample profits for investors, create half a million jobs, and move America closer to energy independence. The American Atlas can indeed be powered with energy from beneath the soil on which it stands, if America's governments—state and federal—make the necessary decisions to permit the reasonable mining of that most plentiful American energy resource.

Surely hydro, nuclear, and solar power must also play their roles, but only coal can be the bedrock from which the American Atlas gains needed strength.

For the distant future, however, the bright glow of fusion holds the hope. American scientists lead the world in taming nuclear fusion, the same process from which the hydrogen bomb evolved. Ex-Congressman Mike McCormack, himself a nuclear physicist and former chairman of the House Science and Technology Committee, says that the feasibility of nuclear fusion could be demonstrated within a few years and possibly available for use before the year 2000. That augurs the possibility of unlimited energy. Fusion—the joining of the nuclei of two light atoms at temperatures above 60 million degrees centigrade—is the same nuclear process that powers the sun. The energy that could be released by the fusion process from a single glass of water would be equivalent to 280 gallons of gasoline. One pound of the heavy water could produce the energy equivalent of 5,000 tons of coal. Because the fuel could be derived from water, the supply would be unlimited. The harnessing of fusion energy, then, could be as historic and far-reaching as the discovery of fire. Is this but another fantasy? A *Star Wars* brought to Earth? Surely it is no more so than DaVinci's dream of flying, of Franklin's urge to harness lightning. Whether it will be available in the twenty-first century is, of course, speculative. But certain facts are clear: In 1977, scientists at Princeton University produced the conditions for a fusion reactor inside a magnetic bottle; the federal government is spending over $400 million a year in fusion-energy research; a specific process known as the Tokamak Confinement Device has been developed, and responsible observers believe this revolutionary process could be commercially available within decades.

When this dream becomes reality, America and the

world will have the capability of lifting man's burdens off his back. Until that day, however, America must find progress with the tools at hand. The American Atlas must see and prepare for the changes sweeping across its body, for the shifting of people and their interests, for the growth of certain sinews, and the painful atrophy of other parts.

The 1980 Census revealed not only that the number of Americans grew from 203.2 million in 1970 to 226.5 million in 1980, but that American living patterns have changed dramatically. Americans now marry later, have fewer children, and choose to live in different places. For the first time in this century, the net in-migration to rural areas has exceeded the out-migration. They are moving out of the cities into the suburban and rural areas; they are moving in record numbers out of the Northeast and Midwest into the South and Southwest. Over 55 percent of the American people now express a preference for living in small towns and rural areas, with only 13 percent preferring cities. Table 9 tells the story.

TABLE 9. Population Change by State 1970–1980 (millions)

State	1980	1970	Percent change, 1970–1980
Alabama	3.9	3.4	12.9
Alaska	.4	.3	32.4
Arizona	2.7	1.8	53.1
Arkansas	2.3	1.9	18.8
California	23.7	20.0	18.5
Colorado	2.9	2.2	30.7
Connecticut	3.1	3.0	2.5
Delaware	.6	.5	8.6
Florida	9.7	6.8	43.4
Georgia	5.5	4.6	19.1
Hawaii	1.0	.8	25.3
Idaho	.9	.7	32.4
Illinois	11.4	11.1	2.8
Indiana	5.5	5.2	5.7
Iowa	3.0	2.8	3.1
Kansas	2.4	2.2	5.1
Kentucky	3.7	3.2	13.7
Louisiana	4.2	3.6	15.3
Maine	1.1	1.0	13.2

TABLE 9. *continued*

State	1980	1970	*Percent change,* *1970–1980*
Maryland	4.2	3.9	7.5
Massachusetts	5.7	5.7	0.8
Michigan	9.3	8.9	4.2
Minnesota	4.0	3.8	7.1
Mississippi	2.5	2.2	13.7
Missouri	4.9	4.7	5.1
Montana	.8	.7	13.3
Nebraska	1.6	1.5	5.7
Nevada	.8	.5	63.5
New Hampshire	.9	.8	24.8
New Jersey	7.4	7.2	2.7
New Mexico	1.3	1.0	27.8
New York	17.6	18.2	−3.8
North Carolina	5.9	5.1	15.5
North Dakota	.7	.6	5.6
Ohio	10.8	10.7	1.3
Oklahoma	3.0	2.6	18.2
Oregon	2.6	2.1	25.9
Pennsylvania	11.9	11.8	0.6
Rhode Island	.9	.9	−0.3
South Carolina	3.1	2.6	20.4
South Dakota	.7	.7	3.6
Tennessee	4.6	3.9	16.9
Texas	14.2	11.2	27.1
Utah	1.5	1.1	37.9
Vermont	.5	.4	15.0
Virginia	5.3	4.7	14.9
Washington	4.1	3.4	21.0
West Virginia	1.9	1.7	11.8
Wisconsin	4.7	4.4	6.5
Wyoming	.5	.3	41.6

(Extracted from *1980 Census of Population and Housing, Advance Reports, PHC 80-V-1,* U.S. Department of Commerce, Bureau of the Census)

These demographic trends are reinforced and accelerated by the flow of both private-sector jobs and federal funds into the South and West. While the nation's economic growth is expected to generate eleven million new jobs over the next seven years, a disproportionately high percentage is projected for the South and West, further exacerbating the economic decline of the Northeast. Federal funds also flow disproportionately from the North to the South. For example, Pennsylvania receives about 87 cents for each federal tax dollar its residents pay, while Georgia gets about $1.16. As political power inevitably follows closely behind population, seventeen congressional seats have shifted from the Northeast to the South and West based upon the 1980 Census.

Should national policy "go with the flow?" Or should it reallocate resources in an attempt to revitalize declining regions of the country?

While federal schemes to entice economic growth into declining areas sometimes have the ring of progress, they are often fraught with insurmountable problems. Many of the reasons why people choose to move South or West are beyond the reach of public policy. Sun, sand, surf, and space offer alluring siren calls. The economic advantages for business to go where their markets are growing cannot be denied. Shabby surroundings of worn-out cities stand in stark contrast to the gleaming vibrance of booming new locales. Different labor attitudes contribute more than many would like to admit. On two different occasions I was deeply involved in efforts to attract new industry to Pennsylvania—efforts which were rebuffed, we were told, purely because of the "unattractive labor climate" in the Northeast. An economic package of tax breaks coupled with development of water, sewer, and transportation infrastructure matched any other offer, but the perceived labor climate killed both prospects. Even though there are marked differences in attitudes and productivity rates between rural and urban areas of the Northeast, they seem to count for little when outside firms begin to measure regions.

No amount of federal dollars can plaster over the disadvantages of declining markets, decaying cities, and dropping productivity. But that is not to say that the federal government should not attempt to stimulate economic activity evenhandedly throughout the land.

The federal government has a duty to be sure that public investment is fairly distributed among the different regions of the country, to create a climate which is conducive rather than hostile to economic growth. But when the federal government passes out favors to certain states at the expense of others, it treads on shaky ground. The American Atlas will not be strengthened by building one part of the body while disregarding or dismembering the other. Atlas will thrive only if all parts are given equal opportunity to grow in strength.

Many northeastern states are missing opportunities by not giving greater attention to development of the nonmetropolitan areas. The evidence is now overwhelming that a majority of the American people prefer to live outside large cities. In the past twenty years, the federal government has funneled over $600 billion into revitalization of America's metropolitan areas, compared to about $175 billion that has gone to her nonmetropolitan areas. Had that money been distributed more evenly, many more prospering small communities would today adjoin environmentally sound, modernized, light industries across the nation. The American Atlas would be more uniformly strong, and those parts that were most conducive to robust growth would have blossomed and prospered most.

For the future, America can achieve better growth and more congenial life-styles by distributing more evenly her public assets and letting each region rise to achieve the potential on which it sets its sights.

Surely, the natural diversity of the land offers differing opportunities for regions prepared to capitalize upon their own strengths. Already, Americans have turned deserts and swamps into sparkling areas for living, work, and play. Such metamorphoses prove that where the will exists, Americans have the ability to create prosperity.

A drive through Florida's Alligator Alley proves that, for Americans, almost nothing is impossible. Cutting across South Florida to connect the Atlantic and the Gulf coasts, Alligator Alley, State Road 84, is a seventy-five mile miracle, albeit taken for granted now by virtually all of the four million people who traverse it every year. Alligator Alley is a twenty-four-foot swath of modern America through primordial swamp. The Everglades of South Florida are 1.7 million acres of desolation—100 miles across by 50 miles wide, a swampy area of grass rising out of peat and muck and rock and marl. Populated by Seminole Indians, their ferociously independent cousins, the Miccosukees, a smattering of swamp-rat whites, alligators, snakes, wild boars, mosquitoes, and other insects, the Everglades historically has been a dank, dark, dangerous no-man's-land. Although the area's surface composition is geologically young, about five thousand years old, the more ancient rocks beneath it knew the hoof of the mastodon. Because the peat base of the eco-basin makes it highly susceptible to oxygenation, fires sweep uncontrollably across it during dry seasons. Without man's intervention, the Everglades would eventually dry up, turning first into a bed of muck and later into a bowl of dust.

But man has made the difference—more precisely, twentieth century American man has made the difference. After World War II, representatives of the state of Florida and the federal government decided both to preserve and to improve that unique portion of America. In 1947, plans were developed for a huge system of canals and dikes to control the drainage and water levels of the Everglades, Lake Okeechobee, and the Kissimmee River valley to the north. By 1949, a $208 million flood-control and water-conservation program was begun. Huge reservoir areas—some as large as Lake Okeechobee—were built to store water for release during dry winter months and prevent the damaging floods that came with the rainy season. The slow death of the ecosystem was reversed, and the preservation of the Everglades was assured.

Within a decade the state, along with several South Florida counties, began thinking about building a highway across the swamp to connect its Atlantic and Gulf coasts. Floating a $17 million bond issue to finance the project was the least of the problems. To get the material necessary to raise the roadbed safely above water, a canal adjacent to the highway route had to be dug through the swamp all across the state. Indian guides, swamp buggies, and airboats had to be brought in to survey and construct the highway. To preserve the smooth flow of water, numerous culverts were built underneath the roadbed. Aboveground, relationships with the Indians and other groups were not so smooth.

At one point, tempers ran so hot that project opponents

threatened the lives of the federal-state coordinator, U.S. Senator Lawton Chiles, and the Florida secretary of transportation. Nevertheless, the project was completed, an extremely difficult engineering feat was accomplished, and South Florida was tied together by a ribbon of concrete poured through a seemingly impenetrable and desolate swamp. Almost immediately Alligator Alley was a success— vehicles using the highway and the tolls they produced were double the original projections. Inspired by that success, and with increasingly heavy usage projected, plans were developed to upgrade Alligator Alley into a divided, four-lane section of Interstate Highway 77, scheduled for completion after 1990.

So it was that a feat that seemed all but impossible in the 1950's was, by the 1980's, viewed as a relatively routine task. Meanwhile, a driver crossing the Everglades who reflects upon the enormity of the changes within his lifetime can only be impressed. Such a highway was made possible, not just for the wealthy few, but for millions of average Americans—made possible by the ingenuity, initiative, and determination of generations of Americans all committed to building a better place for themselves and for their children. It was also made possible by resources that were there to be shaped. The sun and water, sand and shale—the gravel and cement, energy and iron—all had to be part of physical America before Americans could bend them to their use. There could have been no taming of a tiny stretch of that magnificent desolation of the Everglades had there been no Everglades. Nor could there be a vacation journey in comfort through the heart of a foreboding, prehistoric wilderness, had there been no wilderness to preserve.

So it is all across America: The land's magnificent diversity lets Americans experience all there is to see in life— from the sunny beaches and blue waters of the South to the rugged rocks and snowy mountains of the North, from the lakes and rivers of the nation's heartland to the deserts facing western slopes.

Nor has the miracle of man's creation been limited to cutting roads through eastern swamps. In the arid southwestern desert, where only cactus and rattlesnakes once could thrive, twentieth century Americans have harnessed the water necessary to give it life. Beginning with the Reclamation Act of 1902, which provided federal subsidies for irrigation projects to help farm families settle western lands, the process of converting wasteland into valuable earth has been the public policy.

Shortly after the enactment of that landmark legislation, the Theodore Roosevelt Dam rose across Arizona's Salt River to provide irrigation for 250,000 acres, to generate hydroelectric power for 53,000 homes in the Phoenix area, and to make low-cost water recreation available to thousands of people. With the Roosevelt Dam setting the pattern for developing the Southwest, additional dams were constructed, and deep wells drilled to tap the aquifers below.

With the Colorado River's flow ranging wildly from 5.6 million acre-feet* to over 24 million acre-feet annually, depending upon how much rain and snow fell in the far-off Rocky Mountains, plans were developed to manage that mighty flow. Eventually, it became clear that groundwater from the deep wells was being used up more quickly than it was being replaced by nature. By 1936, in the northwest corner of Arizona on the Nevada border, the Hoover Dam was built to capture 28 million acre-feet of water annually and supply hydroelectric power for Arizona, California, and Nevada. As people saw an almost worthless desert bloom and hard-scrabble lives blossom into prosperity, water-reclamation projects sprang up throughout the Southwest. By 1979, over 150 such projects irrigated more than twelve million acres of private land in seventeen western states, producing over $7 billion in crops, and providing water, power, and recreation for millions of families and businesses throughout the region.

Referring to the beneficial impact of water projects on central Arizona, Congressman Morris K. Udall (D-Ariz.), one of the nation's most highly regarded conservationists, stated: "We have seen develop a multi-billion dollar economy and one of the twenty-five largest metropolitan areas in the

---

*One acre-foot equals 325,850 gallons of water.

country. Over a million people now live and work where only a handful were able to subsist before. The government's initial investment has been repaid by the water users and, in addition, many times over through the Federal taxes that flow from the economic activity which the Salt River Project made possible."

The benefits of water were so great that the success of each new project quickly brought demand for still more water. People flocked to the sun and space of the new Southwest which had been brought to life by water. Arizona boomed, especially in the Phoenix area, where the population doubled to 1.7 million between 1960 and 1980, with projections that it would double again within another two decades. Water tables continue to drop, and major segments of the arid Southwest face critical water shortages in the years ahead.

Even as the metropolitan Phoenix area exploded with life and prosperity, downtown Phoenix felt decay with age, crime, and smog taking their toll. Around the city, however, sprang up a series of enormously successful communities— seeming to prove that even in the best of circumstances there must be death for life to spring anew, larger and more vibrant.

Although Arizona's leaders had long recognized the need for further development of their water resources and in 1947 had presented Congress with a plan to divert 2.8 million acre-feet of Colorado River water into Arizona, court challenges delayed the project for almost twenty years until it won U.S. Supreme Court approval in 1964. Finally, in 1968, the long-needed, long-planned Central Arizona Project was approved by Congress and signed into law by President Johnson—a monumental project, which would provide 1.2 million acre-feet of water annually along with power and recreation for more than five million people and businesses.

Now well under way and scheduled for completion by 1988, the Central Arizona Project will provide a 300-mile "ribbon of life-sustaining water" from the mighty Colorado, through aqueducts, dikes, tunnels, and dams, to central and southern Arizona. Its hydropower will drive pumps which will lift the water 800 feet to a tunnel which will transport it 6.8 miles through mountains where 3,000 cubic feet of water per second will splash into open concrete aqueducts nineteen feet deep, twenty-four feet wide at the bottom and eighty feet wide at the top, for its 190-mile trip to Phoenix, and then another 110 miles south toward Tucson. Using the largest precast-concrete pressure pipe in the world, with 24.5-foot-diameter sections weighing 225 tons—the size of a jumbo jet—the aqueduct system, with remote-computer-controlled checkpoints and gates at six-mile intervals, will be monitored from an automated center in Phoenix. The project, which will cost about $2.5 billion, will provide 36,000 man-years of work, and will be the largest, longest water-resources project ever accomplished.

Those parts of Arizona already irrigated by earlier water-reclamation projects have proved the enormous benefits of the effort: Land where three hundred acres were required to graze one cow now produces thirteen lush alfalfa crops a year, four times the output of the alfalfa-growing regions of New York or Pennsylvania. Wasteland that twenty years ago sold for $100 an acre now sells for $40,000 an acre. Fifty miles north of Phoenix, along the aqueduct, beautiful homes and modest trailer parks plant their different living styles among the beavertail cactus and beneath the two-hundred-year-old giant saguaro cactus with its fingerlike green tubes extending fifty feet upward toward the boiling sun.

Within another decade, thousands of homes and dozens of communities will have settled in along the aqueduct on this once-barren land. Brown-speckled cactus wrens will move from their thorny nests among the plants, grow plump, and warble contentedly from beneath the shade of irrigated hedgerows and stately, wide-leaved palms.

As with its namesake, the legendary bird of gorgeous plumage that rose alive out of its own ashes to worship the sun, Phoenix is a modern-day miracle of new life rising out of the barren sand. Phoenix, and the whole Southwest around her, symbolize what twentieth century Americans can do with their raw environment.

Relatively speaking, the projects of the U.S. Bureau of Reclamation represent only a minuscule part of America's management of her resources in this century, yet those projects alone tell a story of astonishing results. From its inception in 1902, through fiscal 1982, the U.S. Bureau of Reclamation has spent not quite $10 billion, less than the most recent cost estimate for the Washington, D. C., metropolitan subway system. While many of the reclamation dollars were spent in less inflated times, the fact remains that, for the price tag, the range of accomplishments is impressive: 322 dams, 14,490 miles of canals, 174 pumping plants, fifty hydroelectric plants.

Together, these projects provide: irrigation for 146,000 farms, producing enough food for 33 million people; 620 billion gallons of water annually to meet the industrial and municipal needs of 18 million people; flood control that has saved nearly $1 billion in flood damages; 40 billion kilowatt-hours of electricity annually—equal to all the electrical energy used by all the people of New York City, Washington, D. C., Dallas, Chicago, and San Francisco—and the equivalent of 70 million barrels of oil.

Additionally, reclamation water areas provide recreation for over 65 million visitors annually in 271 recreation areas, along 12,000 miles of shoreline in 580 campgrounds with 215 swimming beaches and 13,800 boat slips. Water reclamation improves navigation, reduces salinity, provides food for waterfowl, spawning and nesting areas for fish and fowl, and an annual harvest of 20 million fish.

Reclamation projects pay for themselves many times over through the tax revenues generated by their economic activity: over $1 billion in state and local taxes, and nearly that much in federal revenues.

For example, the Central Arizona Project in its first fifty years will provide revenues of about $500 million each from hydroelectric power, water users, and property taxes. Additionally, nearly $1 billion in nonreimbursable benefits will be provided to Indian reservations during the period. The revenues received directly from the project, plus the income taxes generated by the multibillion-dollar increase in economic activity, make the project a sound financial investment of taxpayer dollars—not to mention the incredible improvement in the quality of life in the region.

When, in 1895, Katherine Lee Bates wrote "America the Beautiful," she captured more than a feeling for the beauty of "spacious skies, for amber waves of grain, for purple mountain majesties above the fruited plain." She captured the feeling of a people for their country. And justly so.

From the White Mountain ski slopes of New Hampshire to the elegant August days at Saratoga Springs; from the trout streams hidden in the Allegheny hills to the hiking paths of the Great Smoky Mountains; from water-skiing in the Ozark Lakes to standing silently atop the great Grand Canyon breathing in the beauty that descends a mile below; from the depths of the hemisphere's lowest point in Death Valley to the majestic white-capped peak of Mt. Rainer; from the frozen glaciers of Alaska to the hot volcanic lava of Hawaii; from the seasons of snow to the summers of sun; from mountain peaks to valley floors; from water hyacinth to cactus sage; from North to South and East to West, Americans love the physical beauty of their land. And well they might, for no other nation on Earth bursts with such natural gifts.

Perhaps even more significantly, Americans more than any other people have access not only to the natural treasures of their land but also to an enormous diversity of recreational choices, developed and improved upon by the hand of man. Such facilities—some publicly and some privately owned— offer more to see and do than any individual or family could hope even to scratch in a lifetime of travel and recreation.

Each year more than 250 million Americans visit 333 national parks comprising 79 million acres in the 50 states and the Virgin Islands. Another 66.5 million fish, swim, camp, boat, hike, hunt, and sightsee in the mountains, valleys, streams, dams, and lakes of 286 federally created recreation areas associated with water-reclamation projects. Additionally, some 105,000 state and local parks provide fun for more than 220 million visitors, as parks somehow touch the lives of almost every citizen in one way or another— whether as participants in organized sports, as spectators, or just as Sunday strollers.

Throughout the nation's history, federal, state, and local

governments have channeled many billions in tax dollars into the development, preservation, and maintenance of more parks and recreational areas than exist in any other nation in the world. From fiscal 1917 through fiscal 1982, $2 billion was spent by the National Park Service alone, most of it after fiscal 1961 when congressionally authorized parks began to be acquired, primarily from privately held land sources. In fiscal 1982 alone, federal, state, and local governments combined to spend more than $6 billion for parks and recreational areas across the nation.

Meanwhile, the world's most highly developed public park and recreation systems are but scattered attractions among a galaxy of privately owned vacation spots open to the public. Over 830 amusement parks, from Florida to California—including theme parks such as Disney World, Kings Dominion, Great America, Six Flags, and Busch Gardens—attract around two hundred million Americans each year to immerse themselves in lands of make-believe—many times seeming more real than life itself. Americans take over six hundred million vacation and weekend pleasure trips annually, almost 50 percent of which include staying in hotels, motels, or private campgrounds. More than ever, Americans are fulfilling their desires to play and hike, to ride and learn, to rest in the sun and be refortified—in the usually justified hope that a good dose of lazy days will send them once again back to lives of meaning and purpose, refueled and ready to meet the challenge of each day.

For out of the physical resources of America do Americans extract not only the minerals for material might but also the spiritual and psychological strength for self-renewal.

No description of the sheer physical prowess of America is complete without including the physical capacities and resilience of the American people themselves. Matching the mountains and forests, the cascading waterfalls and verdant valleys, the bulging mineral seams and blossoming prairie floors, are the attributes of health that make Americans strong. But it wasn't always thus. Even though the clean air, hard work, and usually bounteous foods of a rural way of life let those who escaped infant deaths or infectious diseases live long productive lives, at the turn of the century only two out of every one hundred Americans survived to see four score and ten.

During World War II, 50 percent of the draftees failed their preinduction physical exams. By the time of the Korean War, however, the failure rate had dropped to 32 percent, and today in the volunteer army it is down to 11 percent.

By 1978, about 9 of every 100 Americans were surviving their ninetieth year. At the turn of the century, American life expectancy was 47.3 years; by 1980, it was 73.6 years. In 1969, 3,200 Americans had survived 100 years; by 1979, the American population included 13,000 citizens over 100 years in age.

Continued medical advances saved lives that previously were doomed. Thirty years ago, only 50 percent of heart-attack victims survived; today 85 percent are saved. Thirty years ago, kidney failure meant death; today, through kidney transplants, 80 percent lead useful lives. Open-heart surgery, pacemakers, artifical hips, and dozens of other procedures and devices save tens of thousands every year.

But the greatest medical progress in America over the past two decades has occurred, not in hearts opened by surgeons' knives but in minds opened by peoples' knowledge about the kind of life-styles that lead to a vigorous longevity. In America, more than in any other country, the real revolution in health care has been and continues to be the increasing recognition that good health is largely a do-it-yourself proposition.

The twin principles of sound nutrition and regular exercise have swept across America as in no other land, turning more and more Americans into the most truly healthy specimens in the world. Forty-seven percent of American adults exercise—some 70 million of them eighteen years and older. Nearly half of them are women. About 30 million of them are runners. Thirty million others, six through twenty-one, are involved in out-of-school sports. Over 5 million high-school youths are involved in interscholastic sports; 1.6 million of them are girls. Intercollegiate sports involve 525,000 students, recreational sports involve 2.6 million, and college intramural and club sports involve 4.3 million.

Primary types of exercise in which those 47 percent of American adults involve themselves include running, swimming, weight-training, cross-country biking, aerobic dance and other forms of rhythmical jazz dance, tennis, bowling, and hiking.

A whole new branch of sports medicine growing up around exercise and sports has become a $2 billion-a-year specialty. With the overall recreation industry at a value of $244 billion, the personal health industry is also booming, with about one tenth of the national income spent for health services. Health-food stores and general dietary and nutritional consciousness have combined to develop a whole new industry within the food-services and nutritionist-training fields. By 1982, more than 140 U.S. firms were actively involved in the health-and-dietetic-food industry; they ranged from very small companies to giant corporations with large nutrition divisions.

Time magazine devoted an entire cover story to "The Fitness Craze," estimating the dietary element to be a $13.25 billion-a-year business. In a quarter century, Americans have experienced a 23 percent decline in fatal coronary disease and a 33 percent decline in strokes, for which three factors are credited: (1) Earlier detection and treatment of high blood pressure, (2) Decline in adult smoking, (3) Improved exercise and eating habits. The statistics tell the story:

Between 1960 and 1974, the trend toward high cholesterol in American men declined 12.5 percent; in women, 22.5 percent. Between 1965 and 1980, the decline in adult cigarette smoking was 27 percent for men, 14 percent for women.

Meanwhile, between 1963 and 1979, per capita consumption of milk and cream, in terms of pounds consumed per year, had declined 22.8 percent; per capita consumption of butter had declined 33.3 percent, of eggs, 10.7 percent, and of animal fats, 37.8 percent, while consumption of vegetable fats increased 58 percent.

As the distinguished Dr. John Farquhar of Stanford University's Department of Medicine puts it in discussing the findings of the continuing Stanford Heart Disease Prevention Program: "Somehow, we don't seem to fully comprehend how much American medical science has swept the world, with the congressionally created National Institutes of Health the main wellspring of good health information; certainly NIH monies have been dollars well spent." He adds:

"The Nobel prizes in physiology and medicine, by and large, have been going to Americans during the past fifteen years, with the United States leading the field in a number of ways, with American medical productivity providing amazing benefits to people for many years. We have," says Dr. Farquhar, "a health revolution in self-help sweeping the country and leading the rest of the world, with Canada and Australia in second and third position. Yet, while these three countries have had major drops in coronary disease, in other countries it's still going up." He continues: "Western Germany hasn't begun to do anything about it; Scandinavia has done some work in the field; Switzerland has a better record than the rest of Europe.

"On the other hand, Bulgaria, Romania, and the Soviet Union have increased their coronary rates by 50 percent in the past twelve years—and in Poland, it's even higher."

This new American revolution—the revolution in physical fitness—represents a milestone in human progress. More than ever, the evidence is clear: A set of rather simple habits, when followed, add years of vigor to one's life. Moreover, millions of Americans understand that evidence and are acting upon it. Tragically, millions of others are either unaware of it or simply don't seem to care. With Medicaid and Medicare extracting $60 billion a year from American taxpayers for health care, a sizable portion of which could be avoided by the more widespread adoption of personal health-care habits, it raises a rather vexing question: Do American taxpayers have an obligation to care for people who consciously decline to care for themselves? While free people most surely have a right to do irrational things, their call upon the public treasury to support such activities is at least debatable.

Great progress has occurred in making Americans aware of how they can achieve mastery over their own physical well-being, and the trend continues to shoot skyward as millions more each year begin to mend their ways.

The physical well-being and resiliency of that symbolic American Atlas extends beyond the natural and developed resources of the nation to the individual bodies of millions of Americans who glow with health beyond their grandparents' dreams. And while Americans may not yet have found a fountain of youth, the building blocks now seem in place to lead upward toward a fountain of healthy golden age. That magical goal of a hundred healthy, happy years seems not beyond the grasp. For Americans in their cribs today it is a worthy goal. And for their children's children, who knows what might be real.

Taken together, the cumulative impact of: a growing commitment to personal health; America's sheer size, her resources—both natural and developed; the diverse beauty of her regions and the coherent strength of her wholeness; the different values of a hundred nationalities all bedded in a single rock of hope, provide a sum beyond her parts.

America is an Atlas, very much alive, bursting with energy, straining to build, produce, and grow. Powered by visions and values, by the people and the land, America is an Atlas—a cumulative synergism—a whole that is greater than the sum of the parts.

IX

KNOWING MORE THAN EVER

The principle of aristocracy was honor, the principle of tyranny was fear, but the principle of democracy is education.

—MONTESQUIEU

LITTLE GIUSEPPE MARASCO passed through the gates of Ellis Island on a bright spring day in 1910, not knowing what his future might be, yet knowing that he was in America—and that was enough. He could do the rest. A few years later he began his half century of labor as a gardener for Pittsburgh well-to-do. Today, his son is vice chairman of the American College of Radiology.

About the same time that Giuseppe Marasco began spading American flower gardens, young Frank Rommel walked out of an eighth-grade class and into a glass factory where he became a dollar-a-day apprentice. Today, his son is a specialist in physical medicine, one grandson a nuclear engineer, and a granddaughter, a financial analyst in one of America's largest banks.

It's unlikely, however, that Rufus Ruffing thought much about a college education for his son, because a black man in the first half of the twentieth century knew such a dream seldom could come true. Nor could his son, even during a major war, seriously contemplate rising through the ranks to become "an officer and a gentleman," for "gentlemen" were almost always white. But today, Rufus Ruffing's grandson is a midshipman at the U.S. Naval Academy at Annapolis. He will be more than a gentleman; he will be a highly educated American military leader—someday perhaps even an admiral.

The stories of Giuseppe Marasco, Frank Rommel, Rufus

Ruffing and their progeny could be multiplied a million times. Never before and nowhere else on earth has there, within one century, been such an explosion of education—not simply among the so-called upper classes, but throughout the entire population. Never before has the typical 8.27-inch American cranium been filled by so much knowledge.

America's material prosperity, her economic strength, her technological prowess, her spiritual heart, and her intellectual power are built upon a bedrock of knowledge: knowledge discovered, knowledge disseminated, and knowledge acquired throughout the population by the world's largest, most diversified, most pervasive educational system. A system with its problems, yet overall, the world's premier system for developing millions of minds from Head-Start to post-doctoral programs, not only through formal institutions but also through the media and through a broad spectrum of private programs.

Prior to World War I, the average twenty-five-year-old American had completed eight years of schooling; by 1950 he had completed only nine years. By 1975, however, he had completed twelve years. Between 1950 and 1977, the number of U.S. students completing high school increased from about half to four out of five. The number of black students graduating from high school increased from one in ten to three out of four, adding force to the observation of the great educator Horace Mann: "Education, beyond all other devices of human origin, is the great equalizer of the condition of men—the balance wheel of the social machinery. . . ."

Nor did the widening opportunities for education stop at the high-school door: In the past twenty-five years the number of students graduating from American colleges has tripled to almost 1 million annually.

With about 12 million students in college, 15 million in secondary school, 31 million in elementary school, 3.3 million teachers and over 300,000 in supervisory roles, education is the primary activity of over 61 million Americans, not including the continuing education activities of millions more. Nearly three out of every ten Americans are involved primarily in education.

Americans spend over $166 billion a year on formal education, far more than any other country in the world. For example, West Germany spends $30 billion; the Soviet Union, $50 billion; and Japan, $56 billion. Each year, American elementary and secondary schools spend about $107 billion, and colleges spend about $59 billion. Private institutions account for about one out of five educational dollars.

Public colleges receive about two thirds of their funding from the state, 16 percent from the federal government, and only 14 percent from students. Private colleges receive over half their income from students, 20 percent from the federal government, and 12 percent from gifts, grants, and contracts. Although over half of America's 3,142 colleges are private, they educate only about one out of five college students, with the great majority educated in public institutions.

Federal educational expenditures represent a small percentage compared to those of state and local governments, yet the federal financial commitment has tripled over the past decade, rising from $8.7 billion in 1970 to over $23 billion in 1982.

Beyond the statistics and quantifications which tell a most impressive story of America's educational commitment, lie the qualitative questions: How good is American education? How much are Americans learning? Even the qualitative questions, however, cannot ignore the quantitative impact—for a reasonably well-educated citizenry has an impact upon a society every bit as significant as that of a highly educated elite. When America assesses her educational progress and problems, she must keep in mind the significance not only of the quality of the brightest but also of the quantitative contributions of the millions who have edged up from the bottom rungs to the midpoint of the knowledge ladder. The question is not only "How well can Johnny read?" but also "How many Johnnies can read reasonably well?"

Elementary and secondary public schools are increasingly under attack. To a nation that has worshipped education, to a nation that established the first compulsory education laws in modern history, the litany of educational criticisms is profoundly sobering:

- Many students cannot pass proficiency tests to justify promotion to the next grade. Half the students in the first three grades of the Washington, D.C., public school system have failed such tests.
- Standard Achievement Test (SAT) scores for high-school seniors have declined steadily over the past two decades: in math, from 502 in 1963 to 466 in 1980; in verbal, from 478 to 424.
- Classrooms are turning into police rooms. The Los Angeles public school system now has the third largest police force in the country.
- Teachers don't teach. In Pennsylvania during 1980 552,000 teacher-days were lost due to teacher strikes, the most in the nation. Beginning in 1970 teacher absenteeism increased 44 percent, with Fridays and Mondays the days on which absences most often occured.
- Parents don't care. Even those who do are more likely to confront school boards regarding extracurricular activities rather than academic programs. As families disintegrate at a rate of over a quarter million annually, children are turned loose to roam the streets or shift for themselves as best they can.
- Schools are turning into mass-production factories. In 1945 there were over 100,000 local school systems averaging 230 students each; by 1979 there were less than 16,000 school systems averaging 2,600 students each.
- The federal government has imposed impossible requirements upon public school systems. Mandatory programs and paperwork have proliferated to the point where they swamp the system. Instead of concentrating on education, schools are supposed to solve civil-rights problems through integration, affirmative action, and forced busing; to solve nutritional inadequacies through forced feeding; and to solve intellectual inequalities through "mainstreaming"—lumping all students together—then forcing their promotion, regardless of performance.

- Educational associations have degenerated into teachers' unions, focusing their demands on more pay and job protection for teachers rather than on better performance by students. For example, in 1980, the National Educational Association, the largest teachers group, broke from its traditional nonpartisan position to support the reelection of Jimmy Carter because he promised to oppose tax credits for private schools and promised to create a federal cabinet-level Department of Education, thereby further centralizing federal control over public education. The NEA also sought to defeat legislators who opposed such issues as forced busing, abortion on demand, affirmative action, and sex education.

Despite the deficiencies in many public school systems, there are rays of hope: Although SAT scores have declined, millions of students now taking the tests would not have bothered a few decades ago because they had no chance for college. (It is encouraging that for the first time in sixteen years the decline was arrested in 1981.) Although school reading-proficiency tests are sometimes failed, it is most often by the students who, a few decades ago, would have had no opportunity to take them.

Despite the excruciating problems of inner-city schools, even those who fail basic proficiency tests are by and large better educated than their predecessors. By today's standards, twelfth graders reading at the eighth-grade level is a real and serious deficiency. Yet for the grandchildren of illiterate sharecroppers, it is a quantum leap from where their families used to be. The general level of education has risen across the board. Today, virtually all socioeconomic groups have moved up the ladder, the knowledge base to which they are exposed has swelled enormously, and perhaps most significant, the top of the pyramid has widened exponentially.

The superintendent of schools in Diablo, California, James Slezak, has studied and compared U.S. public high schools with several European public high schools, and has noted that while 80 percent of the American student population graduates from high school, only 20 and 16 percent of such students graduate in England and Italy, respectively. He adds: "Comparing reading scores of U.S. fourteen year olds with students of the same age in the Netherlands, Sweden, and the United Kingdom shows U.S. students ahead in every instance. . . . In science U.S. students are doing better than students in Britain, the Netherlands, and Italy." Within the United States, based on standardized tests, elementary-grade children are doing better than their counterparts of the 1960's.

Having studied the top 9 percent of the high-school students in nineteen countries, Sweden's Institute for the International Evaluation of Educational Achievement found that America had "the largest percentage of children from lower income homes (14 percent) of any of the nations surveyed." For example, students from lower-income homes in West Germany represented less than 1 percent of the country's top high-school students.

In the Soviet Union, that professed paradigm of egalitarianism, only about 2 percent of the students have an opportunity for superior educations. Even though most Soviet students graduate from secondary schools, that education takes them through only ten years of schooling.

While over half of America's high-school students go on to college, only 20 percent of the Soviet Union's young people have that opportunity. Most are forced into industry or agriculture, regardless of their personal desires. Admission to college is not based upon an entrance exam, supposedly because that would smack of class distinctions in a society that still plays out its classless charade. Rather, selection is based upon an interview. Despite its model schools for 2 percent of its Communist elite, the Soviet Union is hardly the place to seek solutions to America's educational problems.

Not only are more Americans today receiving more education than their world contemporaries, but more disadvantaged Americans are capitalizing on their own expanded educational opportunities.

When focusing on educational problems and measuring educational progress, a healthy dose of historical perspective is required. Even Plato, in ancient times, despaired over the failures of Athens' students: "The children now love luxury; they have bad manners, contempt for authority; they show disrespect for their elders . . . and tyrannize their teachers."

While American education is not without its defects and problems, it is also not without its pluses and progress. Most important, numerous models exist to point the way for curing the nation's educational deficiencies.

In late 1981 Dr. James Coleman, one of the nation's leading sociologists, released the preliminary report of his federally commissioned study on education. Having analyzed the performance of almost sixty thousand students in over one thousand public and private high schools, his findings meticulously document what many intuitively had felt: Students with similar backgrounds do better if they attend schools that require homework, advanced courses, attendance, and discipline, and provide dedicated teachers.

The Beasley Elementary School in Chicago is living proof of the Coleman study's findings. Located on Chicago's South Side, and attended by children of lower socioeconomic families, this 85 percent-black public school turns out eighth graders whose scores on the Iowa Test of Basic Skills place Beasley among the top 10 of 497 elementary schools. Asked to describe her magic, the school's creator, Dr. Alice C. Blair, replies: "It wasn't difficult. It was based on a strong principal and an emphasis on basics. There's plenty of research available to develop a successful school. I just used it. You must have a strong principal, high expectations, competent teachers, and build a parent contract to force parental interest, participation, and support." On her office wall hangs her motto: IF GOD HAD WANTED PERMISSIVENESS, HE WOULD HAVE GIVEN US THE TEN SUGGESTIONS. At the beginning of a school term Beasley students and parents agree to an "Excellence Plus" contract committing them to strict policies of homework, attendance, discipline, and promotion standards. With a teacher-pupil ratio of thirty-two to one—the same as all Chicago schools—Beasley School emphasizes reading, writing, and 'rithmetic. Sentences are diagrammed, and multiplication tables are memorized.

Asked how good Beasley really is, Alice Blair replies: "I have a grandson enrolled, and I wouldn't put my loved one there if I didn't think it's the best."

Attesting to the success of Beasley Elementary School is the fact that thousands of educators visit it each year, and the Chicago public school system has promoted Alice Blair to deputy superintendent of schools in charge of curriculum and instruction. Reflecting on this opportunity to spread her methods throughout the four-hundred-thousand-student Chicago public school system, she muses: "They're all my children now."

Across town, controversial Marva Collins prowls her private classroom—drilling, demanding, pounding, praising. In 1975 her elementary West Side Preparatory School started in her home with 18 problem students from the public school system; it has grown to 245 students and 6 teachers in two adjoining buildings. Her elementary students, largely from Chicago's poorest black neighborhoods, are taught beginning Latin, Aesop's fables, and Emerson's aphorisms, along with the basic 3R's. Students who had been labeled as unteachable troublemakers were brought above the national testing standards in math and verbal skills. Says Mrs. Collins: "Where do students go when they've been socially promoted, but they can't spell 'social promote'? In my school we go back to the old textbooks that tell kids something, like 'Mr. Toil' out of 1920 that teaches that you can't get something for nothing."

Mrs. Collins emphasizes that she is no miracle worker, that she simply works hard at rigorously practicing the basics of teaching. "The most important lesson," she emphasizes, "is that there's no free lunch, no free ride in this world. If there's such a thing as luck, it's because a man had pluck and went out after it."

Marva Collins is highly critical of what she calls the "downhill slide in public schools," and a group of public-school teachers has reciprocated by attacking her claims as inflated. Nevertheless, educators from the National Council on Education and from around the world visit West Side Prep to see what they can learn. After doing an investigative piece on the school, Morley Safer of TV's *60 Minutes* pronounced Marva Collins "one hell of a teacher."

In her book *Marva Collins' Children,* Civia Tamarkin writes: "She's a terrific motivator. She inspires children."

Most important, perhaps, Harvey Gross, admissions director of Chicago's prestigious Providence-St. Mel's Catholic High School, has tested forty-five of her students, and states that after a year at Mrs. Collins's school, students average about a 1.3 grade-level increase in reading, a 1.2 increase in language, and a 0.7 increase in math. By comparison, citywide public-school students average increases of less than 1.0 in every testing category. Gross emphasizes, however:

"Standardized testing is a very incomplete way of evaluating a student or a school such as Marva Collins's. She is the most extraordinarily gifted primary teacher I've ever known. A number of her kids had been failing in one or many schools. They would have gone on until sixteen, then dropped out—and you know what would have happened to them: They'd have gone on welfare at best, or to the state prison, or they'd be dead!"

Having said that, Harvey Gross, whose private Catholic high school is, scholastically, one of the toughest in the country, concludes: "We'd like to have more of her students. She changes their attitudes about themselves."

Even super-motivator Marva Collins, however, acknowledges her failure to motivate students who enter her school in the upper grades. She now limits her admissions to the first few grades and emphasizes: "Our most important education is elementary," thereby confirming the observation and admitted change of heart of Dr. Mortimer J. Adler, founder of the Great Books program and chairman of *Encyclopaedia Britannica,* that "you can't reform education from the top down; change has to start at the bottom in elementary school."

Meanwhile, at the University of Pittsburgh's experimental Falk Elementary School, a heterogeneous group of mostly middle-class students is taught in an environment similar to that advocated by James Coleman, Alice Blair, or Marva Collins. Says Director Roy J. Creek: "The key here is motivation: of parents, of children, of the school itself." Falk's Demonstration Classroom is closely affiliated with Learning Research and Development at Pitt, has three hundred students, and a nineteen-member teaching staff heavy with Ph.D.'s and masters in education.

Despite its considerable academic firepower, Falk's administrator emphasizes that the school has no magic formula, that it's simply a case of developing a personalized progress plan for each student, then working closely to help him achieve his goals. Clearly, the effort pays off: In the 1982 mathematics examination at Taylor-Alderdice, Pittsburgh's top public high school, four Falk students were among the top ten.

Outstanding performance from a university-affiliated experimental school might be expected, but the mounting evidence of success from one of America's once racially torn public schools is exciting proof that average students do well when fundamental educational principles are rigorously applied. Little Rock's Central High School would hardly seem to be a candidate for a model school. Yet the school where Governor Orval Faubus made his last-ditch segregation stand—the place where black students had to be escorted to school under the protection of President Eisenhower's federalized National Guard backed up by the elite 101st Airborne Division—today turns out students with SAT scores forty-six points above the national average. Coming from all of Little Rock's junior high schools, Central High students represent a cross-section of the entire city. Fifty-three percent black, and described as an academic melting pot, Central High is also acknowledged as one of the nation's best public high schools, with nearly two out of three of its graduates going to college.

Principal Richard Maple says there is no secret: "We have a dedicated staff and a large number of required courses; even our electives are tough—calculus, Latin, Afro-American literature, creative writing. For every graduate, we require a term paper, and it must be well written. We have no social promotions. We have a strong trend toward discipline."

Discipline—a firm, fine thread woven throughout educational success stories—is particularly omnipresent in Catholic and fundamentalist Protestant schools, a presence that greatly reduces disciplinary problems. Father Thomas Gallagher, education secretary for the Washington-based U.S. Catholic Conference, puts it this way: "We have a basic undergirding of discipline. We still function on the philosophy that the school is the extension of the home."

With nearly ten thousand elementary and secondary schools, over three million students, and one out of five students from a minority group,* America's Roman Catholic schools are major participants in America's educational process. The evidence shows, clearly, that students learn in Catholic schools. Across the nation, their scores on the entire battery of standardized tests soar above the national public-school norm. Elementary students in Washington's eighty-two archdiocesan schools score 8 to 34 percentage points above the national norm; students in the Diocese of Pittsburgh and Archdiocese of Philadelphia score 12 to 25 percentage points above the national norms. Most significant, the gap between Catholic schools and national norms widens from the second through the eighth grades.

In his Ford and Spencer foundations-sponsored study, Andrew Greeley, Jesuit sociologist, educator, and author, drew some enlightening conclusions regarding the performances of black and Hispanic students in Catholic schools. Using 1980 data compiled in the U.S. Department of Education-funded study, *High School and Beyond,* Father Greeley discovered that minority students "are less likely to have . . . a disciplinary problem . . . than their public school counterparts," that they "give far higher ratings to the fairness of the disciplinary system," that their "college aspirations are . . . higher," and that "academic outcomes of Catholic secondary education for minority groups are impressively superior to the academic outcomes of public education." He added: "Those who are attending Catholic high school are 20 percentage points more likely to do homework that requires at least five hours a week, 29 percentage points more likely to be confident of college graduation, and to score more than half a standard deviation higher on a standardized academic achievement scale."

---

*Minority, as used by the U.S. Catholic Conference, follows the U.S. government definition which includes blacks, Hispanics, Asians, and American Indians.

The Coleman report corroborates Father Greeley's findings and goes on to state: "Altogether, the evidence is strong that the Catholic schools function much closer to the American ideal of the 'common school,' educating children from different backgrounds alike. . . ." The report goes on to refute the claim that students in Catholic schools do better because they are intellectually and academically superior: It makes clear that discipline, attention to basics, and teacher dedication form the educational structure in which students can learn best.

Although they may differ on the fine points of dogma, Catholic parochial schools and fundamentalist Christian academics are virtually unified in the essence of their approach. Catholic schools emphasize structure, discipline, and values, as do the Christian academies that have sprung up across America in the past decade. Now numbering nearly seven thousand, the latter represent a middle-class religious response to the growing permissiveness and secularism in many public schools.

At the Bethel Christian Academy in Chambersburg, Pennsylvania, well-scrubbed girls in blue jumpers with white blouses and boys in blue slacks, white shirts, and red, white, and blue ties study side by side in individual cubicles facing a cinder-block wall of brightly painted pastel. On the wall before the student is his daily work plan. When he has a question he sets up a small flag, and a teacher moves quickly to his side, speaking encouragingly, in low tones. The room is decorated with student-made signs: GOD IS LOVE (I JOHN 4:16); THERE IS NOTHING TOO HARD FOR THEE (JER. 32:17); A GOOD NAME IS BETTER THAN PRECIOUS OINTMENT (ECCLES. 7:1).

An intercom signal buzzes softly, and on direction from the teacher, the smiling students file quietly into the auditorium where a congressman talks with them about his duties; when he finishes, dozens of hands shoot up, plying him with perceptive questions.

One is so impressed with the orderliness, attentiveness, and courtesy, that one wonders: Can these kids be learning too? A check of the records shows that on the standardized California Achievement Test in one school year they advance a composite 1.7 years in reading, mathematics, and language. A further check reveals that the students come from largely working-class rural families, with about 25 percent coming from families without a strong Christian orientation. Even so, the parents are willing to pay $800 a year to put their children in what they believe to be a solid learning environment.

As Principal Robert Marion puts it: "We have discipline. We deal with the whole person, with a high standard of behavior based on Jesus' principles. We have virtually no problem with smoking or drugs—and whatever difficulty does occur is dealt with swiftly. Our Code of Conduct is clearly defined in our Handbook. We have rules and the students abide by them. We have a few expulsions, but they are rare."

Echoing Father Gallagher, Mr. Marion emphasizes: "We are servants of the home. We expect the parents to back us up."

From Chambersburg's Christian Academy to Little Rock's Central High, from Marva Collins's West Side Prep to Chicago's Beasley School, from Washington's Catholic school system to the University of Pittsburgh's experimental Falk School, the lessons of educational success are crystal clear: discipline, demanding courses, dedicated teachers, strong school principals, and interested parents.

The educational success stories crisscrossing between public and private schools, between religious and secular schools, between mostly white and mostly black schools demonstrate that a good elementary and secondary education need not be limited to expensive, elitist schools—traditionally those public schools in wealthy suburbs, or old-line prep schools with rolling campuses and ivy-covered buildings.

Elitist private schools, which historically have offered superior educations to children of wealthy or otherwise old-line families, continue to serve their function. And they do it well. Even though they remain beyond the mainstream, they too demonstrate that discipline, demanding courses, dedicated teachers, and interested parents provide an environment in which students can learn. South Central Pennsylvania's Mercersburg Academy is one such school. Annual cost in 1982: $7,800 for boarding students, $4,500 for day students. The day rate is in contrast to the $1,788 per pupil cost at nearby John Buchanan public high school—a substantial difference. Even more of a difference is seen in who pays the bill. Public-school educations are financed by all taxpayers, including those sending their children to private schools. Private-school educations are generally financed by parents of the students.

Nevertheless, where today's concerned parents have a choice—or the means—they are often opting for the private alternative. If some form of public funding for private schools should come—from tuition tax credits to vouchers permitting parents to select their children's schools—public-opinion surveys indicate that about one quarter of the parents with children in public schools would switch. Should such a shift occur, it would surely have an immediate damaging impact on many public schools. While the demand for teachers would largely shift from the one sector to the other, public-school overhead costs would be a burden upon a smaller student base.

Given the problems of some of today's public schools, the vexing public-policy question becomes: Should parents be compelled to send their children to public schools to keep such schools afloat? Should they be permitted to choose their children's schools even though such a choice would inflict serious damage on an already beleaguered public-school system?

It seems fair to argue that where public schools are doing a good job, the demand for private alternatives is minimal. How then can parents justifiably be compelled to send their children to schools that are functioning improperly and to pay taxes for their operation if better alternatives exist? Ethically, one answer could be: a well-founded and serious promise of improvement. In some areas, that promise is yet to be forthcoming. Perhaps competition and choice are the prerequisites to the promise, the driving forces needed to stimulate and invigorate lethargic public schools.

It is not as if America does not know how to educate her children. Daily, the fundamentals are demonstrated in thousands of classrooms: public and private, poor and wealthy, black and white, rural and urban. Nor does money seem to be the crucial difference; rather, it is the commitment of teachers and parents, of communities and schools. Where there is commitment, there is learning. Where there is discipline, there is learning. Public schools especially must face the harsh reality that repeated disciplinary offenders must be removed from the classroom. To do less is to inflict punishment upon the innocent—upon those who want to learn —and waste precious educational dollars. Indeed, when punishment is swift and sure, the need for it will rapidly decline.

Returning control to local communities, reducing the size of schools from mass-production factories to humanized environments, and offering parents a choice of schools for their children are three structural changes that could improve the American elementary and secondary educational system.

If the resultant demise of bad schools seems a hard price to pay, the price of their continuing decline is even greater. Choice among schools need not be limited to public versus private. Indeed, the great success of vocational-technical schools has demonstrated that alternatives within the public school system are more than desirable; they are necessary and productive.

In 1963, about four million students were enrolled in vo-tech programs, the large majority in agriculture or home economics. Beginning in 1968, Congress rewrote the vocational education law in an effort to stimulate growth in this form of education and to focus more sharply on job-market opportunities for the remainder of the century. As if tapping a gusher, the result has been a bursting forth of vo-tech programs across America: almost sixteen thousand vo-tech schools, with another eleven thousand offering such programs, and about three million students graduating from such programs annually and ten million more taking elective courses. Moreover, the curriculum has been greatly broadened, ranging from welding to electronics, from cosmetology to computer programming.

Unemployment among high school graduates in Altoona,

Pennsylvania, who neither go on to college nor graduate from the local vo-tech school is above 20 percent, but for vo-tech graduates, it is less than 5 percent, with placement virtually 100 percent in food service, auto mechanics, industrial arts, air conditioning, warehousing, textile production, fabrication, and practical nursing.

With about one out of three of Altoona's high-school students majoring in vo-tech, Dan Clark, the school's director, reports: "We're unable to meet all the requests for cosmetology enrollment, or for carpentry, auto body, electrician, food service, machine shop, and computer programming."

Socrates observed that the truly educated are "those who manage well the circumstances which they encounter day by day." Surely, the vo-tech schools of America are meeting a need for millions of students—providing them with the tools to successfully commence their adult lives.

Milwaukee's public school system has gone beyond vocational education to establish specialty schools ranging from elementary level specializing in creative arts to high-school level concentrating on advanced, college-oriented courses. Within limits, students can select any one of the city's 143 schools and transfer later if they choose. Fifty-three of the schools offer specialty programs and have attracted over twenty-five thousand students—almost one out of every three students enrolled in the public school system.

The Milwaukee experience is especially exciting because it was not designed to provide educational choice but to comply with court-ordered racial integration. Milwaukee solved the problem not with forced busing but by creating the attractive choices offered through its specialty schools. Dr. Calvin McIntyre of the city's Specialty School Curriculum Department says: "Our suspension and absence rates are significantly less than those of regular high schools because we're attracting motivated students and we're further motivating them once we get them."

The problems facing America's public school system can be solved—indeed, are being solved—in many communities such as Milwaukee. The lessons of success need only be more widely learned and applied. The way has been clearly charted, and though far from perfect, it offers real hope for millions of Americans who care about elementary and secondary education. Not only can such schools better equip young Americans for entering the workplace, but they can also lay a firmer foundation for those going on to college.

Never before and nowhere else have so many young people had the opportunity for a college education. With about half of America's high-school graduates now entering college, the twelve million students who circulate through U.S. colleges are building a cumulative pool of college-educated citizens which numbers nearly twenty-three million today and will probably reach forty million by the year 2000.

- More Americans attend college today than attended high school thirty years ago.
- More Americans now teach in colleges than attended fifty years ago.
- More Americans now receive graduate degrees than entered college forty years ago.
- More than twice as many Americans now graduate from medical school than thirty years ago.
- More than ten times as many engineers now graduate from college every year than fifty years ago.
- More than five times as many accountants now graduate each year than thirty years ago.

Much criticism has been written about the quality of education, yet the fact is that more Americans are being given more opportunity to learn more than ever before. More students are attending college, and the body of knowledge being taught is vastly greater than ever. Scientists estimate that knowledge is doubling every two and one half years. Over 70 percent of the medicines in use today were developed after World War II; more than 90 percent of the scientists who ever lived are alive today.

When *Apollo 13* became crippled in space it took the computers at Mission Control eighty-four minutes to discover and solve the problem; it would have taken a mathematician with pencil and paper a million years to make the computations. Man sometimes forgets that computers were not even available a short thirty years ago. When they first became available in the mid-1950's, they were enormously complicated, extremely costly, and highly cumbersome. The UNIVAC I could be installed and programmed only by skilled engineers and mathematicians; it cost over $1 million, and required a tightly controlled air-conditioned and humidified environment the size of a basketball court. Today, college students—via remote time-sharing terminals—routinely tap into computers one thousand times as powerful that cost one tenth as much.

Undergraduate engineering students routinely make calculations that previously could be accomplished only by professional engineers. Junior accountants design sophisticated cost-control systems previously available only to giant corporations. Astronomy students learn more about the galaxy than Copernicus or Galileo could even imagine. Anthropologists carbon-date fossils, linguists translate Dead Sea scrolls, and agronomists grow food in volcanic rock.

World War II triggered a knowledge explosion. No single stroke of the pen did more for higher education than Franklin D. Roosevelt's signing of the GI Bill of Rights on June 22, 1944. From that moment through mid-1981, it has provided college educations for 18 million American veterans. Of these almost 8 million were World War II veterans, more than half of those eligible; 2.4 million were Korean War veterans, 40 percent of those eligible; and 7.3 million were Vietnam War and post-Vietnam War veterans, more than 40 percent of those eligible.

The $51 billion cost was probably one of the best investments ever made by the American people—a quantum leap occurred in the knowledge level of an entire nation. Once unleashed, higher education was embraced with fervor. It was as if Benjamin Franklin's adage had suddenly sunk into a million minds: "If a person empties his purse into his head, no one can take it away from him." A comparison of lifetime earning capabilities showed that a World War II veteran with a college degree would earn more than a quarter of a million dollars more than a high-school graduate, and he would pay additional federal income taxes amounting to six times his GI benefits. Once given the taste for education, his children would be nudged toward college and would be educated largely out of the increased earnings of their college-educated fathers.

The GI Bill, coupled with rising affluence, would expose a nation to the benefits of higher education. Backed by strong public commitment, federal and state governments would provide public funding for higher education through loans and grants. The upward spiral would continue, sending more and more of America's youth to the halls of higher learning. Over the past twenty years a combination of guaranteed student loans, grants, and subsidies for college jobs have provided federal financial aid for about fifty million college students—amounting to more than $35 billion. Today, nearly half of America's college students receive some form of financial aid.

By the early 1980's, America had become a knowledge-based society: one and a half million engineers; a half million medical doctors; a half million lawyers; a million accountants; over a quarter of a million scientists; nearly a quarter of a million writers and reporters.

With the explosive growth in higher education came criticism of decline in quality—seemingly legitimate, yet missing the mark. As with criticism of the public school system, too frequently the focus was on the problems rather than on the accomplishments. America's top college students, the *crème de la crème,* have more knowledge at their fingertips than any previous college generation. So too do America's average college students. Even those in the lower fourth of their classes are exposed to more knowledge—more education—than were most of their parents, who generally did not have the opportunity to attend college.

Colleges can, of course, be improved. Many of the lessons learned in elementary and secondary education concerning the importance of discipline and dedication are equally applicable to colleges, but the central historical fact of higher education in this generation cannot be obscured: Six times as many Americans are receiving higher educations as compared to a single generation ago.

Along with qualitative criticisms other problems exist. Clark Kerr, former president of the University of California at Berkeley, has described the jobs of a university president as ". . . leader, educator, officeholder, caretaker, inheritor, consensus seeker, persuader, bottleneck . . . but he is mostly a mediator."

Like the public school system with extra educational responsibilities thrust upon it, colleges, too, have been burdened with a myriad of nonacademic duties. As educators try—and are often forced—to do too much, the achievement of their basic educational mission becomes more difficult. Pressures to open college doors, not only to all who qualify, but to all who knock, have pushed both schools and students toward easier curricula. The result: Other nations now outproduce America in certain fields. For example, Japan turns out more graduate engineers; one third of West Germany's college students major in math, science, or engineering, compared to less than one fifth in America.

According to a Library of Congress report, a technology gap is emerging. In the coming decade, America will experience a shortage of over one hundred thousand engineers. Shortages will also exist in scientific, computer, and health-related fields.

But these shortages serve to demonstrate the tremendous growth in America's need for knowledge, in her reliance upon college-educated people. Even so, this seemingly insatiable need for higher education has hardly slaked the American thirst for knowledge. Beyond the colleges, millions of Americans search for information, skills, and knowledge in dozens of different ways. Almost as if addicted by the promise of education, Americans want to learn.

Each year thousands of high-school graduates opt to learn a trade rather than enter college. To respond to that demand, nearly six thousand proprietary schools have sprung up. They range from cosmetology and barbering to business and office occupations, from flight training to plumbing, from computer programming to power mechanics, from drafting to commercial art. Each year nearly 230,000 students graduate from such schools, ready to enter the job market with specialized occupational training so they may apply their skills to be more productive for their employer and in the process earn a better living for themselves.

Other high-school graduates join the armed services to do more than see the world. High on their list of reasons for signing up is their desire for education. Upon enlistment, a recruit can qualify for one of a wide range of training opportunities including electronic specialist, diesel repairman, flight mechanic, ground controller, procurement specialist, disposal expert, transportation coordinator, and heavy-equipment operator.

Beyond initial training, both enlistees and officers are exposed to continuing military education and encouraged to enroll in after-hours civilian technical schools and colleges. The Defense Department pays 75 percent of the cost for first termers and 90 percent for career people.

Altogether, over $10 billion is spent annually on the training and education of America's two million military personnel, about $5,000 per service person. Upon reentering the civilian population, whether after a single enlistment or a career, they bring with them knowledge they almost certainly could not have acquired had they not served their country. Indeed, that service is most often also a service to themselves, for in the process, they have prepared themselves for the remainder of their lives.

The famous educator John Dewey observed: "Education is not preparation for life. Education is life. . . ." And more and more Americans are reaching out for learning experiences. The rising demand for lifetime learning is being satisfied in many different ways.

Public television and radio are providing educational services to millions, reaching into both classrooms and homes. Of the 166 public television stations, 140 offer structured courses ranging from elementary school to college. About one hundred thousand Americans formally receive education for credit through public television, and another million informally participate in adult-education series through public television. Virtually all public television stations provide high-quality educational programs, such as Carl Sagan's *Cosmos* and Alistair Cooke's *Masterpiece Theatre,* both of which have viewing audiences of around ten million. The McNeil-Lehrer thirty-minute news program, which focuses in depth upon one issue every evening, has attracted an audience of six million, and is credited with stimulating the commercial networks to expand their news coverage to both longer and more in-depth programs.

America's 264 public radio stations offer educational programs which reach over seven million listeners each week. Yet this is only the rarified tip of the media's educational impact upon America. Through commercial television, radio, newspapers, books, and magazines, Americans are exposed to—and take advantage of—a broader, deeper slice of knowledge than any other people on earth. Routinely, Americans watch and read about wars in faraway lands, about de-icing techniques to keep airplanes aloft, about the impact of the money supply on inflation and interest rates, about barriers to international trade, about nuclear strategies and the domino theory, about the discovery of a 3.6-million-year-old *homo erectus* in Tanzania, about the impact of détente upon the price of wheat in Kansas, about the questions to ask when considering a coronary bypass, about how to lose twenty pounds or add an addition to your home, about how to make friends or bake a cake, about life in the twelfth century or what it will be like in the twenty-second century, about Islam or the Moonies, about great white sharks beneath the sea or vast black holes in outer space.

Over 116 million Americans watch the nightly television news; almost 28 million listen to the radio at any given moment of the day. Americans buy 62 million daily newspapers, 41 million weekly papers, 290 million magazines per issue, and 6.3 billion books annually.

Reinforcing America's opportunity for lifetime learning, over 15,000 public and branch libraries, augmented by about 50,000 mobile library locations, serve nearly 10 million Americans every week. Another 350 million American visitations occur each year to the nation's 4,000-plus museums to browse and to understand the ascent of man.

Beyond America's leisure-time interest in learning more about the world in which we live lies a growing dedication to mastering the skills of our vocations.

Each year American industry spends over $40 billion on formal training programs for its employees, two thirds as much as that spent annually on all of America's colleges and universities. From welding to computer programming, from reading a balance sheet to balancing investment strategies, from calculating structural stress to structuring personal stress, Americans are learning how to do their jobs better. Continuing education isn't an appendage, it's an essential part of thousands of American businesses.

Xerox Corporation has a campus nestled in the hills near Leesburg, Virginia, where, at one time, a thousand student-employees receive marketing and technical training. Not only does IBM train its technical and marketing people at its campus in Armonk, New York, but it also requires every one of its managers—junior and senior—to receive one week of formal management training every year. At its famous General Motors Institute at Flint, Michigan, GM operates the corporate equivalent of a U.S. service academy—training future corporate engineers and executives for expanding responsibilities. For training of dealership employees, GM operates thirty-one centers around the United States and ten more around the world and has contracts with forty-three community colleges.

From Motorola's training center in Phoenix to Arthur Anderson's accounting school in St. Charles, Illinois, from Dana Corporation's center in Toledo to the Westinghouse educational center in Pittsburgh, American businesses are educating their employees to do a better job. The six thousand member companies of the American Society for Training and Development conduct continuing, formal training programs for their employees, and several thousand other companies take advantage of the educational tools within their grasp.

At noontime, the employees of Better Tires, a small tire store and recapping facility in southcentral Pennsylvania, gather periodically around the firm's video-display machine to watch color tapes of how to properly mount and dismount tires, of how to buff and patch, of how to clean and seal, in order to do their jobs safely and productively and, in the process, serve their customers better.

A thousand miles away, in Muscatene, Iowa, the Bandag Corporation produces a continuous flow of videotapes for its recapping franchises across America, to ensure that even the smallest of operations can benefit from the latest in the industry's knowledge. Beyond the thousands of businesses educating their employees on dedicated corporate campuses or in converted company lunchrooms, nearly a thousand academic institutions offer nondegree short courses in management training. Beyond those opportunities rise the premier management learning institutions of the world: America's graduate schools of business.

Dr. Nikos Photias speaks from a full and unique background which includes: finance minister of Greece, director of the Doctoral Program for the School of Business and Government at The American University, economist, and consultant. He has stated: "The one American institution respected throughout the world is the American business school. Students from around the world flock to America to receive their MBAs or Ph.D.'s in business, because they know there is no better place to go."

As America's institutions continue to grow in size and complexity, and as management becomes even more of both a science and an art, America's graduate schools of business continue to broaden. They become graduate schools of management—not only for business but also for governmental, military, social, health, educational, and even eleemosynary institutions.

Never before, and nowhere else on earth, have so many citizens of a single country had spread before them the almost limitless opportunity to learn. Never before, and nowhere else, has there been so much knowledge to be learned.

At a White House dinner honoring Nobel Prize winners, President John F. Kennedy remarked: "This is the most extraordinary collection of talent, of human knowledge, that has ever been gathered together at the White House—with the possible exception of when Thomas Jefferson dined alone."

Across America, there is not only an extraordinary collection of talent at the intellectual apogee but also an extraordinary collection of human knowledge disseminated throughout the entire citizenry. And while the capacity for individual genius may not have increased since Jefferson's day, even Thomas Jefferson would have known much more today than he did in his lifetime, because there is so much more to know.

Though genius may flower even in rocky soil, genius suppressed is genius denied. The world never knows what is lost from talent underdeveloped. The privileged few have always had the opportunity to develop their capacities, but only in America are the poorest of the poor among the privileged many who have that chance.

With Isaac Newton, Americans can say, "If we see more, it is because we stand on the shoulders of others." But beyond the broadened and deepened knowledge base upon which Americans stand, is the unparalleled opportunity to immerse themselves in that knowledge.

As more and more Americans seize the opportunity for some form of education, as more and more Americans look beyond their schooling to a lifetime of learning, the life of an entire nation is enriched—materially, intellectually, spiritually. And with the newfound knowledge that lifts millions of Americans come the beginnings of a higher wisdom, a wisdom that lets Americans see beyond their daily doubts and fears to the brilliant years that lie ahead. A wisdom that whispers in their ears: *With what you know, you may believe, not only in yourself, but in your country, too.*

BELIEVING

The discovery of purpose is the discovery of strength.
—ALBERT SCHWEITZER

MORE THAN EARTH and sky, more than facts and figures, more than economic strength and military might, America is a belief. Rooted in all her different strengths, America is a belief in tomorrow—an optimistic belief—a spirit, a quest illimitable, toward which Americans strive. It is a yearning, reaching search, achieved, yet never satisfied. Two hundred years of experience have shown that, for Americans, tomorrow can be better—materially, intellectually, and spiritually. As that evidence has accumulated, consciously and subconsciously in both head and heart, it has forged a national habit, an expectation of achievement and progress. The expectation has become the father of the effort which has turned belief into truth. This has been not a static reality but a good and gleaming goal, a purification of life sought after, a belief worthy of pursuit. And once pursued, achieved; and once achieved, it has assumed the laserlike purity of intensely focused energy, creative and life-giving.

America has burst forward with the awesome concentrated power of a great Niagara, created by millions of individual rivulets, each giving strength to the nation's forward flow, yet gathering strength from the mighty force itself.

Different at the core from those of other lands, life taught Americans that they could afford to believe—that for them, even failure was seldom final. What they missed for themselves, they saw others like them get, and in their neighbors' getting, lay a promise for themselves.

On a dark Sunday night in January 1981, a flash flood swept through Austin, Texas. Middle-aged Peter Vescovo watched helplessly as the raging waters smashed through his auto dealership, destroying over one hundred new cars, his new showrooms, and the business he had spent most of his lifetime building. As network television cameras recorded the devastation from a nearby hillside, a reporter asked Peter Vescovo what he planned to do. With a smile and a shake of the head, he gave his quintessential American five-word reply: "Clean up and start over." Eighteen months later he celebrated the formal opening of his new building with its sparkling showroom bursting with shiny new cars. He had done what he said he was going to do. No temporary catastrophe would permanently put him under.

Halfway 'round the world, middle-aged Aaron Levstein trudged through the deep snow of Leningrad in the 20-below-zero bitterness of a January night. Pausing as he neared the Astoria Hotel, he turned up his collar, pulled his old rabbit-fur hat down over his ears, and hunched his neck into his tattered coat. Then moving swiftly past Soviet guards, he entered the hotel and strode to the elevator. A few minutes later, in soft whispers beneath the blare of a purposely loud radio, he told his story to members of an American congressional delegation.

In the eyes of the Soviet rulers, he was guilty of two unpardonable sins: He was Jewish, and he had applied for a visa to emigrate from the Soviet Union to the United States. Although he had taught mathematics for almost twenty years and had never been political—that is, he had never spoken out on public issues nor criticized the government —nevertheless, he had lost his job two weeks after applying for a visa. Within a month he and his family had been ordered to vacate their apartment and had moved in with relatives. After searching unsuccessfully for another position teaching mathematics he finally found a job as an elevator operator. All that had happened seven years earlier, and his subsequent visa requests had been denied repeatedly "for reasons of the state." In that clandestine meeting with

American congressmen, he shrugged his shoulders and said: "I, and others like me, we are hostages. Our lives are not our own. We can do nothing but sit and wait. If we are ever set free, it will be for a price. When the Soviet Union wants something—grain, return of a captured agent, some new technology—only then will we be traded. For me, I would like to be worth one pound of grain—nothing more."

While Aaron Levstein waits, wasting in a limbo of resignation and disbelief, Peter Vescovo works, rebuilding upon a foundation of faith, hope, determination, and belief.

Though vastly different, both responses are reasonable. There is little reason for Aaron Levstein to believe; his life is beyond his own control. Peter Vescovo, however, has every reason; for him, and for millions of his fellow Americans, there is a basis for belief.

Out of a thousand daily experiences, large and small, Americans have learned to believe: to expect, to achieve, to fulfill.

The smallest baby who cries is fed; the child who sits on Santa's lap later finds his stocking full; the youth whose teenage life suddenly seems to turn upon the possibility of obtaining a driver's license eventually slips behind a wheel; the high-school senior who hopes for college six months later unpacks his belongings into a dormitory dresser drawer; the college graduate who, with an empty feeling in the pit of his stomach, fills out the application for his first full-time job gets the call to report for work; the young adults who go house hunting a few months later make their first down payment; the parents who wish for their children what they never had watch those dreams come true; the grandparents who burst with pride recounting the achievements of their progeny talk of last summer's vacation or next winter in the sun.

Most Americans find satisfaction in their daily lives, whether it be a farmer bagging an eight-point buck in the woods behind his barn on the first day of deer season or a financier tramping the African bush on safari, a housewife feeling fulfilled in the glow around her family's table or a woman rising in the corporate world, a leader squeezing three days into one or a follower putting a good day's work behind him so he may relax among his friends. Even the

plight of those washed ashore cannot obscure the abundance of the mainstream in which millions live and thrive
—though sometimes complaining, momentarily unmindful
of their favored places atop the world's ascent.

As each belief is turned into reality, new opportunities
and possibilities emerge. With their own eyes, Americans
see dreams come true, and from these personal experiences
grows a powerful basis for belief.

For Americans, dreams need not be an escape from life,
but a plan for life. For Americans, dreams become the images of future realities, the essence of what might be if one
adds mind and muscle to the hope.

Reason may tell what ought to be, but only experience
teaches what can be. For Americans, reason and experience
mesh in harmony, but for millions of others around the
world, the melody of reason too often may be drowned in
the dissonance of a bitter daily life.

While experience teaches Americans to reach and strive,
while it promises that effort will be rewarded, that work will
produce results, it etches different lines in other lands. It
tells the Russian farmer not to work harder, for the fruits of
his efforts will be taken from him. It tells the Central American peasant not to speak his mind, for the price of words
could be his life. It tells the Afrikaner to hate a different
color or be ostracized.

Even in the same country different times teach different
lessons. A century ago, in the same Moscow that taught
Aaron Levstein not to hope, a young composer gathered a
few friends and his teacher, the director of the Moscow
Conservatory, around a piano on Christmas Eve to hear his
new composition. They listened silently, and when he had
finished not a word was spoken. The director, the world-
famous music critic Nicholas Rubinstein, asked the young
composer to step into the hall with him, alone. He solemnly
pronounced his judgment: "Your composition is so worthless, unplayable, disconnected, bad, trivial, common—so un-
skillfully written that it could not even be improved."

To this critique, the young composer defiantly replied: "I
shall not alter a single note." Devastated for days, nevertheless he persisted, and a year later his composition was per-

formed publicly, not in Russia, but in America. Peter Ilich Tchaikovsky's First Piano Concerto in B-flat Minor was first performed in a Boston Concert Hall. Nicholas Rubinstein eventually acknowledged that his initial judgment had been the worst musical mistake of his life. Out of the free, creative musical ferment of his time, Tchaikovsky's music, though rejected by the foremost musical authority of his native Russia, was permitted to survive and eventually to be acclaimed as one of the world's greatest piano concertos. In today's Soviet Union, rejection of a composition by the Minister of Culture would mean that it never would be performed. Period. Like others in the Soviet Union, composers conform or they don't compose.

In America, however, experience teaches that talent is free to breathe; that rational judgments are free to work, and that efforts can produce results because no intervening hand will thwart their natural consequences. People are free to strive, to try, to experiment, and to change—to try again, and start anew. People are able to believe that they will benefit from their efforts, that they will be the reapers of what they sow. Secure in that knowledge, Americans apply their energies to whatever dreams they have, and by so doing, they produce their own realities.

Experience and reason let Americans unleash their energies in harmony with their fondest dreams and deepest feelings. Man, emotionally, wants to believe. Man needs to believe. The oppressiveness of a society, or a government, or an economy, or even a religion, which by its actions tells man that life is not worthy of belief, can only serve to destroy this deepest need.

Throughout history, man's need to believe has proved a powerful, necessary force. From Old Testament prophets to New Testament Christians, from Columbus's confidence in his course to Washington's commitment to his revolutionary cause, from Lincoln's dedication to the Union to Churchill's faith in the Western Alliance—the greatest strides have been so powered.

The entire North American continent was traversed and tamed by people who believed in themselves and in their futures, who set specific goals for themselves and believed intensely that they were achievable: Clear the land and plant a crop; build a cabin, school, or church; send a child to college; start a business; learn a trade; save, invest, build, learn.

America is millions of minute personal goals bundled together, swelling the forward movement of a nation, forging national goals seemingly beyond reach, yet reachable. Whether putting cars in every garage or televisions in every home, children in college or astronauts on the moon, reducing poverty or increasing longevity, winning wars or defeating disease, America has achieved her goals to the degree to which her people have believed in them. Where that belief has faltered, where the national will has slackened, America has missed her mark.

Two world wars have been won, education extended, economic depression obliterated, prosperity expanded, civil rights strengthened, and health care broadened, because Americans have believed deeply in those causes. For lack of such commitment, the Korean and Vietnamese wars were lost, Central America became a Communist battleground, America's inner cities have become cesspools of crime, some schools have become de facto juvenile detention centers, and several of America's greatest industries have been eclipsed by foreign competitors.

Where America fell short, her belief had faltered, her will to achieve had been paralyzed, and the harmony of belief had been replaced by the dissonance of disbelief. Wars were considered unjust, enforcement of laws, discipline, and standards of morality became passé, while the values of saving, investment, and productivity gave way to the something-for-nothing attitude of consumeritis.

Out of the mixture of success and failure, out of the examples of growth and decline, out of the exhilaration of accomplishment and the despair of the defeat, has come the common thread of knowledge: Where America believed, America achieved.

And so it is with individuals, too. Men and women, by their efforts, breathed life into their dreams.

When in 1976, Louise Fletcher accepted an Oscar for her performance in *One Flew Over the Cuckoo's Nest,* millions of television viewers saw her employ sign language to communicate her gratitude to her deaf parents, Reverend and Mrs. Robert C. Fletcher. Before the world, she told them: "I want to thank you for teaching me to have a dream. You are seeing my dream come true."

When thirty-five-year-old Lou Gehrig stood at Yankee Stadium's home plate dying of amyotrophic lateral sclerosis, he was able to proclaim from his heart: "I consider myself the luckiest man on the face of the earth." He had achieved his boyhood dream of becoming a New York Yankee. He had walked off Columbia University's campus to join a Yankee farm club. He not only became a Yankee, he became the captain, with a .340 lifetime batting average over a fifteen-year span. Playing in 2,130 consecutive games, almost twice as many as any other man who ever played the game, he became the "Iron Horse" of baseball.

Although the "Iron Horse" died at a time when his life should have reached its peak, he attained in death a different apogee. His dream, fulfilled, became an inspiration for thousands of young Americans—not so much that they could become major-league baseball players, but that they could dream their own dreams, knowing that theirs, too, might be fulfilled.

Too often, the world sees the glow of success without knowing what tremendous efforts have been expended along the way. Bobby Clark made it to the Philadelphia Flyers of the National Hockey League despite diabetes; Bobby Jones made it to the Philadelphia 76ers of the National Basketball Association despite epilepsy; Ike Skelton (D-Mo.) made it to the Congress of the United States despite polio. Their beliefs, coupled with hard work, carried them to seemingly impossible heights.

One wonders: Are our beliefs beyond our control? Are they simply based upon inherited chromosomes, or upon a thousand early experiences which shaped us to respond in predetermined ways?

What makes different people respond differently to similar situations?

Unhealthy bodies may be too weak to believe, and bodies filled with unhealthy experiences may, emotionally, be too crippled to believe; but most Americans have both the body and spirit to set them free to choose their path. Most Americans are sufficiently free—physically, mentally, and spiritually—to will their course in life; free enough to set their goals and dreams, knowing they have a reasonable chance of achieving them if they but reach with concentrated strength.

The dreams-come-true of famous figures may be the stuff of which men write, but the more meaningful story lies not in the dreams achieved by the famous few, but by the unknown multitude.

Whether a Fletcher or a farmer, a Gehrig or a grocer, a Churchill who inspired the Western world or a teacher who motivates a dozen youngsters, everyone's dreams and aspirations define the outer limit of his reach.

By believing in himself, his country, and the people around him, man creates an environment of achievement. By believing in the enduring principles of religion and philosophy—in the life-building rather than in the life-destroying forces of the universe—man gives meaning to his life. By believing, man becomes a positive force, energized by and energizing those about him.

America's most American philosopher, William James, explained: "Truth is made, just as health, wealth, and strength are made, in the course of experience."

Faith precedes facts. Our beliefs help determine what the outcomes will be. From Paul's admonition to the ancient Hebrews ("Faith is the substance of things hoped for, the evidence of things not seen") to Theodor Herzl's twentieth-century statement on his dream of a Jewish homeland ("If we will it—it is no longer a dream") belief forever has remained the essential precondition for dreams come true.

Those who disbelieve thrive perversely on the ills and vices of sullen cynicism or even violence. By disbelieving, they destroy their roots, close their hearts, and deny their identity. They tarnish all they touch. They condemn themselves to darkness, and cast doleful shadows where they walk.

Yet even in the face of bitter reality, others believe. One family watched its mother—a saint—go under the knife nine times to have her legs progressively sawed off, so the gangrenous, blood-clotted limbs might not claim her life. As she was reduced to stumps for legs and glued into a wheelchair for life, the members of that family, in their collective agony, were witnessing the despicable evidence that God could not be just. Yet they could not, not believe. As they felt a raging helplessness, as their minds cried out in disbelief, they could not help but believe. They knew beyond the point of knowing that a power beyond imagining forced them to believe. For them, the purest truth of all was that even when she could no longer speak, her Madonna's smile and pleading eyes said: "Believe—with all your hearts, believe." They did, and she survived.

And when she was well again from the waist up, for another dozen years she radiated energy and love to all whose lives she touched. Magazines wrote and ministers spoke about the "woman in the wheelchair" who wheeled herself to work each day, who worked her turn at the Woman's Club's volunteer library at night, who hosted her Sunday School class, whose door and heart were open to the neighbors and friends who climbed her wheelchair ramp. When they cut off her legs, she believed her life had taken on new meaning. God had given her new purpose: to show that life was worth living, that one could surmount whatever tragedy life imposed, that by her example, others could believe and hope. She succeeded. The richest years of her life were spent in her wheelchair, as she enriched the lives of countless others.*

The evidence of the power of belief extends from biblical to modern times, from theological to psychological experiences, from ascetic to practical satisfactions, from physical to intellectual achievements.

From Émile Coué's prescription for self-mastery through autosuggestion, to Norman Vincent Peale's power of positive thinking, millions of people in this century have been persuaded that by their beliefs they can mold their lives. Especially in America, living proof abounds. Among athletes, believing in oneself has become the first article of

---

*Her name was Grace Greinert Shuster, my mother.

faith. As baseball's worst team, the Atlanta Braves, were breaking a major-league record by winning their first thirteen games of the 1982 season, Manager Joe Torre explained: "The only thing that's different about us is our attitude."

The Library of Congress has 254 books dealing primarily with belief. Clergymen and coaches, psychologists and sales managers, stock-market analysts and students of behavior modification are all preaching and teaching the same message: Believe in belief.

Although skeptics may dismiss belief as nothing more than a psychological trick to fool oneself into being more highly motivated, the evidence of the power of belief is rooted both in the works of the great philosophers and in modern-day science.

Immanuel Kant looked beyond the sterile world of logic to tell us: *"Was willst du, das kannst du"*—What you have the will to do, you can do—and Santayana observed: "It is not wisdom to be only wise . . . but it is wisdom to believe the heart."

Recent scientific studies indicate that belief can actually cause the brain to release pain-fighting chemicals. Fifty dental patients were injected with a placebo but told they had been given a painkiller. The brains of one third of the patients responded by releasing endorphins, a recently discovered natural painkiller similar to morphine.

Today hypnosis is used routinely in a variety of medical procedures including childbirth and surgery. One of the world's foremost authorities on hypnosis, Dr. Martin Orne of the University of Pennsylvania's Medical School, states: "I have used hypnosis with great success in the easement of pain—organic pain—of terminal cancer."

The scientific application of hypnosis proves that belief can induce real change in people. Although positive thinkers can proclaim the efficacy of believing, literal-minded skeptics have sometimes sought to dismiss their assertions as so much hocus-pocus. More than a few sophisticated eyebrows were raised thirty years ago when Norman Vincent Peale advised, "Fill your mind with thoughts of faith, confidence, and security. This will force out or expel all thoughts of doubt, all lack of confidence." The hard scientific evidence of recent years, however, has lowered most of those eyebrows while opening the eyes of some of the most sophisticated. When, with no anesthesia but the power of belief, babies are born and teeth are extracted without pain, even the most hard-bitten pragmatist must find cause to believe in belief. In the face of such evidence it becomes reasonable to believe in the power of belief, unreasonable not to do so.

Once one crosses the threshold to acknowledge that sheer belief can change a person physiologically, it becomes more difficult to argue that belief cannot also change a person psychologically, intellectually, or spiritually. If, by belief, one can be changed, the belief of ten thousand persons can change a town, or ten million a country.

Dr. Jerome Frank, professor emeritus of psychiatry at Johns Hopkins Medical School, states: "Our beliefs determine our behavior. Faith heals. Negativism destroys. Man must believe to make sense of life."

Our beliefs determine our emotions. Depending upon our feelings, we are filled with joy or sorrow, love or hate, energy or lethargy, harmony or discord.

Scientists are now proving what philosophers have long been teaching, and what popularizers have recently been selling: Belief works. The leap to faith—believing what the heart whispers and the mind intuitively senses before it can be proved—is not so difficult once science has demonstrated that belief alone can change the senses. If pain can be deadened, recall heightened, body temperature dropped, and pulse beat quickened—purely by willing that it be done—then the possibility for willing whatever else we would can no longer be denied. Suddenly the biblical admonitions in the Book of Mark take on a new meaning: "All things are possible to him who believes. . . . Believe that you shall receive them, and they shall come to you."

One may debate the fine points of religious salvation, but throughout history the evidence has been clear that religious belief has saved lives here on Earth, whatever the outcome may be in the hereafter.

In 1949, while serving as a missionary in China, Father Robert W. Greene of Maryknoll was captured and held pris-

oner by the Communists for three and one half years, one
full year of which was in solitary confinement. With no com-
munication with the outside world, with the only source of
light and air a small iron-barred window above his reach,
Father Greene maintained his sanity by telling himself,
aloud, over and over: "My name is Bob Greene. I'm a priest.
I will survive and live to again serve God." He did. After
being condemned to death in an Easter Sunday, 1952, Communist "People's Court," in an open field before thousands
of people, his sentence was commuted to "expulsion" to the
United States.

Lieutenant Charles M. Hill, Jr., was shot down and
wounded in 1952 by the North Korean Communists who
held him prisoner and incommunicado for nearly a year, 162
days of which was in solitary confinement. He maintained
his sanity by tying knots in his shoelaces to fashion a crude
Rosary, using it as he prayed that his wounds be healed and
he be returned. He was freed in the final days of the 1953
prisoner exchanges at Panmunjom.

In 1956, after a four-year study of Chinese Communist
brainwashing of U.S. prisoners of war in Korea, which included interviews with nearly one thousand such returned
prisoners, Major William E. Mayer, U.S. Army psychiatrist,
reported that American prisoners who had retained their
faith generally had survived. Those who "lacked religious
conviction and faith in America, all too often," he said,
"would crawl off in a corner, refuse to eat, and—without
having any disease whatever—simply die."

Man's need to believe has been established scientifically
and religiously, philosophically and pragmatically. Belief
is the *raison d'être* for living—the reason for being. Belief gives man purpose, and purpose fuels the universe.
Belief gives man responsibility—a burden to be sure, except
that life's heaviest burden is having nothing to carry.

While belief may give man meaning, the meanings of
different beliefs can send man down quite different paths.
Choosing what to believe can determine where one will
spend his life—geographically, economically, psychologically, spiritually. Even if one rules out the negativism and
nihilism of the wreckers and destroyers, the positive alterna-

tives offer more choices than any individual could begin to grasp.

Narrowing and winnowing, weighing and selecting, man chooses his beliefs and, by so doing, sets his course for life. By balancing one's beliefs between what is and what might be, between dreams and reality, between the firmness of the Earth and the rainbow in the sky, between heart and head, the self and soul, the present and the past, man defines his future.

Starting at the core with self, man builds his beliefs outward like a series of ever-widening concentric circles, to family—past, present and future—to friends and co-workers, to communities, organizations, and the institutions he embraces.

At the outer rim of those circles of belief there is yet a larger circle—one more distant than family or community, yet closer than the air one breathes; a circle that encompasses all others within it, that holds the other circles in their place, that lets them grow and thrive, turn and change, breathe and be reborn again; a circle that, like the balance of the universe, holds all the planets in their place. That circle is America. Much more than a government or a piece of earth, or even the progression of a people, it is a belief.

By believing in America, one confirms the wholeness of a chosen land. Chosen since the 1600's by more than fifty million legal immigrants, who saw her as that spot on Earth where life could best be lived. From the beginning, America has been the shining city on a hill—the place where tomorrow can be better—the destination for history's largest stream of people flowing from around the globe toward life's most promised land.

By believing in America, one affirms the future. Belief becomes the motive force to work and build, to make the nation prosper. As the nation's minds and hearts focus on the future, Americans more willingly pay the present price in sweat and silver to buy a better day for those who will follow. Building for tomorrow, they touch the inner scars and blighted extremities of the nation, and in the process, make America more worthy of belief.

By believing in America, one finds the strength to keep the nation strong. Unafraid of the predators that prowl the Earth, a secure America can thrive behind her awesome shield. Unrattled by the fear that weakness brings, America can add her firm resolve to the balance wheel for peace. Supporting those who are her friends, and teaching by example that friendship pays, America can nudge all nations toward the rule of law. Recognizing that war is a constant thread of history, and only strength deters a tyrant, Americans reach out for peace with heart and mind and soul, putting their strength and power on the side of living rather than dying—on the side of law, rather than on the side of the jungle rule of bloody conflict. By being a peacemaker strong enough to draw a line before a tyrant's step, America best protects her own while giving hope to others. As they see a friendly hand outstretched from a powerful arm, they too will believe in America as man's best hope on Earth.

By believing in America, one asserts his will to preserve her for the future. Extracting from her hills and fields the foods and minerals to feed her factories and families, Americans, nevertheless, keep an eye on the horizon. Knowing that conservation builds wealth to pass along, Americans can balance their present prosperity with future preservation. By taking, then reclaiming, they can possess, but still preserve. By using, then renewing, they can consume, but still conserve. By setting seedlings where trees are felled, spreading lime and potash on soil that yields bounteous crops, recycling scrap, and redesigning mills, machines, and management styles, America saves. In the saving, she adds reason to believe that the future will begin atop a powerful structure waiting to be tapped.

By believing in America, one acknowledges the wisdom of a nation fed on knowledge. Knowing more than ever, and knowing that knowledge is a driving force that pushes the nation on, Americans can pour themselves into the bubbling crucible of education, from which will emerge the tempered steel to build intellectual bridges to the future. By believing in knowledge, man acquires it. In the acquisition, he learns that knowledge fuels belief.

Belief in America becomes the mental gyroscope that

keeps one on an even keel, that lets him strike out in whatever direction he may choose, secure in his surroundings of a land and people providing stability for those who strive.

Belief in America becomes the outer circle that holds in place the many inner circles of belief that each man draws unto himself.

Belief in America becomes the great foundation stone upon which millions of divergent lives may safely be constructed—each embracing what, for him, is true; each reaching for different stars in a different part of the sky, yet knowing they are protected by the rock upon which they stand, the air they breathe, and the opportunity wistfully awaiting their touch.

America: a land where dreams can still come true.

America: a dream worthy of belief—a belief worthy of a dream.

Snowflakes, thick and wet, flutter down from cleaner, clearer skies. Like narrow strips of cotton, they cluster and cling atop bare branches sheltering the empty, life-worn sidewalk lying underneath. All is silent—too still, too white, too pure, except for the soft crunch of my boots upon the virgin snow.

With legs and heart I retrace those steps I took thirty-eight years ago, as an eleven-year-old lad carrying a precious, hand-painted shaving mug tucked tightly in his left arm. The boy who believed he could be a congressman became one. Even as a college student he had learned the magic of belief.

It started around the campfire of the University of Pittsburgh's freshman camp located in Western Pennsylvania's Allegheny foothills. It was the final night of freshman orientation.

Following the singing of several college songs came the highlight of the evening: a talk by the previous year's graduate who had been named the outstanding senior of his class. Selected by a committee composed of students, faculty, and administration members, he had been chosen as the kind of person the "university aims to produce in scholarship, character, and leadership." Each year the recipient's name was chiseled in a large stone alongside the campus walk.

The outstanding young man, who had been captain of the university's debating team, told the new freshmen their next four years could be the most important, most formative years of their lives. He explained that they could become either streetcar students who returned to their homes after classes, or fully committed students who participated in campus life, thereby gaining the full measure of a college education.

The lad who seven years earlier had made that journey to the congressman's house listened intently in the shadows of the flickering campfire. But for an academic scholarship, he probably would have been laboring in a Western Pennsylvania steel mill instead of entering a great university.

As he weighed the words of the outstanding graduate exhorting them to make the most of their college years, as he studied the faces of his new classmates and the dancing flames of a campfire that removed the chill of an early September evening, he set his four-year goal: to be named the outstanding senior of his class.

Never mind that as a product of a small mill town's public school system he would be competing with students from many of America's most highly rated private and public schools. Never mind that he had never even set foot inside that university, or any other, before that very week. Never mind that he decided on the spot that, like the campfire speaker, he would become a college debater even though he had never even heard a debate, let alone participated in one. The very audacity of his dream exhilarated him.

Four years later, after immersing himself in his studies, after serving as president of several campus organizations and along the way winning the national intercollegiate debating championship, he stood in silent awe as his name was engraved upon the university's campus walk—as he was named the outstanding senior of his class. The dream he had embraced around the freshman campfire had come true. He had converted that dream into a goal composed of many precise subgoals and had set out to achieve them. Along the way he discovered that each effort returned many times its cost. He discovered that the satisfactions one got from supposedly hard work made the work not hard at all. The efforts extracted virtually no sacrifices; they only produced satisfactions. He learned that a dream is a goal you give your heart to, that a goal is a dream with muscle added.

To him it was a stunning revelation; it was as if he had discovered one of the world's great mysteries, had inadvertently stumbled upon a magic truth—that one can make something come true by believing it can come true; that belief can cause events to happen. In the years that followed, he saw that maxim occur time and time again. He experienced the power of belief. For him, it became as real as the laws of physics, yet not so simple or assured.

He learned that not all dreams come true, but more important, what is never dreamed can never be fulfilled. He learned that even unfulfilled dreams have a way of branching into new possibilities; that positive beliefs sometimes unlock exciting new challenges of which one may have been totally unaware; that even when a positive belief comes head to head with a stubborn, immovable reality, it finds new paths that lead to other opportunities, like a sunflower that blossoms by leaning toward the sun.

Throughout his life he never lost his sense of wonder each time a dream came true. He knew that belief was the precursor of achievement, yet he always was deeply moved when he witnessed that truth. He never lost his sense of awe over the magic of belief—he never fully understood it, but he could not doubt what he repeatedly experienced.

For me—my dream came true. Whether it be worthy or wasted is a chapter not yet written, and for others to decide. Much more important, for millions of other Americans their dreams have also come true. For them, it is families and homes, educations and careers, all built upon a bedrock of belief—in themselves, their country, their priceless freedom that let them fashion futures out of the raw earth, out of the technology, out of the knowledge that was theirs to tap and use.

And even for those who still struggle in hard and heavy times, the hope for better days shines through. The light that lets them see their chance for opportunity stands not far off, and holds the promise for a prosperity in which they too can share.

Former Congressman and Judge Samuel A. Weiss, the

object of my boyhood mission, is gone. Most of the people
—not just neighbors, but neighborly neighbors—who lived
in the modest homes along the way from his to mine, who
gently touched my early life when touching counted most
—are gone. But many of the names on the houses, though
shuffled about, remain the same. They are the sons and
daughters of those who peopled a small Western Pennsylvania town during searing years which dragged America
through hard times and distant death. Struggling through
those years to keep family and country together, they never
lost faith—at least not for longer than it took to remember
who they were and from whence they came. Through it all,
they had *believed*.

And now a new time for testing faces another generation.
Awash in material abundance, intellectual capacity, military
might, and physical strength, it is almost embarrassing to
ask: Will we meet the thrilling challenges of today and tomorrow as our parents and grandparents met the awful challenges of yesterday?

With a modicum of modesty, we might insist that we
shall do more! Not simply because of what we are, but because of what they were. We shall conquer worlds they
knew not of, because it is on their shoulders that we stand.

In our time too, we shall prevail, for we are Americans
—and we believe.

Yet, in our moment of reality, new dreams are dreamed.
The old ones, once achieved, somehow are assumed to have
always been there for the grasping. Minds stir, imperfections become dissatisfactions, man forgets how, really, things
once were. New goals, new desires, new destinies slowly,
silently take shape, first amorphously like a far-off fog rising
from a river bottom, then closer, clearer, as the sun of opportunity breaks through. Man begins to strive anew; new
dreams become reality, if not for him, then for his sons and
daughters. The joys of success strengthen man's resolve, and
the tears of failure soften his heart and help him understand.
The young reach out to touch the stars. Their days ascend.
Life goes on as dreams turn into reality, and reality reaches
toward new dreams. America, changeless in the bedrock
that sustains each generation, ever-changing in the oppor-

tunities that she unfurls, holds hope and promise for her people. America: More than rock or people, she is a dream come true, yet not fulfilled, an ideal that is real, yet beyond realization; but most of all, she is a belief that takes 230 million different shapes yet fuses in a single form for love, for hope, for a shining future—knowing full well the better day will come, and when it does, the dream will turn into reality—and thence begin anew.

Fed from fields we did not clear, watered from wells we did not dig, sheltered in homes we did not hew, protected by a peace for which we did not fully pay, educated by knowledge we did not discover, we nonetheless lay claim to our success. It is a claim that will be substantiated not by what we achieve atop foundations built by others but by the lasting structures we erect for those who follow. So that in their hour on this Earth they may look back and say: See, this our forebears did for us.

ACKNOWLEDGMENTS

MORE THAN THE obligatory claim of responsibility must fall upon my shoulders, for this book was not ghostwritten. From split infinitive to misused noun, the burden is mine. Whatever its weaknesses, however, they would be much worse but for the advice and help of Howard Cady, Professor Donald Gallehr, Lu Ann Holstine, Robert Siegrist, and many others.

Without the excellent resource material available through the Library of Congress, congressional committees, and executive branch departments, the research necessary for this book could not have been obtained.

—BUD SHUSTER

APPENDIX

AS A RESULT OF PRESS SPECULATION ABOUT MY INVOLVEMENT WITH THE PRESIDENT AND THE WHITE HOUSE DURING THE PERIOD LEADING TO THE PRESIDENT'S RESIGNATION, MAYOR ALLAN HANCOCK OF ALTOONA, PENNSYLVANIA, A LONG-TIME SUPPORTER OF MINE, REFERRED THE QUESTION TO WILLIAM TIMMONS, ASSISTANT TO THE PRESIDENT FOR LEGISLATIVE AFFAIRS DURING THE WATERGATE PERIOD. FOLLOWING IS HIS REPLY.

June 24, 1977

Dear Mr. Hancock:

Some time ago you referred a press inquiry to me asking what role Congressman Bud Shuster played during the final days of the Nixon impeachment proceedings. As President Nixon's Assistant for Legislative Affairs, I felt it best to defer a reply until the passage of some time.

As you know, during the impeachment period Congressman Shuster was the President of the Republican Freshman class which numbered over 40 Members of Congress. The President recognized that his leadership position among the younger Members could be crucial in the House of Representatives.

The President invited Congressman Shuster, along with a few other Members, for dinner and an evening aboard the Presidential yacht Sequoia in July—to the best of my recollection—as we entered the crucial period. Congressman

Shuster had taken the position that he believed it was his constitutional duty to reserve final judgment on the impeachment question until the Judiciary Committee presented its findings and debate was completed before the full House. My office, of course, was solicitous of Congressman Shuster's assistance along with other leaders; however, he maintained his independence throughout the proceedings.

Mr. Shuster did agree to keep us appraised of the mood of the younger Members and was open and forthright in so doing. During July and early August of 1974 I was in touch with him frequently and sometimes several times a day to determine the probability of impeachment in the House and shifting sentiments of Members of Congress.

When the tape of June 23, 1972 was heard by House Members, Representative Shuster advised us that impeachment was virtually certain. As I recall, the Congressman urged the President to resign for the good of the country.

To his credit, Mr. Shuster did not exploit his position as a leader of the new Members to gain media attention, as he could have during those explosive days.

Because his counsel remained private, reasoned and candid, I feel he was one who played a significant role in that ultimate outcome when the President resigned for what he felt was best for the country. I am sorry my reply has been so long in coming and hope this letter will help put Mr. Shuster's position in proper perspective.

Sincerely,

William E. Timmons
9501 Newbold Place
Bethesda, Maryland
20034

Mr. Allan Hancock
Penn Alto Hotel
Suite K
Altoona, Pennsylvania 16601

SELECTED
SOURCE NOTES

Chapter I

Page
23   *Compton's Encyclopedia,* Vol. 24, p. 252.
25   Laurence LaFore, *The End of Glory* (Philadelphia: J. B. Lippincott Company, 1970).
26   *Compton's Encyclopedia,* Vol. 11, p. 220.
30   J. Hector St. John, (aka Michel Guillaume Jean de Crèvecoeur) *Letters From an American Farmer,* London: 1782.

Chapter II

Page
42   Director of Review and Analysis, Office of the Controller of the Army, OCS.
42   Mark Clark, *From the Danube to the Yalu* (New York: Harper & Brothers, 1954).
43   *New York Times,* Jan. 26, 1950.
44   As told by Charles "Chip" Bohlen, then U. S. Ambassador to Moscow.
47   Lawrence Baskir and William Strauss, *Chance and Circumstance: The Draft, the War, and the Viet-*

nam Generation (New York: Alfred Knopf, 1978), p. 169.

49   Earle G. Wheeler, Chairman of the Joint Chiefs of Staff, Top Secret *Memorandum for the President*, July 1968, declassified per Shuster request, March 9, 1981.

50   Peter Braestrup, *The Big Story*, Vol. 1, (Boulder, Colo.: Westview Press, 1977), pp. 147–154.

50   *Review of the News*, March 18, 1981, pp. 65–66.

50   Hanoi Radio, July 20, 21, 24, 1972.

52   Martin Kasindorf, *The New York Times Magazine*, Feb. 3, 1974.

Chapter III

Page

60   Gerald R. Ford, *A Time to Heal* (New York: Harper & Row, 1979), p. 429.

62   Cord Meyer, *Facing Reality, from World Federalism to the CIA* (New York: Harper & Row, 1980), p. 93.

63   U. S. Congress, Senate, Select Committee to Study Governmental Operations with Respect to Intelligence Activities, *Supplementary Detailed Staff Report on Foreign and Military*, 94th Cong., 2d sess., April 29, 1976, S. Rept. 94-755, Part 1, p. 427.

64   *Washington Post*, Oct. 24, 1976.

66   *New York Times*, Sept. 20, 1974.

66   *Philadelphia Inquirer*, April 24, 1976.

66   UPI, Plains, Ga., Dec. 23, 1977.

67   Jimmy Carter, Second Carter/Ford presidential debate, Palace of Fine Arts Theater, San Francisco, October 6, 1976.

68   Richard Scammon and Ben Wattenberg, *Public Opinion*, April 1978.

71   *Congressional Quarterly Almanac*, Dec. 1979, p. 11.

76   David Yankelovich, *Boston Globe*, July 31, 1980.

Chapter IV

Page

78 Howard C. Frey and George Shumway, *Conestoga Wagon 1750–1850,* 3rd ed. (York, Pa.: George Shumway, 1968).

81 The World Bank, *World Redevelopment Report 1980* (Washington, D. C.: August 1980), p. 34.

84 Union Bank of Switzerland, *Prices and Earnings Around the Globe, 1979–1980,* Vol. 69.

84 Agency for International Development, Unpublished Statistical Compilation, May 15, 1981.

85 United Nations, Dept. of International Economic and Social Affairs, *Compendium on Housing Statistics, 1980.*

85 U.S. Dept. of Housing and Urban Development, *Characteristics of New Housing, 1979–1980.*

85 *Economic Report of the President,* 1980.

85 U.S. Dept. of Housing and Urban Development, *Housing Costs in the United States and Other Industrialized Countries,* 1980.

85 Union Bank of Switzerland, *Prices and Earnings Around the Globe, 1979–80,* Vol. 69.

85 National Transportation Policy Study Commission, *National Transportation Policies Through the Year 2000,* June 1979.

86 U.S. Central Intelligence Agency, National Foreign Assessment Center, *Handbook of Economic Statistics,* 1980.

97 Ernest Hemingway, *A Moveable Feast* (New York: Charles Scribner's Sons, 1964), p. 3.

97 U.S. Bureau of the Census, May 22, 1981.

97 U.S. Dept. of Housing and Urban Development, *Annual Housing Survey,* 1979.

98 Testimony of Dr. Robert L. Rizek, Director of Consumer Nutrition Center, U.S. Dept. of Agriculture, before Subcommittee of Committee on Agriculture, U.S. House of Representatives, March 18, 1981.

100 The World Bank, *World Redevelopment Report, 1980* (Washington, D. C.: August 1980), p. 34.

Chapter V

Page
102 Ayn Rand, *For the New Intellectual,* 1961.
103 U.S. Dept. of Commerce, *International Economic Indicators,* May 1981.
104 George Kurian, *The Book of World Rankings* (New York: Facts on File, 1979).
108 Jean-Jacques Rousseau, *Discourse on Political Economy,* 1755.
111 Prime Minister James Callaghan's Parliamentary Report to the Labor Party's Annual Conference, Blackpool, England, September 28, 1976.
111 National Westminster Bank of England, *Public Consumption and Economic Performance* by David Smith, Principal Research Officer.
112 Henry George, *Progress and Poverty,* 1879.
113 U.S. Department of the Treasury, June 16, 1981.
113 John Stuart Mill, "Representative Government," *Great Books of the Western World,* Vol. 43, (Encyclopedia Britannica, 1952), p. 383.
116 U.S. Bureau of Labor Statistics, January 1981.
119 John Maynard Keynes, *The Economic Consequences of the Peace,* 1919.
120 *The Limits of Growth,* a Report from The Club of Rome (New York: Universe Books, 1972).
120 Ibid.
121 Oscar Martin, U.S. Patent Office, Historical Division.
122 *The Global 2000 Report to the President,* Vol. 1 (Washington, D.C.: U.S. Government Printing Office, 1980).
123 Herman Kahn, and Ernest Schneider, *Globaloney 2000,* "Policy Reviews," Spring, 1981, The Heritage Foundation.
124 Ben Wattenberg, "What Population Explosion?," *Washington Post,* May 19, 1981.

124   Austin H. Kiplinger, *The Exciting '80's, The Kiplinger Letters,* 1979, and *The Kiplinger Washington Letter,* Dec. 26, 1980.

125   The Futures Group, report prepared in cooperation with Peat, Marwick, Mitchell & Co., for Futures Development Studies for the National Transportation Policy Study Commission, May 1978, Glastonbury, Conn.

125   Robey Clark, President, American Association of Petroleum Geologists.

125   *Paul Harvey News,* June 3, 1981.

125   U.S. Bureau of Census.

125   U.S. Bureau of Labor Statistics, Growth Division, June 9, 1981.

Chapter VI

Page
128   U.S. Department of State, *Treaties and Other International Agreements.*

129   Frank Donovan, *Mr. Monroe's Message* (New York: Dodd Mead & Company, 1963).

134   U.S. Agency for International Development, *U.S. Overseas Loans and Grants, and Assistance from International Organizations: July 1, 1945–Sept. 30, 1980.*

136   Quincy Wright, *A Study of War* (Chicago: University of Chicago Press, 1942).

137   *United States Military Posture for FY 1982,* an overview by General David C. Jones, USAF, Chairman, Joint Chiefs of Staff.

137   *The Military Balance 1980/81,* compiled by The International Institute of Strategic Studies, London, and published in *Air Force Magazine,* December 1980.

138   John M. Collins, Senior Specialist in National Defense, Congressional Research Service of Library of Congress.

Chapter VII

Chapter VIII

172 U.S. Department of Commerce, Bureau of the Census, *Statistical Abstract of the United States,* 1980.

172 U.S. Department of Agriculture, Alien Investment Office.

172 U.S. Department of Commerce, Bureau of Economic Analysis, International Investment Office.

172 U.S. Department of the Treasury, Office of Securities Market Policy.

176 U.S. Library of Congress, Congressional Research Service, *Opening Federal Lands to Non-Fuel Mineral Development,* Issue Brief #IB81158, Nov. 19, 1981.

177 George Kurian, ed., *The Book of World Rankings* (New York: Facts on File, 1979).

177 *Fisheries of the United States,* National Marine Fishery Service/NOAA, U.S. Department of Commerce, 1980.

178 Testimony of U.S. Deputy Secretary of Commerce Joseph A. Wright, Jr., before the U.S. House Committee on Science and Technology, July 28, 1981.

178 Ted Littman, Manager, Government Relations, Rockwell International (prime contractor for *Apollo 11* vehicle).

180 U.S. Department of Energy.

181 Eliot R. Cutler, "The U.S. Role in World Coal," *Wall Street Journal,* March 18, 1981.

186 U.S. Library of Congress, Congressional Research Service; U.S. Department of the Interior, National Park Service; Florida Highway Department; U.S. Bureau of Indian Affairs; *Encyclopaedia Britannica*

189 U.S. Library of Congress, Congressional Research Service, *Reclamation Reform,* Issue Brief #IB81031.

189 *Congressional Record,* Vol. 123, No. 49, March 21, 1977.

191 U.S. Department of the Interior, *What is Reclamation?,* Bureau of Reclamation, 1979.

194   U.S. Travel Rate Center.
196   *U.S. Government and Industry Data*, August 1981.
196   *Time* magazine, November 2, 1981.
197   Personal interview.

Chapter IX

Page
199   *The American School Board Journal*, June 1980.
200   *The Wilson Quarterly*, Autumn 1979, p. 128.
200   U.S. Department of Education, National Center for Education Statistics, *Digest of Education Statistics*, 1981.
201   U.S. Bureau of Labor Statistics.
204   *The American School Board Journal*, June 1980.
204   Dr. Fred M. and Grace Hechinger, "A Long Tug of War," *The Wilson Quarterly*, Autumn 1979.
204   Peter Atetov, Deputy Director, Institute of Pedagogy, Soviet Academy of Education.
204   W. L. Patty and L. S. Johnson, *Personality and Adjustment* (New York: McGraw-Hill, 1953), p. 277.
205   Congressional Research Service, Library of Congress.
206   Dr. Elmer Casey, Director of Testing, Chicago Public Schools.
207   Harvey Gross, Admissions Director, Providence-St. Mels Catholic High School, Chicago, Illinois.
207   Dr. Mortimer Adler, "We've Grown Weaker, and Europe Stronger," *U.S. News and World Report*, July 31, 1981.
209   Andrew M. Greeley, *Minority Students in Catholic Secondary Schools*, Chicago: National Opinion Research Center, 1982.
215   Dr. Calvin McIntyre, Milwaukee Public School System.
215   Dr. Jack Van Impe, *The '80s, the Antichrist and Your Startling Future*, Royal Oak, Mich.: Van Impe Ministries, 1982.

216   Dr. Tim La Haye, *The Beginning of the End* (Whea-
        ton, Ill.: Tyndale House Publishers, 1972).

216   U.S. Veterans Administration, May 11, 1975.

217   U.S. Bureau of Census.

217   Clark Kerr, "The Godkin Lectures," Harvard Uni-
        versity, 1963.

217   *United States Supply and Demand of Scientists and
        Engineers: Effects on Defense Research and
        Technology, Part I, Current Situation and Fu-
        ture Outlook,* Edith Fairman Cooper, analyst in
        social science, Science Policy Division, Con-
        gressional Research Service, Library of Con-
        gress, November 6, 1981.

219   U.S. Department of Education, *The Condition of
        Vocational Education,* National Center for
        Educational Statistics, eds. Mary A. Galladay
        and Rolf M. Wurfsberg, GPO document, 1981.

219   U.S. Department of Defense, Office of Training and
        Education.

220   National Newspaper Publishers Association; Neilsen
        survey; Arbitron ratings; Library of Congress.

221   Robert Craig, Vice President, American Society for
        Training and Development, Washington, D.C.

221   *American Management Association Directory of
        Education.*

NOTE: Quotations from educators, where not otherwise
        footnoted, are based on personal interviews.

Chapter X

Page
227   Edward Garden, *Tchaikovsky,* J. M. Dent and Son,
        Ltd., New York, 1973.

231   William James, *Pragmatism,* 1907, p. 218.

233   George Santayana, "O World, Thou Choosest Not."

233   John Levine, M.D., Ph.D., Newton Gordon, D.D.S.,
        and Howard Fields, M.D., Ph.D, "Naloxone
        Dose Dependently Produces Analgesia and

Hyperalgesia in Post-Operative Pain," *Nature* magazine, April 19, 1979, Vol. 278, No. 5706, p. 740–741.

233   Norman Vincent Peale, *The Power of Positive Thinking,* (New York: Prentice-Hall, 1952).

INDEX

ABOUT THE
AUTHOR

CONGRESSMAN E. G. BUD SHUSTER writes about America from a unique perspective—as an early participant in the electronic computer industry; as holder of an MBA and a Ph.D. in Management and Economics; as a six-term member of the Congress of the United States in which he has served on the Budget Committee and its Defense Task Force; the Public Works and Transportation Committee and its Subcommittees on Economic Development, Surface Transportation, Aviation, and Water Resources; the Education and Labor Committee and its Subcommittee on Higher Education; as chairman of the Republican Policy Committee, and as a delegate to NATO's North Atlantic Assembly. He has also chaired the National Transportation Policy Commission and is the only Pennsylvanian in half a century to twice win both the Republican and Democratic congressional nominations.

He is the recipient of numerous awards, including Watchdog of the Treasury award for his efforts to control government spending; Guardian of Small Business award for his efforts on behalf of the free enterprise economy; the Golden Age Hall of Fame award for his efforts on behalf of senior citizens; the National Security Leadership award for his support of a strong national defense; the Significant Sig award, the highest award presented to alumni by Sigma Chi Fraternity, and special awards from the Pennsylvania Academy of Science and the American Society of Highway Engineers. Congressman Shuster has been a principal author of much of America's transportation legislation during the past decade, and is the only Pennsylvanian ever elected to the capital's prestigious Chowder and Marching Society.

A descendant of early Pennsylvania Dutch settlers, he was a

Phi Beta Kappa graduate of the University of Pittsburgh where he was named the outstanding senior of his class. He received graduate degrees from Duquesne University and The American University, and has been a University of Pittsburgh trustee.

After service as a U.S. Army infantry officer and counterintelligence agent, he entered the computer industry in which he was involved in the installation of some of America's first large-scale UNIVAC computer systems as well as in the development of COBOL, the first English-language programming system. As a vice president of RCA's Electronic Data Processing Division, president and chairman of a computer terminal company, and a founder of a computer software company, Bud Shuster was actively involved in the American technological explosion commencing in the 1950's.

A runner and self-confessed handball addict, he resides with his wife and five children on a farm in Bedford County, Pennsylvania, when not in Washington. Congressman Shuster looks at America from the grass roots up, from the dark days of the Great Depression and World War II through the present, and into the future.

What he sees is cause for hope.